Soul of Erie

Sports in the
City by the Lake

For my Aunt Judy,
who was an outstanding writer, editor
and the strongest, most courageous,
most spiritual person I have ever known.
You will be forever in my heart.

Acknowledgements

I am grateful to the following people and organizations for helping to make this book a reality with their time, work, encouragement, interest, advice and/or resources:

Henry Adaso, Willie Alford, Greg Baney, Allania Banta, Tom Barnes, Vicki Bendus, Fred Biletnikoff, Dustin Bingham, Lou Bizzarro, Lou Bizzarro's Ringside Restaurant (including the staff), Mike Bizzarro, Valeria Boyd, Dan Brabender, George Brown, Joe Bufalino and Sherry Bufalino.
Jon Cacchione, Kareem Carson Sr., the Cathedral Preparatory School and Villa Maria Academy athletics department, Dan Chojnacki, Glen Conner Jr., Glen Conner Sr., James Conner, Michael Conner, Richard Conner, Aaron Cooney, Tiffany Cory, Joe Cuneo and Kevin Cuneo.
John Dahlstrand, Monica DiNicola, Ron DiNicola, Sophia DiNicola, Johnny Dogun, Stella Dogun, Edinboro University Athletics, Don Elbaum, Kipp Elbaum and Lance Elbaum.
The Erie Bayhawks, the Erie City School District, the Erie Otters, the Erie SeaWolves, the *Erie Times-News* archives, Drew Eubank, Gary Ferch, Aaron Fitzpatrick, Stephon Fitzpatrick, Bill Flanagan, Brad Fox, Josh Freeman, Brian Fuller, Joe Gaeta, Mark Gaeta, Mike Gallagher and Greg Gania.
The General McLane High School football and boys basketball teams of 2006-07, Michael Gresham, Matt Glass, Mary Jo Goldcamp, Dylan Grafius, Kathryn Grimaldi, David Hahn, Veronica Harden and Stefanie Herrmann.
Greg Hoffman, Melinda Holliday, Denise Horton, Gary Horton, Chris Janulewski, Bob Jarzomski, Jovon Johnson, LeAnn Johnson, Mike Johnson, Taylor Johnson, Curtis Jones Sr. and his family, Matt Jones, Derrick Jordan and Sandra Jordan.
Carmen Joyce, Jason Keim, Robert Kennerknecht, Clint Kent, Adrienne (Kloecker) Kalivoda, Keith Latzo, John Leisering, Anthony LoPinto, Gary Magorien, Joe Magorien, Dan Mason, Molly McCracken, Diane McCullough and Matt McCullough.
Laura McIntosh, Carla McKrell, Jon McKrell, Matt Mead Photography LLC, Mercyhurst University Athletics, Mike Mischler and his family, Miss Lynn, Brice Myers, Brett Neumann, Chad Noce, Courtney

Oberlander, Dan Olson, Don Orlando and Quentin Orlando.
Peter Overare, Julie Pace, Greg Parker, Adam Parkhouse, Kelly
Patterson, Jim Peluso, Maria Peluso, Peggy Peluso, Dean Pepicello,
Gus Picardo, Brian Polito, R. Frank Photography, Duane Rankin, Tom
Reisenweber, Tony Robie, Tim Romanski, Abby Rose, Dywon Rowan
and Levonne Rowan.
Alex Rupert, Dave Rupert, Mike Ruzzi, Cindy Sanford, Joe Sanford,
Craig Schauble, Vanessa Schauble, Alex Schmude, James
Schweikert, Bob Shreve, Mike Sisti, Kelley Smith, Snodgrass Photo,
Mark Soboleski, Kelley Steadman, Andy Steinke and Josh Stevens.
Brett Trott, Marilou Trott, Steve Tuholski, Mark Vatavuk, Rich
Valahovic, Gerry Weiss, Jim Wells, Jim Wertz, Doug White, Brad
Whitman, Sonya Whitman, Terry Williams, Mel Witherspoon, Alex
Womer and Jolene Young.

Credit and thanks to Eli De Leon for taking and providing the author
photograph on the back cover, as well as Gannon University Athletics
for providing the photographs for "Way Back When" and the front and
back covers.

Special thanks to:

Gillian Kieft, for her editorial excellence, measured view on the scope
of this project and steadfast efforts to make this book the best it could
be.

Joe Mattis, for his work on "Calmness and Courage" and "Way Back
When," as well as his consistent support, advice, encouragement and
help with creating connections to make this book possible.

Steve Orbanek, for his work on "Back to Back," as well as his valuable
counsel, connections and outstanding design of the covers of this
book.

Emmanuel Overare, for his candid interview for "Every Point Counts,"
as well as his substantial encouragement and voice of reason
throughout the creation of this book. His unfailing support helped
make this book possible.

The Stories

Introduction

In the fall of 2001, one of Erie's defining legacies was put to rest in a matter of moments.

As reported by the *Erie Times-News*, the closing of the International Paper Company plant in Erie was given just a brief rundown during the company's quarterly earnings report in October 2001.

It was the rusty nail in the proverbial 2x4 that was delivered to 760 employees who'd be out of work when the plant was to close the following June.

It was no secret the company had been struggling, and massive layoffs had already occurred in multiple plants across the country.

And yet, Erie had seemed safe, and employees even had reason to be optimistic. International Paper Company had hired 50 new workers as recently as July of that year.

But those 50 weren't immune to the layoffs, nor did it matter that the Hammermill Paper Company — which was purchased by International Paper Company in 1984 — had been founded right here in Erie by the renowned Behrend family.

"It's part of who and what we are, so part of our identity is now on the line," then Erie Mayor Joyce Savocchio was quoted as saying in the *Times-News* following the announcement.

I remember clearly when the paper plant closed its doors. A few guys from my church were laid off. I was 11 years old, and our nation was still reeling from the September 11 terrorist attacks, but I knew the plant's closing was a big deal.

Even my grandparents, who were from Canton, Ohio, knew what it meant to Erie.

I was born in Canton, but my family moved to Erie when I was just four years old. My dad — who has roots in Allegheny County dating back to around the time Abraham Lincoln was president — was hired as a physician at Saint Vincent Hospital in 1994. Our family of five lived in one of the red brick apartment buildings on Lewis Avenue while we waited for our house in Millcreek Township to be built.

My dad is a family practice physician, but he also is a sports medicine doctor. He covered athletics for East High School, Mercyhurst College (now Mercyhurst University), and, later, Edinboro University. He also occasionally provided medical care for the city's minor league baseball team, the Erie SeaWolves.

With my dad's job offering me a front row seat to some of the finest competition the city had to offer, I became an Erie sports fanatic. I was a fixture at high school, college and semipro games, and I pored over the *Times-News'* sports section each morning while I ate breakfast. This continued through my adolescence, and I was overjoyed to cover the scene as an intern/stringer in the sports department of the *Times-News* while attending Edinboro University. Even after I left Erie to become a sportswriter in the state of Indiana, I kept an eye on my hometown's sports scene. The newspaper business is another industry that has fallen on hard times, and in 2019 I returned to Erie to work in a more stable field.

When I came back, I found that the city's population had decreased and more manufacturers had left Erie. Nearly two decades after the paper plant closed, Erie is among the many American towns still trying to identify themselves in the 21st century economy. The coronavirus pandemic certainly hasn't helped matters.

But, as I've settled back into my hometown, I've also gotten back in tune with Erie's sports scene. And man, what a delight! In 2020 alone, McDowell boys basketball coach Kevin O'Connor and star William Jeffress led the Trojans to the PIAA quarterfinals before the pandemic ended the season prematurely (Jeffress is now playing for the University of Pittsburgh on a scholarship); the Cathedral Prep golf team and North East girls golf team won state titles; the Gannon women's basketball team won the Pennsylvania Scholastic Athletic Conference championship and the Mercyhurst women's hockey team captured the College Hockey America crown; and the SeaWolves were confirmed to remain in Erie after more than a year of uncertainty about their future in town.

And even though there have been changes — most notably the merger of Strong Vincent, Central Tech and East high schools into Erie High School — the spirit of competition, unshakable grit, athletic excellence and unity through sports has remained a constant in Erie. That's what *Soul of Erie: Sports in the City by the Lake* commemorates. Despite what Netflix or the weather advisory will have you believe, Erie is much more than the home of the "pizza bomber" or a habitat for abominable snowmen. It is a place where boys and girls shed blood, sweat and tears under gym and stadium lights on their way to becoming men and women. It's a town where, no matter what is going on in the world, people still make it a priority to check local sports scores and trek to games to cheer on their alma maters. And it's an area — including the suburbs and county towns — where sports mean so much more than wins and losses.

This book exemplifies the physicality, attitude and soul of Erie. The people, teams and places in these pages vary by age, gender, ethnic background and socioeconomic status, but are bound together by the life lessons they learned on their respective playing fields.

We're also tied together by our determination, which is a nice way of saying that many of us carry a chip on our shoulder. Erieites will complain about the snow, bicker about local politics and dream of moving to Florida when they get older. (It's telling that Erie Apparel makes and sells T-shirts that read "It's Okay to Love Erie.") But, let anybody outside of the county bad-mouth Erie, and see how quickly our pride comes out. We're quick to remind fans of the Western Pennsylvania Interscholastic Athletic League of Erie's formidability in football.

But I have to tip my cap to our neighbors to the south. If it weren't for them, I'd have never thought to write this book.

I received *Pittsburgh Sports: Stories From the Steel City* as a holiday gift one year. I was captivated by its stories by area writers and former athletes that reflected the hard-scrabble nature of Pittsburgh in the steel era. It was, as *Pittsburgh Sports* editor Randy Roberts intimated in the introduction, about so much more than sports.

At some point in my adolescence, I had the thought that it would be a thrilling endeavor to write a similar book about Erie. When I was 17, I set myself to the task, and even interviewed Erie boxing great Lou Bizzarro for a story. However, that was the year I decided to join the McDowell football team, so I put the idea on the shelf. After football came college, the aforementioned gig at the *Times-News*, a career and a plethora of other responsibilities that come with adulthood.

But, nearly a year after I returned to Erie, I realized there was nothing stopping me from making my dream a reality. I had the time. I'd hoped I had the resources. I still kept in contact with some of the people from my days as a sports fan and writer in Erie, but nearly seven years had passed and I'd lost touch with others. I'm blessed to say this experience allowed me not only to reconnect with friends, colleagues and coaches of years' past, but it also reminded me of the sense of community that makes Erie remarkable and reinstilled some of the values I learned while growing up here.

While I wrote roughly a third of this book, there are many amazing Erie sports figures who lent their talents to its creation. Their accomplishments far outweigh my own, and I am grateful to them for making Erie sports history come alive in these pages.

The stories of this book stand on their own in order to allow the reader to pick up the book and start at any point. However, the order is intentional. In particular, "Fred's Hill" and "Every Point Counts" comprise a two-part tale bound by blood ties, while "Boro Built" continues the tale of an outstanding athlete from "The Little Things." I believe the book is strongest when read from cover to cover.

There are many stories which highlight the diversity of life and sports in Erie. However, some of the essays — specifically those about high school state champions — intentionally underscore the commonalities in values that lead to ultimate victory.

Because of the human-interest nature of these stories, one doesn't have to be from Erie or even be the biggest sports fan to enjoy this book. But, it sure helps! For Erie residents, you'll be treated to reading about your neighbors, classmates, friends and family members. There are even a few global legends that make appearances, which shows just how vital Erie is to the sports world.

This book is very personal to me, and fittingly many of my friends and even some family are included in one way or another. Yet, I contend that each and every person written about deserves to be in this book on their own merit.

To be sure, this is not an all-encompassing anthology of Erie sports. Anyone who knows Erie knows that would be impossible. I did my best to hit a lot of high notes and included stories spanning gender, competition level and location within Erie County. And yet, there are volumes' worth of fascinating stories to be told.

Among them are the state-title-winning boys and girls basketball teams of Girard High School; the life and careers of professional athletes such as Essie Hollis (basketball) and Andy Lorei (soccer); the triumphs of East basketball star and Strong Vincent coaching legend Shannon Pullium; the rise of McDowell track and field superstar Sheena Gordon; Erie's rich bowling tradition, including the Professional Bowlers Association career of Bob Learn Jr.; the World Series heroics of Tom Lawless, who played at Strong Vincent and Penn State Behrend before enjoying a career in Major League Baseball; and the wrestling excellence of the Carr family, including Olympians Jimmy and Nate Carr.

I could go on and on. In fact, the list of deserving athletes, teams and organizations is so extensive that even offering up names here is insufficient.

Also, because this book features first-person essays and relies heavily on interviews for its third-person narratives, the stories here are all from post-World War II Erie, and the majority are set within the last 30 years.

Yet, I'd like to believe that, whether tangibly written about or not, Erie's legends are included in this book in spirit. It's that spirit — that passionate, powerful and ultimately positive spirit — that remains the defining principle of Erie.

No matter what happens in the coming decades, as long as that spirit is present on the playing fields of this area, Erie will continue to be an outstanding place to live.

Aaron McKrell, January 4, 2021

Photo provided by the Jones family

Former East High School basketball star Matt Jones (right) poses for a photo with NBA legend Magic Johnson. Jones led the Warriors to District 10 championships as both a player, in 2000, and a coach, in 2010.

Sitting atop the Universe

By Aaron McKrell

You never know you're in the happiest times of your life when they're happening. It's only when you look back, years later, that you can recall the rush of joy you felt during a certain experience and realize, "Wow, I don't think my life has ever been better than it was in that time."

For me, that time was spent in the heat of the hallowed Hammermill Center on Friday nights, and in the legendary Erie Veterans Memorial Stadium on mercilessly cold Saturday afternoons.

As a sports medicine physician for Saint Vincent Hospital, my dad covered the football and basketball teams of the predominantly African American East High School. This meant he was away on Friday nights and some Saturdays. Ever the family man, my dad brought along my brother, Dan, and me. My brother is four years older than I am, but we were pretty close as we bonded over our love of sports. No matter what we bickered about at home, I can't recall a single argument that was had at one of those games.

Yes, those were happy times. But more than anything, they were influential times. Though I didn't realize it at the time, I soaked up lessons about class and race that shaped me into the person I am today. It's these experiences, even more than the joy I felt, that made sitting on those cold stadium seats and hard wooden benches worth it.

I grew up just minutes from the city, in Millcreek Township. My family of five lived in an affluent neighborhood called Westbury Farms. It was not unusual to drive by and see sprinklers watering perfectly manicured lawns or children riding their bikes up and down the street. It was the picture of American suburbia.

My siblings and I wanted for nothing. There was always food in the fridge and name-brand clothes on our backs. We never had to worry about going without heat, water or electricity. However, my parents took measures to ensure that we wouldn't be entitled or spoiled.

My dad comes from a rural background where hard work was a way of life. My mother comes from a family of working-class Italian Americans, where she learned the value of stretching a dollar out of necessity. We also were raised in a Christian home, and were taught the values of kindness and generosity.

I was never handed money. I did chores each week and earned an allowance of $4.50. If my chores were not done well enough, I was not given the allowance. And yet, I must admit, the creature comforts I enjoyed still affected me. I expected a certain number of Christmas gifts to be under the tree each year. I took family vacations to the Atlantic Ocean for granted. I remember once asking my dad the financial status of our family, and he became stern with me. I don't think he wanted me to get it into my head that having money made you better.

Growing up in suburbia is a luxury. However, without exposure to the rest of the world, living in privilege can lead to classism. More than that, if your only exposure to different cultures is the stereotypes you see on TV, you may develop racial prejudices.

That's why my experiences at East High games were so vital. The people I met there — both Black and white, of various creeds, backgrounds and socioeconomic statuses — opened my eyes to a world beyond white-picket fences.

I started off my East fandom with a bang. At six years old, I was all set to go to my first game. I asked my dad which team I should cheer for.

"Aaron, you gotta root for East," he told me.

That's it. I was hooked. An East High fan for life. I still have an East hoodie, polo and football jersey hanging in my closet. The merger of the three city schools into Erie High School happened in 2017, but East is alive in my mind, heart and soul.

I was just a little kid, and my brother couldn't make it to the game for some reason. So, with my dad on the sidelines, my brother's friend Pete Krzak came along to keep an eye on me. I generally made a ruckus, running up and down the aisles playing drums on the seats while Pete laughed. East was playing Mercyhurst Prep, which held the lead and wasn't exactly being sportsmanlike. Partway through the game, a brawl ensued. Like full-on, bench-clearing, helmets-off, fists-thrown brawl. I'd never seen anything like it. I think my dad had to explain to me afterward that this wasn't how high school football games usually went.

That didn't keep me from coming back, though. Week after week — while my classmates were at Gus Anderson Field watching the McDowell Trojans play — I was rooting for East at Erie Veterans Memorial Stadium. I still vividly recall that beautiful, bowl-shaped coliseum, and the paint peeling from the murals of Erie football legends on the walls.

East had some standouts, namely David Dickerson, a running back, Hardin Moss, a tight end, and Andre Dawson, who ran the ball and played in the secondary. And yet, they didn't have much success in my youth. That, too, was a lesson for me. You show up and play the game, or in my case, to root for your team, even if you're arriving for what is almost assuredly a losing battle. You show up, because you just can't quit. You forge ahead, hoping for and trying to make better days. That lesson has been important for me as I've faced life's adversities throughout adolescence and adulthood.

No matter how tough things got, I never quit on my Warriors. I'm loyal. And what can I say? I have a thing for the underdog.

East's basketball team, however, was another matter. They were good. Real good. My dad didn't do as much for the basketball team as he did for the football team, but we went to the games to watch for pure enjoyment. In 1999, Millcreek was abuzz for the McDowell boys basketball team, led by the outstanding Justin Shouse. The Trojans pulled off a thrilling victory over New Castle High School to make it to the state title game. My second-grade classmates were ecstatic, and my teacher Mrs. Loomis, a McDowell grad, was overjoyed.

And yet, I was quick to remind anyone who would listen that East was good, too. While my classmates wanted to be Michael Jordan and Scottie Pippen, I was in the boiler room of my basement, pretending to be East forward Kyle McGinnis on my Little Tikes hoop. McGinnis was long and athletic, and might as well have been a Titan from Greek mythology in my eyes.

East made it to the semifinals of the PIAA District 10 Class AAA Playoffs that year to face General McLane. It was a close game. East was down by four with one possession left. Jabbar Jamison, a junior guard, released one of the purest shots I've ever seen from behind the three-point arc. It sailed into the hoop, nothing but net. And yet, he was not fouled, so the Warriors lost by one. It was heartbreaking. My dad took me for dessert afterward, which was a ritual of ours. There's nothing like an ice cream sundae to soften the sting of defeat.

The next year was the Warriors' year. They were coached by the excellent Bill Gausman, who was hard-nosed but fair. Their lineup was solid across the board. Jamison ran the point, while Marc Jones was the shooting guard and his older brother, Matt, was the small forward. McGinnis reprised his role as the power forward, and freshman "Big Mike" Johnson, who was about 6-foot-5, occupied the middle. I loved Big Mike. He was always kind to me. I remember shaking his hand, which was more like my little hand disappearing into his giant one. The Warriors were thrilling to watch. They combined athleticism and a free-flowing style of play with acute attention to detail and the fundamentals. It was basketball the way it's supposed to be played. They all had game, but Matt Jones was the star. He was 5-10, but the guy could dunk like he was 6-6. I've never seen a rocket launch, but watching him rise to the rim was my version of Cape Canaveral. Midway through the season, East played Cathedral Prep and won, 65-54. This was huge, as Prep usually had its pick of city players and often beat the Warriors. I sat at the scorer's table with East's athletic trainer, known to many as "Miss Lynn." A wonderful, passionate lady with a huge heart, Miss Lynn was overflowing with excitement as she watched the Warriors oust the Ramblers. She shook me with glee as East pulled off spectacular play after spectacular play.

At one point during a fast break, Matt Jones jetted down court. McGinnis stopped at half court and lobbed an improbable alley-oop. Jones arose with perfect timing and slammed it home with authority. The way the place shook from the crowd's reaction, you'd have thought the fault lines cracked under the arena.

I loved the Hammermill Center. It was like a cathedral, which I suppose is appropriate because it's the arena for a Catholic university. It had an if-these-walls-could-talk classicism to it. When I sat at the highest row, looking down at it all with a cup of fruit-flavored Tootsie Rolls in my hand, I felt as though I was sitting atop the universe.

As the regular season ended, we left the comfort of the Hammermill and ventured into uncharted territory. East traveled to play Corry in the first round of the District 10 playoffs, and used a third-quarter spurt to win, 62-54.

Next, the Warriors played Sharon at Meadville High School, where I screamed myself hoarse as they edged the Tigers, 54-51 in overtime. On one play, someone took a shot and the ball bounced high off the left side of the rim. Matt Jones rose into the air, caught it with one hand, and jammed it back into the hoop in earth-shattering fashion. He injured his ankle on the way down, and my dad had to check on him. He was fine, and all set to go for when East played Franklin for the PIAA District 10 Class AAA Championship.

My dad, brother and I traveled to Edinboro University's McComb Fieldhouse, which, for a nine-year-old kid from Millcreek, might as well have been going to a different state. I don't remember much about that game, except that East won, 56-50, and that my brother and I were elated. Our men had done it. They were champions.

The Warriors made it to the second round of the state playoffs before falling to Montour, but it was still a great run.

As I got older, I started going to more McDowell games and less East games. It was a social thing. I played football for McDowell in my senior year under the formidable coach Mark Soboleski. I loved my high school football experience, and I enjoyed my team immensely. I was far from the most talented player, but I worked hard and got playing time in half of our regular season games once we had comfortable leads.

My most cherished moment of that season came at the end of McDowell's 43-23 victory over Cathedral Prep on opening week. Our wide receivers coach, Brad Whitman, made sure I saw time on the field. On the last play of the game, I finally got to play a down at Veterans Memorial Stadium. After all those years in the stands and on the sidelines, it remains one of the most thrilling and satisfying moments of my life.

And yet, I never forgot the Warriors. They still hold a special place in my heart. When I look back on those years, I'm struck by what made the difference for me. I said "hello" to the players and interacted with the fans. There were a few rowdy fans, as you'll have anywhere. Mostly, though, everyone was friendly. Part of that may have been because I was Dr. McKrell's son. Everyone loved my dad, because he is a man of upstanding integrity, kindness and respect. Though, I also think that's just how people on the east side are.

The guys on East's basketball team comported themselves with the utmost dignity. I don't ever remember them complaining to an official or jawing at another player. They were role models to me, guys I could respect, look up to and imitate on my Little Tikes hoop. Matt Jones, who comes from a large, Christian family, was my hero, and I am blessed today to call him my friend.

I had a college professor who said the only way to eliminate — or at least minimize — racism is to push for integration at a young age. I don't mean to say that this exposure kept me from having moments of racial insensitivity. If we're being honest with ourselves, I think we all have.

I also don't mean to say that these experiences turned me into an all-knowing man in regard to matters of race. I know that, as a white male, I am afforded many privileges that people of color are not. I will never know what it's like to live a day as a Black man or woman in America.

Still, I feel blessed to have been able to go across town and share a common joy of sports with people from different backgrounds. This exposure prevented any misconceptions I may have developed had I stayed in my safe little room in Westbury Farms.

The influence didn't stop there. These experiences led me to embrace

NBA legend Allen Iverson at a time when so many didn't attempt to understand him and decried him for his image and fashion choices. In turn, my love for "The Answer" developed into a life as a diehard Philadelphia 76ers fan. (I do not hold anyone at East responsible for the unspeakable suffering I've endured while rooting for my beloved Sixers.)

Those times at Vets and the Hammermill enabled me to understand people from all walks of life and influenced close friendships I maintain today. They also impacted my musical preferences, leading to a love affair with Hip Hop that continues to this day and led to nearly a decade as a rap journalist.

When I graduated from college and moved away from Erie in 2013, these experiences stayed with me. They enabled me to relate well to the African American athletes and coaches I met and wrote about as a sportswriter for *The News-Dispatch* in the charming, diverse town of Michigan City, Indiana. And they carry a lasting influence on which societal issues matter to me, who I vote for and the way I will raise my own children someday.

There are, of course, many factors that go into making a person who they are. It would be a stretch to attribute all these life events and values to my East High fandom. But I am confident that's where it all started, and I have my father and the Warriors to thank for it.

When I think about both my dad's and East High's influence on my life, one memory in particular sticks out to me. My dad and I were in the car on our way to East, where he would perform physicals on student-athletes. On the way there, we passed some houses in need of repair. My dad gently explained to me that the people who lived in those houses were just like us. The only difference was that they didn't have as much money. It may seem like a condescending thing to say, but my dad was truly imparting a valuable lesson to his son. The content of your character is what matters most. I learned that watching East High on hot Friday nights and cold Saturday afternoons in Erie.

Photo by Mike Gallagher (provided by Keith Nies)

Cathedral Prep basketball standout Keith Nies (left) meets Los Angeles Lakers legend Kobe Bryant at the Cleveland Cavaliers' Quicken Loans Arena in 2014. Nies and the Ramblers faced off against Bryant and Lower Merion High School in the 1996 PIAA Class AAA boys basketball state championship game.

Mamba and Me

By Keith Nies

Keith Nies was a four-year letter winner and varsity basketball player at Cathedral Preparatory School. He was a three-year starter and three-time state finalist, playing on the 1993 Ramblers team that captured the state championship. He was a three-time All-Metro League selection and was part of more wins than any other player in school history, with 96. He went on to letter four more times as a player at Mercyhurst College (now Mercyhurst University) and became Fairview High School's winningest basketball coach in school history (238 wins). He is the director of special education for the Fairview School District. His wife, Jayme, is a teacher in the Fort LeBoeuf School District. Together, they have two daughters, Ava and Ivy.

Heroes come and go, but legends are forever.
In the minds of many, crossing paths with a legend is both unfathomable and unattainable. It's a wonderful fantasy, but a fantasy it often remains.
In 1996, I was one of the fortunate few who stood sneaker to sneaker with an icon. Let me take you back to a time in which a dream for many became a reality for me.
I was a starting guard on the Cathedral Prep basketball team, which enjoyed tremendous success in my time there. By my senior year, we had been to the PIAA state championship twice and took home the trophy in 1993. By March 1996, we had found ourselves once again in the PIAA Class AAAA western final.
For the fifth time that season, we faced crosstown rival McDowell. We had split our two Metro League regular season games with the Trojans before beating them in a tiebreaker for the Metro crown. McDowell paid us back in the District 10 title game, though we both advanced to the state playoffs.
The western final was as closely contested as every other game against McDowell that season. We traded leads of two, three and four points with the Trojans throughout. We held a one-point lead with 10

seconds remaining when the Trojans inbounded the ball. McDowell's Jake Delsandro had the ball on the wing and was driving to the foul line when I came up for help defense and stripped the ball from him. I was fouled and made both free throws to give us a 47-44 lead with a few seconds remaining.

The Cathedral Prep faithful were on the edge of their seats. McDowell fired a shot from half court that bounced off the front of the rim as time expired. As the crowd erupted and Hershey Kisses filled the arena, my teammates stormed the court to begin the long-awaited celebration of becoming the kings of the west. As we hugged, high-fived and cried tears of joy, we quickly realized how close we were to our dream of becoming state champs.

Like a stiff winter wind coming off Lake Erie, the attention of our team soon shifted in the direction of our next task at hand. We sat restlessly on locker room benches as our talented and energetic coach, Marcel Arribi, addressed the team. One question weighed on the mind of every individual in the room: *Who's next?*

Prior to our matchup with McDowell, we knew there was the possibility of getting a chance to compete and showcase our talents against one of the premier high school basketball players in the nation: Mr. Kobe Bryant.

It's not as though we were scared. When it came to our squad, there wasn't a team or player we ever feared. We never backed down from facing the best competition, and we spent countless hours in the gym to be prepared for any challenge that would arise. Throughout our careers, we competed against future NBA players Ron Artest, Tim Thomas, Shammgod Wells and Melvin Levitt, to name a few. So, when we learned that we'd be facing 6-foot-6 Kobe Bryant and his 31-3 Lower Merion team, we were more than eager to rise to the occasion.

The same night we defeated McDowell, the Aces of Lower Merion ousted Chester High in the PIAA Class AAAA eastern final. The Aces' win set up Kobe's shot to end his career in style by capturing the gold medal that had eluded him for three years.

The game-day headline in the *Erie Times-News* read, "Ramblers play Aces for PIAA jackpot." It was aptly titled. Capturing the state gold would be the epitome of our high school basketball careers. All the years of blood, sweat and tears would come down to one defining moment on a Saturday night in Hershey, Pennsylvania.

To make the most of that moment, we had to maintain focus amidst the buzz surrounding the game. We were still on the ultimate high of beating McDowell, but we had to quickly shift from jubilation to preparation.

First and foremost, our focus was on stopping Kobe. A McDonald's All-American, Kobe was ultra-athletic and had scored nearly 2,900 points in his career. His per-game stats were out of this world: He averaged 30.8 points, 12 rebounds, 6.5 assists, four steals and 3.8 blocks per game as a senior.

After viewing Kobe's 39-point performance in the eastern final on film, Cathedral Prep assistant coach Wes Alexander lavished praise on him to the *Times-News*.

"He's the real thing," Alexander told the newspaper. "Every inch of him is legitimate. The kid has no weaknesses. He can run the floor, bring the ball up, shoot, rebound, go after the ball, the whole package."

In an interview with a local TV station, coach Arribi compared Kobe to Michael Jordan on the high school level. He did, however, point out that every player has their weaknesses.

While watching Kobe on film, I noticed how well he could score both inside the paint and from beyond. If you were smaller, he'd use his height advantage down low, and if you were slower, he'd take you to the outside.

Beating Kobe would mean beating the guy who earned player of the year honors from *USA Today*, *Parade*, *Gatorade* and the *Atlanta Tipoff Club*. But that wasn't all. Surrounding Kobe was a host of athletic and talented players that made the matchup with the Aces seem like a daunting task. However, we'd been in similar situations before. Known for our great man-to-man defense, unselfish play and fundamental basketball, the Prep teams of the '90s found success against some of the best teams in the country.

Fear was not a factor. Indeed, I remember stating, "I don't think myself or my teammates are going into this game being scared or tentative because we're playing against an All-American. That kind of picks up the intensity for us. He's a great player and we're going to have to do some things to stop him. Basically, we're going to have to do what got us there."

Not only had we prepared for a lifetime to play in a game of this magnitude, we also expected to be there. A four-year member of the Ramblers, I already had been to the state final twice. My teammates and I were confident and thought we had the weapons to beat a team as good as Lower Merion.

Hungry, gritty and glowing with confidence, our 1996 Ramblers team featured six future college basketball players, including a future LaSalle University point guard in sophomore Julian Blanks. We also benefited from seniors Brian Szewczykowski, who led the team with

12.3 points per game, and John Trocki (10 points per game). They both were deadly from behind the arc and gave opposing teams fits. I averaged 11 points per game and brought considerable experience with well over 100 high school games played. Bob Vahey, Mike McMahon and Doug Lecker rounded out our strong, tight-knit senior group.

Combined with a bench that featured future college players RJ Fiorelli and Graham Witherspoon, my teammates and I believed in each other and were ready for any challenge that came our way.

Still, everyone kept asking us the same question: "How are you going to beat Lower Merion when they have Kobe Bryant?"

For two years, our undersized teams of average athleticism had utilized a matchup zone defense against elite competition to great effect. Our game plan was to use this defense to try to take Kobe out of the game as much as possible. We aimed to limit his touches and slow him down as much as we could. If Kobe was going to beat us, he was going to have to earn every point he scored. Wherever he was on the court, we were going to try to surround him with two players — one in front and one in back — at all times. Our coaching staff knew Kobe could take over and control the game at any point in time. In their minds, if we had any chance to win, it had to be by forcing his teammates to beat us. We also were to rely on our skill, shooting abilities and togetherness to claim victory.

For many, March 23, 1996, is etched in history as Kobe Bryant's final high school basketball game before heading to the NBA. However, for our team, that night in Chocolate Town serves as a lifetime memory of friendships, teammates, competition, the agony of defeat and the opportunity to compete against a future Naismith Memorial Basketball Hall of Famer.

A sellout crowd of 8,242 fans watched as our Ramblers jumped out to a hot start and held Kobe scoreless in the first quarter. We frustrated him, and he complained about the slippery texture of the ball.

Things didn't stay that way for long.

Kobe's high-powered athleticism and smoothness came to light in the second quarter. With a balance of gracefulness and pure intensity, Bryant went on an eight-point spurt that kept the Aces in the game. In true Mamba fashion, he combined extraordinary skill with intense competitiveness to reveal his unparalleled basketball prowess.

Though the way we defended him limited his outside game, he still excelled on fast breaks and in the paint. He slammed home a put-back dunk and threw down an open-court jam. He also dribbled the ball between his legs and behind his back before whipping a

flawless, no-look pass in traffic to a teammate in the open court.
Still ahead, 21-15 at the half, we were inspired and confident that we were just 16 minutes away from capturing the gold.

Kobe and the Aces thought differently.

Spurred on by jaw-dropping, open-court plays by the young Mamba, Lower Merion ripped off the first 11 points of the third quarter. The game's pace had intensified, and we fell behind for the first time all game.

We didn't fold, though. Trailing 37-31 after three quarters, our squad battled and clawed back to tie the score three times in the final frame. With the score tied at 39, Kobe picked up his fourth foul on a charge call with 3:53 remaining. Both teams had a chance to regroup during a media timeout. Coming out of the timeout we regained the lead with a lob inside to Trocki, who laid it in to make the score 41-39.

That was the last lead we held.

Lower Merion tied the score at 41, and a fifth foul on Szewczykowski led to two made freebies from the charity stripe that gave the Aces a lead they did not relinquish.

They led 45-41 before I sank two free throws to cut their lead to two. After a Lower Merion miss, we took a timeout to gather ourselves. Tension filled the arena with 1:11 left on the clock. As we broke from the timeout, the Rambler faithful were on their feet in anticipation of a dramatic finish. A missed shot and a secured offensive rebound gave us a second chance. However, after passing the ball around for 20 seconds, we missed a shot from about 12 feet out. The miss gave way to a Kobe-led fast break capped off by a no-look pass and a layup.

The Aces led 47-43 with 18 seconds left. After a key turnover, Kobe was fouled and — in what would be his final shots in a high school uniform — made one of two free throws to seal the 48-43 win for Lower Merion.

Kobe finished with 17 points, about 13 less than his per-game average. Not bad for a group of kids from a town in the snowbelt.

As the final horn sounded, I witnessed Kobe run around the arena, celebrating having won the state crown and his final hour as a high school basketball player. My teammates and I walked off the court as one, disappointed and saddened.

Twenty-five years later, the memory of Cathedral Prep competing against the legendary Kobe Bryant is one that is forever etched in Erie basketball history. As many of my teammates and I have gone on to successful careers of our own, we all have witnessed the fascinating Hall of Fame career of the talent with whom we once shared the same court. When I look back on that moment, I am filled with gratitude. For many of us, competing against Kobe in 1996 was the pinnacle of our sports career.

People often ask me what it was like playing against Kobe Bryant. I simply say, "Competing against Kobe was special and something that will forever be remembered."

On that day in 1996, who could have known what Kobe would become? I couldn't have foreseen that the tall, lanky kid I was guarding would become an icon, and be known around the world as "Black Mamba," or mononymously "Kobe."

In 2014, it was my privilege to reunite with Kobe during his NBA farewell tour when he came to the Quicken Loans Arena to face the Cleveland Cavaliers. It was a night I will never forget.

Kobe, looking as fly as he always did in a black suit, was in a small media room during a pregame press conference. I sat patiently tucked in the corner of the room, completely in awe of the Black Mamba. During the conference, Kobe was asked if he remembered the 1996 state championship game. Indeed, he did. As he recalled the game in detail, Erie media veteran Mike Gallagher directed his attention to me. Kobe nodded.

"Oh yeah, I remember you," he said to me.

That would have been a once-in-a-lifetime moment for any sports fan. It took on a deeper meaning to me for the time we spent on the court together.

Shortly after the game, Kobe and I had a chance to meet one last time and share a moment together. It was a moment that was both surreal and genuine, and was, above all, special. Gallagher gave Kobe a Cathedral Prep shirt for his trophy case. Then, Kobe shook my hand and we chatted about the state title game.

"I thought we had you guys," I told him.

"It was a good game," he said. "You did have us there, and we happened to pull through."

I told him how I had followed his career through the years, and that I admired not only how great he had become, but how much passion and hard work he had put into his craft.

He thanked me and departed shortly after. He was wearing yellow sneakers that were tied around his neck, and he was on his way to meet LeBron James. I later found out that he signed and gave those sneakers to LeBron.

In our short meeting together, I found Kobe to be authentic, original, charismatic and true to the moment. In a time when Kobe would have been being pulled in a million directions, he took the time to chat with an old high school competitor. That speaks volumes about who he was as a person.

Chatting with Kobe brought back so many memories of that 1996 season. Yet, in order to know how I really felt that night, it is important to understand what Kobe meant to me throughout his NBA career. As I went on to enjoy a 15-year career as a high school basketball coach, the Mamba was someone I referenced often to my players, not because of his talent but because of his work ethic. Kobe became a Hall of Famer and a five-time NBA champion because of his will to win, strong work ethic and intense personality. It is for those reasons he was so admired.

On January 26, 2020, Kobe, his daughter Gianna, and seven others died in a helicopter crash in Calabasas, California. When I first heard about it, I didn't believe it. I was in shock. My phone started blowing up with text messages and incoming calls. Person after person told me Kobe had passed. I searched the internet to confirm what I was being told. Once I found out it was true, I felt empty. He wasn't a family member or someone I loved, but I competed against him, so I had a relationship with him that many didn't. I felt like there was a piece of me that was gone. Yet, I also felt fortunate and honored that I got to play against him, especially in his high school finale.

As a husband and father myself, I felt for his family. And I knew the sports world had lost an icon. Kobe was just 41 years old when he died, and he had so much more to give to the world. Specifically, I think he was going to do great things for women's basketball because he was involved in the burgeoning career of his daughter, Gianna. His charisma, professionalism and willingness to help younger athletes will be missed in the coming years.

Those years will go by, and I will grow older. One day, I will tell my grandchildren about what it was like to play against Kobe Bryant. I will tell them about how a group of teenagers from Erie, Pennsylvania, faced off against one of the greatest basketball players who ever lived.

To this day, when I see him on television and in highlight clips, I am reminded of his legendary status. The thing about legends is they don't really ever die. Kobe lives on as his "Mamba Mentality" has been adopted as a mindset by tenacious athletes around the world. And "Black Mamba," or "Mamba" for short, is a nickname that will echo throughout gyms across the country for generations to come.

As for me, I will always remember him as my competitor Kobe.

Photo provided by Sonya Whitman

Villa Maria Academy swim coach Sonya Whitman (above) trains for her swim across Lake Erie in 2007. Whitman swam the Great Lake in a then women's record of 14 hours, nine minutes.

Swim, Sonya, Swim

By Sonya Whitman

Sonya Whitman, a native of Bradford, Pa., swam and played water polo at Gannon University, where she graduated in 2004 with degrees in both advertising communications and business administration. She earned her master's degree in public relations at Syracuse University in 2005. In addition to coaching swimming at Villa Maria Elementary and for the Fairview Fins Swim Club, Whitman founded and coached Fairview High School's girls water polo team. She is currently the head swim coach at Villa Maria Academy, and led the program to PIAA State Championship victories in 2019 and 2021. She and her husband Brad have two children — Jack and Brooke — and live in Erie, where she is the practice manager at Hertel & Brown Physical Therapy.

"What made you *want* to swim across Lake Erie?"
I've been asked that question countless times, and although I'm frequently tempted to come up with some deep, meaningful explanation, the answer has always been, "Because I could."
Every time I say it out loud, it sounds so selfish to me. As it turns out, my dream of swimming across Lake Erie was in no way something I did just for myself.
I have swum competitively since I was eight years old. I was a three-sport athlete in high school and a dual athlete at Gannon University. I broke swimming records, was named an Academic All-American in water polo and earned a master's degree from Syracuse University, which is one of the most prestigious communications schools in the country. After graduating, I began competing in triathlons and even won some of those races.
Blessings were abundant in all aspects of my life. I had a fantastic job in Saint Vincent Hospital's marketing department with coworkers who became my second family, and I was in a happy relationship with my now husband Brad. However, something was missing.
Part of me was drawn to a bigger challenge waiting for me out there. Something not just great, but historic. It's not that I wasn't proud of my accomplishments or that I felt they weren't good enough; I just don't

know how to settle.

I love competing and I hate losing. Competition drives me. The idea of winning a race and that profound satisfaction of earning a victory or a personal-best time because I worked for it is what feeds my soul and fills my cup.

I grew up with older brothers who were amazing athletes. They were my heroes, and I credit them with forming my competitive spirit. I remember the newspaper clippings my mom kept in scrapbooks featuring their names in the headlines. Most importantly, I saw how people admired them largely for their unparalleled work ethic and unwavering belief that they could achieve anything they set their mind to.

I wanted that for me, too. So, from the time I was very little, I was determined to keep my mom busy making a scrapbook full of my achievements. It's safe to say I made my family proud, but I was still looking for something extraordinary.

I was going to swim across Lake Erie.

Yet, I wasn't just going to do this thing that only a handful of people had done. I was going to be the fastest woman to ever do it.

Enter project 'Swim, Sonya, Swim.'

The record time to beat was 15 hours, two minutes, set by Sara McClure in 2005. Training began in October 2006 with 5 a.m. swims in the pool at Nautilus Fitness Center. Soon after, I added a second pool session after work. As soon as it was bearable, I swam in the open water of Lake Erie with a wetsuit on. As water temperatures increased, I dropped the wetsuit and the swims got longer.

Learning how to transition from slicing my strokes through a calm pool to maneuvering my body through waves which were pounding me in the face was quite a challenge, both mentally and physically. My longest training swim was from Beach 10 to Walnut Creek Access, which was more than 10 miles. The elite group of Lake Erie crossers say that if you can endure that swim, you're ready.

My thought after that practice?

Bring it.

After months of preparation, our first attempt to cross Lake Erie was on Saturday, August 4, 2007. Mark Farrell, my uncle, was generous enough to bring his boat up to Erie to be our captain, and we motored out of Lampe Marina toward Long Point, Ontario, in the wee hours of the morning. Brad and I were accompanied by one of my coworkers, Stacy Knapp, and one of my best friends and teammates from Gannon, Jamie Heynes. These two ladies would rotate with Brad as kayakers who were to guide my path. Also, in addition to my uncle, a

camera man from WJET and Dr. Laura McIntosh were on board.
My adrenaline was pumping. My heart was pounding. I could not wait
to start this journey. We were halfway across the lake in the boat, and
we all were soaked and partially seasick because of how rough the
water was. I saw everyone on board start to look at each other like,
"Who's going to be the one to tell her?"

When Brad sat down next to me and put his arm around me, I hung
my head and bawled uncontrollably before he even spoke a word. I
knew that day wasn't going to be the day.

Take two: Monday, August 6. We waited until it was light out before we
ventured across the lake in my uncle's boat. Jamie had to work, so
another Gannon teammate and best friend of mine, Tara Skasik
Quinn, took her place. It was a much smoother ride to Long Point this
time, and when that Canadian peninsula appeared, the butterflies in
my stomach multiplied. It was really happening. I stripped down to my
suit, waved goodbye to the crew and kissed Brad for good luck before
I dove in.

I did a brief warmup swim from the boat to land before the official
start. I stood up out of the water, pressed play on my underwater MP3
player and started my watch to record my time. I waded back into the
water as "The Final Countdown" by Europe blasted through my
headphones. Around 8 a.m., I dove in headfirst with Brad and Stacy
kayaking on either side of me.

Truth be told, I don't remember a whole lot of details about the first
half of the swim. It flew by and I felt unstoppable. About once an hour,
I took a quick nutrition break. With the help of Dr. McIntosh, I followed
a nutrition plan created by registered dietician and friend Sandra
Luthringer. I would drink a Boost shake, eat a banana or a Clif bar, top
it off with some salt tablets or Clif Shot Bloks and get a drink of water.
During my stops, I would tread — I didn't get in the boat or even hang
on to a kayak.

I'd touch base with my kayakers to check my speed and see how far
we had traveled. Sometimes, I would have to switch out my goggles
for a different pair loaded with another MP3 player full of new songs.
My coworkers, the coordinators of every detail of this day, had put
together a surprise playlist for me. Songs such as "My Wish" (Rascal
Flatts), "Unwritten" (Natasha Bedingfield) and "Lose Yourself"
(Eminem) empowered me as I sliced my way across Lake Erie, one
stroke at a time. My friends also included motivational speeches to
keep me going. I saved this playlist for the middle of the lake and
listened to it until the battery died. It was such an awesome reminder
that I was far from being alone out there.

About halfway across the lake, nature showed its fierceness. Brad warned me that the lake would get rough in the middle of the day. I was prepared for that and pushed on through. He also said it would calm down. It did not. Two- and three-foot waves turned into five- and seven-foot waves. Dr. McIntosh had to add ibuprofen to my nutrition stops because of the persistent ache that was growing in my shoulder. She also had me apply Biofreeze on my shoulder, using a cloth so as not to get the substance on my hands or in my eyes when I wiped them.

I eventually got so used to the waves tossing me around that I didn't notice the giant freighters passing us by. At one of my stops, Brad pointed one of the 100-foot-long vessels out to me and said, "See that boat?" I noticed it was close but wasn't too excited about it. He casually mentioned that we came within about 20 yards of it, one of three that crossed our path that day.

The kayaker on my left was always the lead. They held the GPS and had the responsibility of keeping me swimming in a straight line. For most of the day, Brad was in that spot. After midday, I was pretty sick of watching him point to the west as there was a nasty wind working hard to push us off course to the east. For most of the second half of the swim, I felt like I was swimming the long way across the lake, toward Cleveland!

While I was on a routine stop during the one and only break Brad took from the kayak that day, I remember him hanging over the side of the boat, shouting out to check on me. I let him have it.

"You told me it was going to calm down after lunch!" I yelled. "This is bleep, you bleep liar! All I want is some bleeping blueberry pancakes!" I was not nice, but he just smiled and said, "You're doing fine. Keep it up!"

At that point, I wasn't going to give up. I was more than halfway across, so I put my face back in the water and prayed to God. I asked Him to carry me the rest of the way across the unfriendly lake that day. I asked Him for strength, patience and to occupy my mind so I wasn't thinking about how hard this was.

There are a few other scenes burned in my brain. Tara was in the lead kayaker position late in the afternoon, and I had my eye on her every fourth stroke. One, two, three, breathe…Tara, pointing to the west. One, two, three, Tara. One, two, three…no Tara. I popped my head up to see her treading in the water next to me! A big wave had tossed her right out of the kayak.

Sooner than we had hoped, darkness set in. There's dark, and then there's middle-of-Lake Erie dark. It's hard to describe, but it's a creepy, lonely place I'll never forget. Brad's headlamp was the only thing I could see. I remember feeling something soft and slimy slide over my shoulder. The next time I stopped, I started to ask Brad about it. He interrupted me: "It was a dead fish." Gross.

Finally, we saw light — the shore was within reach! We could see the huge floodlight from one of the local fire trucks and see the crowd on Freeport Beach. As we got closer, my uncle peeled off toward the marina so he and the rest of the crew could meet us on the beach. They left Brad and Tara guiding me the rest of the way, their headlamps the only lights we had.

Suddenly, the light on the beach disappeared. The firetruck was called away to an emergency. People on shore grabbed spotlights from their cars, while others knocked on the doors of houses close by to ask if they could borrow lights. Since the boat was long gone, Brad and Tara panicked slightly until there was enough of a glow to give them a guiding light.

I could see the proverbial light at the end of the tunnel, and I felt a burst of energy. We agreed I would skip my last nutrition stop since we were almost there, but Brad stopped me anyway. I was about to yell at him again, but he told me to listen.

I could hear, "Swim, Sonya, swim!" All of my friends and family waiting for us on the beach were chanting for me. It was a moment I'll never forget, and one that made it all worth it.

When we finally got to shore, the ground was so rocky that I was tripping all over. I was trying to check my watch for the finish time without cutting my foot or breaking an ankle. Brad hopped out of his kayak to help me. I jumped into his arms and he carried me out of the water. He was my rock all day, and the finish was no different.

We finished shortly after 10 p.m., in 14 hours and 9 minutes, a new women's record. My 86-year-old grandmother was one of the first to greet me — with a bouquet of roses — followed by my mom, my brothers, Brad's family and so many relatives and friends who had gathered to support us. The news cameras and microphones were shoved in my face, and I couldn't believe it was over. I was so relieved, so proud and so grateful for my family, my support team and my faith.

We took a quick trip to the hospital just to get checked out. While I replayed the day in my mind and praised God for this gift of accomplishment, someone stopped in to visit and asked if anyone had told me yet. Told me what? Come to find out, I swam a "little" extra. What was supposed to be 23.8 miles turned out to be about 26.5. The wind, waves and current had pushed us off the straight-line course, and the extra distance we covered was considerable.

So…satisfied? Yes. However, I vowed to take on the task again should anyone break my record in less than five years. Had I not experienced less-than-ideal conditions and a few extra miles, I might have thought that was the best I could do. There will always be a part of me that believes I could have done it faster.

Then, four years later, almost to the day, my record was broken. Melanie Reade Nickou set a new record in 2011 with a time of 13 hours, 35 minutes. At that point, I had accomplished many more amazing things in life that I was just as proud of. Brad and I were married and we had an amazing little boy. I decided that records are made to be broken, as I was far too busy with a new challenge.

I became the head coach of the Villa Maria Academy swim team in 2011, and I was as committed to bringing success to that program as I was to swimming across Lake Erie. I pushed the girls hard. I tried to help them understand that the things they were capable of were simply a matter of how strong they were mentally and how badly they really wanted it — lessons I learned firsthand in the middle of Lake Erie.

Throughout my life, I was incredibly blessed with coaches who brought out the best in me from high school through college in every sport in which I competed. I wanted nothing more than to share that same positive influence with these girls. I wanted them to feel the deepest satisfaction of achieving the extraordinary, the same way I feel in my soul every time I stand on Freeport Beach and look at Lake Erie.

In 2019, the Villa Maria Academy Victors won the program's first-ever Pennsylvania Interscholastic Athletic Association swimming state championship. (Another state title would be earned in 2021.)

In that moment, accepting that trophy, I knew my swim across Lake Erie had played a vital role in inspiring me to reach new heights.

In turn, my dreams became a reality not just for me, but for my family, my friends, Brad and our future children, and all the swimming Victors who I have coached along the way.

Photo provided by Stephon Fitzpatrick and courtesy of the Erie City School District

The 1978 Tech Memorial High School mile relay team: (from left) Stephon Fitzpatrick, Dwayne Blanchard, Amos Tate and Terry Williams. The foursome won the relay to spur the Centaurs to victory at the 1978 PIAA Class AAA track and field state championship meet.

Fred's Hill

By Aaron McKrell

It's funny how something so forgettable to one person can hold so much meaning to another.

Take the red brick hills in Erie's Glenwood Hills neighborhood, for instance. For some, driving up those slopes may be nothing more than a little extra pressure on the gas pedal.

But those hills — particularly the one on Glenside Avenue — symbolize a daunting, difficult, yet ultimately delightful journey to the alumni of the 1978 Technical Memorial High School boys track and field team.

They called it "Fred's Hill," because even though those slightly uneven red bricks were property of the City of Erie, there was no question as to whom they truly belonged.

Fred Trott, the legendary Tech Memorial track and field coach, lived near the long, steep hill. He had his athletes sprint up the hill on frigid spring afternoons in Erie, only to jog to the next street and down the adjacent hill before running over to Glenside Avenue for another uphill sprint.

The Centaurs built their legacy on that hill, brick by brick, on the road to becoming the first high school track and field team in the city to win a state championship.

In doing so, they cemented Trott's legacy as one of the greatest high school coaches of any sport in Erie County history and set a precedent that the next generation — including their own children — would continue.

At the time, though, these young athletes weren't thinking past the next race. It was the late 1970s, an era of newfound peacetime in America, booming industry in Erie and an unfortunate trend of leisure suits, bell-bottomed pants and platform shoes.

Hop in the Cutlass and cue up the Stevie Wonder. We're going back.

A Simpler Time

Tech Memorial track star Stephon Fitzpatrick knew the pain of two whoopings for the price of one screwup.

He said Erie's neighborhoods in the 1970s were so close-knit that parents of friends would act as authority figures if needed. If a kid did something wrong, they'd take heat from their friend's mother. By the time they got home, a phone call had already been placed to ensure a second round of discipline.

"Growing up, it didn't matter who your family was," Stephon said. "Everybody looked out for everybody's family in the neighborhood."

With just three TV stations being broadcast into their homes, Stephon and his friends spent most of their time outside on Erie's east side.

The same held true for Gary Ferch — a jumper on Tech Memorial's track and field team — on the west side. They rode bikes and played sandlot sports day after day with their same groups of friends.

"Anything we could find, we made fun (out) of it," Stephon said.

The relative peace may have been a result of Erie's stable economy. Jobs were aplenty, and General Electric, Kaiser Aluminum and AMSCO were staples of employment in Erie. Though layoffs weren't uncommon, there were so many manufacturers in Erie that most folks could land on their feet.

Still, not everybody was able to benefit. Terry Williams, another Tech track standout, was one of many who had to work to help his family make ends meet. He and Stephon bussed tables and washed dishes at Elby's Restaurant in the Millcreek Mall. The $80 Terry brought home at the end of the week went a long way in helping his family.

"It was rough times back then, but as long as you had friends and family everything worked out," Terry said.

He was known to his friends and family as "Nooney," a nickname his mother gave him when he was young. He's still not sure why.

"I tell everybody I was born at noon and I had a bad knee, but honestly I don't know," he said with a laugh.

Though one's memories are often prone to romanticization, by multiple accounts the '70s were a simpler time for Erieites.

"It was an absolutely wonderful time to grow up," Gary said. "I wouldn't change anything."

The Mathematician

As blue-collar industries boomed in the city by the lake, the seeds for track and field dominance had already begun to sprout in Erie County. While Class AAA high schools in Eastern Pennsylvania routinely captured state championships and Aliquippa High School ruled the roost in southwestern Pennsylvania, Erie County had had its own moments in the sun.

North East High School was the first school in Erie County to win a track and field state championship. Led by coach Bob Wall, and then coach Ted Miller, the Grapepickers' boys program won state titles from 1962-64. Academy High School also turned out stalwart programs and star athletes in the 1940s and '50s. One such athlete was Fred Trott.

Trott competed in football, wrestling and track and field at Academy and then Edinboro University before becoming a teacher and assistant coach in the City of Erie. He taught math while coaching future Pro Football Hall of Fame inductee Fred Biletnikoff and his brother, multi-sport superstar Bobby Biletnikoff, at Tech Memorial. He became Tech's head track coach in 1966, and by the time Gus Picardo signed on as Tech's athletic director in '69, Trott's track dynasty was well underway.

"(Trott) put his heart and soul into the program, and it showed," Picardo said.

Trott kicked off a streak of nine straight City Series titles that made Tech's track program a popular after-school option. Gary recalled there were more than 100 athletes on each of the boys and girls teams. The numbers didn't water down the competition either.

"If you didn't make the top three (in an event) and you were four, five or six, you were working your butt off to crack that top three," Gary said.

While North East remained a force and Tech always kept an eye on McDowell High School, the Centaurs emerged as the ones to beat at the starting blocks.

It all went back to Trott, who coached his teams with quiet intensity and extraordinary dedication. Melinda Holliday, who taught at Tech Memorial and later coached the girls track and field program opposite Trott, recalled his relentless pursuit of excellence. Even when it was snowing, Trott and Holliday were out on the field to lay down markings for upcoming meets.

Especially when Tech's opponent was North East.

"You knew that if you could succeed against Ted Miller, you were good," Holliday said.

The same standard Trott held himself to, he expected of his athletes. "His practices for track practice were by far the hardest practices I've ever had being an athlete," Gary said.

Trott didn't yell or swear at his athletes, but used a less-is-more tactic to motivate them. If one of them wasn't giving their all, he gave them a disappointed nod that spoke volumes:

I know you can do better than that.

They'd look him in the eye with a wordless response:

I think I need to step it up just a little bit more.

When they did, Trott would come up to them and say three words. "Proud of you."

It was more powerful than any obscenity-laced tirade ever could have been.

"You didn't want to let him down," Gary said.

The Grind

As serious as Trott could be, it was his values that made the difference. His wife, Marilou Trott, was at nearly every one of Tech's track and field meets and saw firsthand how he fostered an atmosphere of unity amongst his team.

Trott, a devoted Catholic who was a fixture at St. Luke Catholic Church every morning during Lent, took his cue from the One to whom he prayed.

"He respected everyone (on) his team (in) the way he wanted to be respected," Marilou Trott said.

Trott's humility was not lost on his athletes.

"He was one helluva guy," Stephon said. "He was the greatest, man."

Trott's approach inspired his athletes to compete not just for themselves or each other, but for him and his coaching staff.

Not that they needed much extra motivation. There was so much talent on Tech's teams in the '70s that it was a battle each day to keep a spot in the lineup.

"There weren't any easy days," Terry said. "We knew we had something from our work ethic, and we didn't want to lose."

The Centaurs were bolstered by a stable of strong coaches, including throw coaches Frank Kupniewski and Chuck Villa and distance coach John Esser. Trott coached the sprinters and jumpers.

Tech was solid across the events. Gary and his brother, Bill Ferch, were strong contributors in the jumping events, while David Haft excelled in throwing. But the Centaurs truly shined on the track, specifically in the marquee sprinting events.

Terry and Stephon were joined by Danny George, Amos Tate, Willie Jordan, Greg Riley and Ray Dickerson to create some of the best relay teams the state had to offer.

And then there was Dwayne.

In street clothes, Dwayne Blanchard didn't look like much of a track athlete. He stood 5-foot-3, and his upper body was unremarkable. And yet, his quads and hamstrings looked as though they were built for winning state championships.

"You would look at him and say, 'Well, he can't beat me,' because he was so short," Terry said. "But when he came out of (those) starting blocks and you (were) looking behind at him, that was it."

Dwayne was the fastest runner on the team, but he didn't coast on his speed. The son of Academy track legend Grove "Doc" Blanchard, he would work even harder under the tutelage of his father than he did with Trott. He was humble and led by example, lifting up those around him.

"He would try and pull you along," Gary said. "He never expected you to run a (9.5-second) 100-yard dash, but he expected you to put in the nine-five work."

(At the time, the race distances were measured by yards. The measurements were changed to meters in 1979).

Just as Dwayne expected a lot from his teammates, he was always there for them both on and off the track.

"He always had your back, no matter what," Stephon said.

They were a tight group. The comfort level they had with each other meant they never had a problem telling another to step it up. They took their cues from Terry, who was co-captain along with Dwayne. When they weren't up to par, Terry was there to push them harder.

"'Come on dude, you gotta do better than this,'" Stephon recalled Terry telling him. "'You gotta step it up.'"

"Don't worry about it, I got your back, Terry," Stephon would say. "I got ya."

Stephon, who was two years younger than Terry, kept on his captain's heels. He was right there, in his green Tech Memorial sweatshirt, determined to beat his leader in the 400 run.

"You ain't gonna beat me," Terry would tell him.

"I'mma get you one of these days," Stephon would shoot back.

But Terry reveled in his teammates' success. He was OK with a teammate beating him in a race if it meant they were getting better. And he always knew his own value on the track.

"Running track gave me a lot of pride, and it made me happy because it made you feel like you were worth something," Terry said. "And the more I felt good about myself by running track, the harder I worked out."

One Big Family

The Centaurs conducted practices like they were meets, holding themselves to stringent time limits. Trott, ever the mathematician, created what he dubbed "computer workouts" before computers were commonly used in society. He had timetables and measurements for precisely how far and how long they should run.

This included the cyclical runs up and down Fred's Hill. He'd sit at the very top, blow his whistle and his athletes would storm up the hill time and time again.

"How many more laps we got to go?" they'd ask Terry.

"Don't ask," Terry would reply. "Just wait 'til we get done because if you ask how many more, he's gonna make you do more."

No matter how hard it was, they always enjoyed the grind. And they always had a coach who was willing to give them a ride home after practice, invite them to dinner or let them stay the night at his house.

The Trotts had three kids of their own: Brett, Lance and Lori, who they nicknamed "Cricket." Brett attended Academy, Lance went to Cathedral Preparatory School and Cricket was at Mercyhurst Preparatory School. The boys competed in track and field and football, while Cricket had a stint in track before focusing on art and music.

All three got to know and love Trott's athletes and came to regard them as brothers.

"We were all just one big, happy family," Marilou Trott said.

The athletes felt the same way and viewed Trott as a father figure.

"He did everything that a parent would do for you," Terry said. "That's how good he was."

The fact that the Trotts were a Caucasian family and many of the athletes were African American had no bearing on their relationship. The same held true for the white and Black athletes who competed together on the team.

They were, as Stephon said, "like brothers."

Word Up!

There were a few visible differences, though. Trott was old school and favored button-down shirts and neckties. His athletes, however, dressed with the times. They'd leave their houses decked out in flowered shirts, bell-bottomed pants, knee-high socks and platform shoes. They wore their hair in Jheri curls, Afros or long and straight. And they carried themselves as animatedly as their fashion style suggested.

"We were all clowns, man," Gary said.

They were Pennsylvania kids who listened to the Ohio Players, disciplined students who got down to The Temptations and extraordinary athletes who dug the Average White Band.

The late '70s was a relatively unburdened time in America, free of the tensions of the Vietnam War and the Watergate scandal. The Tech teens were fairly carefree, doing donuts in Doc Blanchard's Cadillac and hanging out with kids from high schools across the city at parties. But come race time, the friendships were put on pause as the Centaurs cued up Cameo's "Word Up!" before their meets:

"Yo, pretty ladies around the world/Got a weird thing to show you, so tell all the boys and girls/Tell yo brother, yo sister, and yo momma too/'Cause we're about to throw down and you'll know just what to do..."

"When we grew up, music was music," Stephon said.

It was also the era of drive-in movie theaters. *Jaws* and *Star Wars* were massive hits with audiences across the nation. While the former flick scared teens out of the water, the latter dazzled audiences with its groundbreaking special effects.

One night at Erie's Peninsula Drive-In, Dwayne and Stephon made some sparks of their own. They had taken out Doc's 1967 Ford Mustang and couldn't get it to start. Stephon poured gasoline in the carburetor, which caused flames to erupt from the vehicle.

Stephon looked at Dwayne. Dwayne looked at Stephon. Then, they did everything they could to put out the fire. They succeeded and got the car back to Dwayne's father in one piece.

Doc shook his head. He was just glad they were OK.

Neither snow nor rain ...

That wasn't the last time two Tech track athletes appeared sheepishly before a father figure.

The Centaurs made their way to the PIAA Class AAA boys track and field championships in 1977. They were solid in their first day of competition, with senior Kirk Loomis placing sixth in the javelin. However, Trott was a stickler for the rules, and he made no bones about the fact that all athletes were to be back at the Shippensburg University dormitories in which they were staying by curfew. Terry and Dwayne had left to meet a few girls from Academy, and they stayed out past curfew. When they got back to the dorms, Trott was outside waiting for them. He gathered the entire team and loaded up the bus for the ride back to Erie. The Centaurs did not compete the next day. They got the message.

"(Coach Trott) showed you even though you were the best on the team, you weren't any different from anybody else when it came to punishment," Terry said.

The mishap of '77 behind them, the Centaurs went into the '78 season focused on improvement. Rather than looking at the big picture, they aimed to run each race one second faster than before and clear each jump one inch higher than the last time. Holliday said that even though the athletes were "icons" to their classmates, they maintained a humility about them.

"They were just normal guys, but they had amazing athletic abilities," she said.

Those abilities were on display as the Centaurs faced top-notch competition in large invitationals. One such invite was the Kane Invitational in Kane, Pa., 94 miles southeast of Erie. The meet was held amidst ice and sleet, which was not uncommon for a spring track meet in the area.

"It's a pretty unique individual that wants to go run track and field in Erie, Pennsylvania," Gary said.

The conditions were far from ideal for sizing up competition. Yet, Corry High School track and field coach Joe Sanford was still able to get a feel for Tech's extraordinary talent. He likened most of their sprinters to "a group of gazelles" with their tall, lean builds in stark contrast to Dwayne's short stature.

But Sanford knew he was seeing something special as he watched Dwayne fly around the icy track, going so fast that he navigated the first turn like a car skidding around a corner. Sanford knew the hard work Dwayne must have put in to excel, but couldn't help but marvel at his grace.

"It just looked effortless," Sanford said.

During the 220 relay, a spike from Dwayne's cleats caught the back of Stephon's cleats, tossing Stephon into the air. He fell and couldn't get up, and he thought his track career was over. Even as the swelling from his injury decreased, he wasn't sure if he could return to form. Terry and Gary weren't having it.

"Come on, you can do this," they would tell him. "There's nothing to it. Just do it."

Their motivation expedited Stephon's recovery process. Terry, meanwhile, had injured his knee playing a pickup game of scatter dodgeball in his neighborhood. Both he and Stephon, though, were all set to go for the District 10 meet.

The Centaurs were the clear favorites in the district, and those in the track community knew they had a good chance to compete well at the state level. So long as they performed well at the district meet.

"That's the key," Sanford said.

The Centaurs excelled, both at the district qualifier at Fairview High School and by capturing the D-10 crown at Oil City High School the following week.

Now, there was only one thing left to do.

"Nooney, Nooney"

Looking back on it, Tech Memorial's goals at the 1978 state meet were pretty modest. The Centaurs were hoping to do well across the board and finish in the top five. Their reservations regarding their chance to win it all are understandable. Eastern Pennsylvania schools dominated track and field to the point that if a team from western PA won, it was viewed with either reverence or head-shaking confusion. Sanford said this mindset is prevalent to this day.

"They expect to win state titles, and when someone from the west wins — especially if they're not from Pittsburgh —there's a respect level there," he said.

If any team from the west was going to win that year, the thought was that it would be Aliquippa.

Though one thing was for certain: Dwayne was going to run the 100 in less than 10 seconds.

"He was our bread and butter," Terry said.

There was one person who thought Tech had a good chance of winning it all: Fred Trott. While he shared this thought with Marilou, he was tight-lipped when it came to his athletes.

"He wasn't one that would give out information, because I don't think he wanted you thinking too much about it," Gary said. "He just wanted you to concentrate on your job."

Instead, Trott prepared his athletes for the state finals as he did every other meet. He made sure they stretched their muscles, put heat pads on their legs, stayed out of the sun and ate honey to boost their performances.

"We ate so much honey," Terry said.

The Centaurs wasted no time wowing the crowd on the first day of the meet. Dwayne practically sparked flames on the track as he blazed past the competition in the 100-yard dash preliminary.

"You could have heard a pin drop," Gary said. "People couldn't believe how fast this kid was."

Still, there were those who doubted him. A group of men from Philadelphia were in the crowd at the state meet and were placing bets with each other on who would win events. Almost all of them underestimated Dwayne because of his size. Before the 100, only one of the half-dozen or so guys put his money on Dwayne.

Dwayne fattened the man's pockets by taking gold in the 100 in 9.67 seconds, and then won the 220 in 21.35 seconds. He had single-handedly earned 20 points for the Centaurs, but he was far from finished. He also was part of the 440 relay team — the equivalent of today's 4x100 meter relay — along with Stephon, Amos Tate and Terry. The foursome ran the race in 42.82 seconds to take fifth out of sixth places and earn two points for the Centaurs.

Terry reaggravated his knee during the 400, so Willie Jordan was on standby in case the man called "Nooney" couldn't run in the mile relay. Gary sat in the stands watching just a few feet from Trott. As calculating as he was, Trott may very well have known how close his team was to winning the state championship. If he did, he didn't share it with the rest of them. They had no idea they were within punching distance of taking the title.

Stephon led off. When he hit the 110-mark on the track, he heard someone whistle. It was Doc Blanchard, signaling for him to kick it into gear. Stephon dropped his head and took off. Danny and Dwayne maintained the lead Stephon built, and then it all came down to Terry Williams.

Terry had one thought.

I can't let these guys down.

And they couldn't — they wouldn't — let him down either. As Terry spilled his heart out onto the track, he heard the crowd chanting a name. His name.

"Nooney, Nooney, Nooney, Nooney..."

"That's a heck of a feeling, man," Terry said. "It really is."

His knee proved to work just fine, and he was the first to cross the finish line. Tech had earned 10 more points by winning the race in 3 minutes, 17.37 seconds, just .77 seconds shy of the then state record of 3:16.60.

Gary looked over at Trott, who had started to cry. It seemed he knew what they didn't yet; the Centaurs were state champions.

It was the pinnacle of Trott's career, but it was obvious to those around him that the tears he was crying weren't for himself, but for the boys he had helped mold into young men on the track.

"It wasn't about him," Gary said. "It was about the kids."

The athletes joined in their coach's celebration — and tears — as the surprise of their win gave way to celebration. They jumped up and down, savoring the moment for which they had worked so hard.

Marilou Trott, who couldn't be at the meet because she had to work, still remembers getting the phone call telling her they had won it all.

"That was a joyous moment, it was," she said.

Tech had earned 32 points in the meet, edging Haverford High School by two points to take home the hardware. It was only afterward that Trott told his athletes the meet had come down to that final relay. The Centaurs had once again pushed themselves past the limit. They finished first when all they needed was a second-place finish to win the title.

"You could see in coach's eyes, that made his career right there," Terry said. "It couldn't (have happened) to a better person."

Dwayne was named the No. 1 high school athlete in Pennsylvania by Hertz that year. The team received a commendation from the City of Erie, as well as gold state championship rings.

But for Terry, nothing meant more than Trott's words to him at an awards assembly in Tech's auditorium:

"You are the apple of my eye."

Both of them started to cry.

Photo by Aaron McKrell

Terry Williams (left) and Stephon Fitzpatrick stand atop the hill on Glenside Avenue in 2020. As track athletes, the two regularly sprinted up the hill, nicknamed "Fred's Hill" for Tech coach Fred Trott.

Days Gone By

The 1979 team, led by Dwayne and Stephon, earned a runner-up finish at the state meet.

Though they were disappointed in their placing, consolation for the Centaurs came at the National Track and Field Championship in Atlanta. There, Dwayne left another naysayer in the dust, and Tech earned even more respect with a 16th-place finish.

As the years went on, the athletes ventured down separate paths and saw less of each other. They also saw a change in Erie. As more manufacturers closed their doors and jobs left Erie, the athletes noticed a decline in the neighborhood solidarity they had enjoyed in their youth. And as more students continue to leave Erie for college and find jobs elsewhere, they're not sure how a turnaround will happen.

"It's not expanding," Gary said. "It's shrinking the other way."

But at least one thing has remained constant through the years: Erie continues to churn out strong teams and athletes, particularly in track and field. Terry joined Trott's staff at Tech as an assistant in the late '80s. Together, they coached future NFL wideout Dietrich Jells to an individual state championship in the 100-meter dash in 1989.

Following that season, Trott passed the reins of the program to Terry and moved to Florida with Marilou. Two years later, Terry coached Jells to another individual state title, again in the 100.

Despite the distance, Trott continued to receive Christmas cards, well wishes and friendly letters from his former athletes. When Trott retired, Gary read an article about him in the *Erie Times-News* and typed a letter to Trott to tell him what he meant to him. Trott sent him back a handwritten letter of appreciation.

"One of the best pats on the back you could ever have as a coach is (to) have one of your former athletes say, 'If it wasn't for you, I wouldn't be where I'm at today,'" Gary said.

Gary became a coach himself, coaching football at East High School and Blessed Sacrament School. Terry had a 35-year career at General Electric, while both Stephon and Dwayne served in the Navy. Dwayne died at age 27 in 1988. But he's still in the hearts and memories of his former teammates.

"He was a good kid," Terry said. "I miss Dwayne."

The lessons they learned from Dwayne, from each other and from Trott stick with them to this day. At or nearing retirement, they can look back on their lives with pride and the knowledge that they worked for what they got.

"If you want to be great, you got to work at it," Stephon said. "That's what we did. We worked hard. That was our thing."

And though they don't see each other as often anymore, when they do meet it's as if they're 17 years old all over again.

"That's the comfort of being friends and not just acquaintances," Gary said.

Dwayne was inducted into the Metropolitan Erie Chapter of the Pennsylvania Sports Hall of Fame in 1999, one year after Trott was inducted. Trott died at the age of 80 in 2017.

Before his death, he occasionally talked about Tech Memorial's 1978 state championship to Marilou. He would tell her it was probably one of the most thrilling times of his life.

"He wasn't a braggart at all, ever," Marilou said. "He just wasn't that kind of man. But he was so proud inside. He truly was."

Postscript: The Legacy of the Mile Relay

Joe Sanford was at the 1978 state meet. He watched as Tech Memorial's mile relay team clinched the state championship in the final event of the day. The importance of that race is something he never forgot.

"You better have some skin in the game when it comes to the last event," Sanford said.

He learned that not only from Trott, but from Ted Miller, who strategically brought in athletes with fresh legs into the 1600-meter relay.

Sanford, ever humble and determined, soaked up this knowledge from these two titans of Erie County track and field.

One day, many years later, he'd find out just how valuable those lessons would be…

Photo provided by Joe Sanford

The McDowell High School boys track and field team (above) poses with the 2007 PTFCA State Championship trophy. The Trojans went on to win the 2007 PIAA Class AAA outdoor state title, becoming just the fourth school in state history to win indoor and outdoor championships in the same year.

Every Point Counts

By Aaron McKrell

There is a picture on Stella Dogun's refrigerator of four, unsmiling teenage boys in track uniforms.

The photo shows the boys in contrast to how they usually were: silly, lively, vibrant. It was taken at the Pennsylvania Track & Field Coaches Association State Championships, just moments after the 4x200-meter relay race.

The boys ran for McDowell High School. They had won their heat with the second fastest time in the state. However, in the next heat four teams clocked faster times, dropping McDowell's squad to sixth.

"We were like, 'We got some work to do,'" said Peter Overare, who was on the relay team. "And then they took the picture. That captures our mentality."

The athletes of the 2007 McDowell boys track and field team had a tireless work ethic, which was driven by a selfless determination to help their brothers-in-cleats.

"We were all doing it for each other," said Josh Freeman, a senior on the team. "They say track's an individual sport, but it never was for us."

The Trojans had an uncommon unity across the track and field events. In particular, a handful of them — seniors Brice Myers, Aaron Fitzpatrick, Emmanuel Overare and Josh Freeman, junior Johnny Dogun (Stella Dogun's son) and sophomore Peter Overare — formed extraordinarily tight-knit friendships that bolstered their performances on the track and transcended athletics. The result of that team-wide closeness was an undefeated season, two state championships and one of the greatest athletic teams McDowell High School has ever assembled.

"I really feel that bond was the reason for the win, or both wins," said head coach Joe Sanford. "They loved each other."

The chemistry that would boil over into gold medals wasn't formed in 2007, though. It happened years before, when a family moved from London to Erie, Pa.

An American Dream

David and Felicia Overare wanted the best lives possible for their children. So, a handful of years after they moved their family from Nigeria to London, they skipped across the pond to Erie. Stella Dogun, whom David had met in medical school in Nigeria, was already practicing medicine in Erie. David, who had previously been a doctor in the U.K., began his medical residency in Erie while the Overares moved in with the Doguns.

The Overares had four children, including two sons: Emmanuel and Peter. They became close with the Doguns' only child, Johnny, and Peter and Johnny even shared a bed in their grade school years. Around that time, they met Brice Myers at Grandview Elementary School. Brice also met Aaron Fitzpatrick at Grandview, though they didn't become friends until they were in middle school. That's also where they met Josh Freeman, as they all were in the same grade. Though they didn't know it then, these initial meetings were the foundation of something much greater than a "hello" in the hallways.

Father & Son

Stephon Fitzpatrick was a Tech Memorial High School track and field legend. He and his friends pulled off a thrilling victory in the mile relay race to capture the 1978 PIAA state title and bring track and field glory to the City of Erie. Stephon led off the race and ran his lap in 48.5 seconds.

When his son, Aaron, came of age to run track, Stephon was eager to pass the baton.

"I wanted him to do better than what I had done," Stephon said. Stephon told Aaron that one day he would face the same pressure Stephon had been under, and that he would rise to the occasion.

"I said, 'Yeah right, dad, whatever,'" Aaron recalled.

Aaron didn't feel pressure, but was motivated by his father's excitement.

"I felt more of a challenge, like I wanted to go after it," he said. "He was extremely encouraging in the fact that he wanted me to exceed what he had done."

Aaron, along with Emmanuel and Brice, competed in the middle school track meet McDowell held each year for seventh and eighth graders.

However, he suffered an ACL injury in his freshman year, which sidelined him while Brice, Josh and Emmanuel joined the team. The Trojans were led by Joe Sanford, who had been coaching track and field since 1975 and also coached football. He had won state championships with the McDowell girls team in 2001, 2004 and 2005. The key to Sanford's program was discipline.

"I was a firm believer in discipline," he said. "A saying that I often repeated was that discipline will win games."

It was a component that both Brice and Josh lacked. Brice went out for track simply for something to do, while Josh was balancing his indoor track schedule with baseball and volleyball workouts.

As such, they missed several practices. One day, they came to practice late and Sanford had had enough.

"(He was) just like, 'If you don't want to be here, go home,'" Brice said. "So I went home."

Neither Brice nor Josh returned for the rest of the season.

Something Special

Sophomore year rolled around and Aaron was healthy. He joined the team for the indoor season. Right away, Sanford and sprint coach Bill Hoffman, both of whom knew of his father's success, told Aaron he was going to compete in the 400-meter dash.

"Coach Hoffman said, 'You don't know it yet, but you're gonna be pretty darn good,'" Aaron said. "'You're gonna follow in (Stephon's) footsteps.'"

Sanford also reached out to Brice and Josh to return. Brice, who had already wanted to come back, agreed. Josh, who was initially upset after being chastised by Sanford, realized the coach had been looking out for him. He, too, decided to return.

Johnny, a freshman, also joined the team after being intrigued by Emmanuel's excitement about it the previous year.

"I'm like, 'Bro, why do you like this so much?'" he said.

Early on, a bond began to form, something that Peter noticed when he watched his brother compete.

"You could just tell the fun that they were having, and they were having success in it," Peter said. "And I wanted a piece of that."

Even though the athletes themselves didn't see it yet, the coaching staff knew early on that they had potential.

"The whole thing was starting back with discipline, because we knew as a staff that those guys were gonna be great," Sanford said. "It was just a matter of when they would be great, and how great they would be."

After practice one day, the coaches took the boys team into the dance studio where the throwers practiced. As the athletes sat on the mats, the coaches told them they were going to win a district title.

Then, they had the juniors and seniors leave while the freshmen and sophomores stayed behind.

"'This bunch in particular, you guys are gonna do something special,'" Aaron recalled being told. "'You need to stick with it.'"

Randy Gunther, the jumps coach, emphasized the need for unity.

"'Work hard,'" Aaron recalled him saying. "'Get to be friends with all these guys.'"

The Squad

Brice still hadn't fully bought in. He didn't lift weights and took repetitions off in practice during the indoor season.

A switch flipped when he was getting beat off the blocks one day in practice. Brice grew frustrated because he knew he could be better.

"Coach Gunther came over and was like, 'You know why that's happening, right?'" Brice said.

Brice said, 'No,' and Gunther pointed to the weight room.

"'That's the difference,'" Brice recalled Gunther saying.

Brice responded by not only hitting the weights, but by immersing himself in his events. He began to listen to his coaches' encouragement and bought into Hoffman's training regimen. He also studied books on hurdling and learned about fast-twitch muscles and their effect on sprinting. And, he went to the track by himself for more training on the weekends.

His unassuming demeanor led Aaron to call him "the silent leader."

"I always looked at Brice as the sergeant of the squad," he said. "He just knows what he's doing, he's gifted, he's athletic. He's encouraging to everybody else."

Aaron, too, was a leader, but he was more vocal than Brice.

"He was an exceptional leader in the sense that he was also leading by example and trying to be first in line in every workout," Johnny said. "But he also (was) verbally making sure we're all on the same page and everyone felt inspired."

Emmanuel, meanwhile, led mostly by example.

"Emmanuel was a really reserved and quiet individual," Sanford said. "But, I'll tell you what. When he competed, that didn't show. There was an inner part of Emmanuel that sprang to the surface."

Like Emmanuel, Johnny mixed a low-key demeanor with intensity. "Johnny was very soft-spoken, but the effort that he exuded was just amazing to me," Sanford said.

Josh exemplified two values which Sanford prized.

"It was consistency," Sanford said. "He was always there, and the other thing was his hard work ethic."

When he joined the team as a freshman, Peter added his own personality into the mix.

"He was a different type of personality than Emmanuel," Sanford said. "Little bit more lively, little bit more like Brice to tell you the truth. But, I think what fueled him was once he knew he could be successful, he was on board."

McDowell also had excellent pole vaulters in seniors Eston Winn and Mike DiFucci, and strong sprinters in senior Nate Krizanik, juniors Nick Adamski and Robert Ward and sophomore Alex Schmude.

Brett Cassidy and Matt Harrison further bolstered the Trojans as solid alternates who flexed between the sprinting and mid-distance events.

Chad Noce and Dan Kwiatkowski muscled up as the top throwers on the team. They were constantly pushing each other to improve and set a standard for their throwing counterparts to follow. Yet, they still managed to have a good time.

"We just tried to keep everyone loose, keep everyone smiling and focusing on the reason why we were actually there," Chad said. "It's obviously great to compete (and) better yourself, but it's all about having fun, too."

Twins George and Powell Brown kept things light among the distance runners. George said they had been through adversity in their youth, so they understood the importance of being positive.

"We knew what it was like to be down at times," he said. "So, the big thing was, why be sad when you could be happy?"

Spaghetti Dinners and Barbecues

The common thread amongst all these different personalities was a tireless work ethic. Sanford noted that, while the athletes had a loose feel in warmups, they were all business during repetitions.

"Once the practice started, they flipped a switch," he said.

Stephon had forged lasting friendships with his teammates at Tech Memorial, and encouraged Aaron to do the same at McDowell. Aaron took his dad's advice, and the team held spaghetti dinners at the Overares' house and barbecues in the Fitzpatricks' backyard.

"All the different personalities just happened to fit and gel really, really, really well," Aaron said. "I knew we were gonna be good friends from the get-go."

Peter, younger than the rest, loved hanging out with the crew.

"They talked to me and treated me like I was one of them, and that meant a lot," he said. "That gave me a lot of confidence."

Their bond carried onto the track, where they engaged in intense competition.

"It was all friendly," Emmanuel said. "But, at the same time, not so much we want to beat them, but push each other to become the best athlete you could be."

Peter was watching the upperclassmen excel, doing his best to compete with them, and looking up to Emmanuel as his role model. He said his experiences in practices with them helped him tremendously.

"It showed me how hard you have to work," he said.

Brice always kept Aaron on his toes. He'd walk past, uttering sly comments under his breath.

"I got you in that 400, Fitz," he'd say.

"What?" Aaron would reply. "That's my race!"

"I'mma get you in it, though."

The athletes zeroed in on the 4x400-meter relay, which consisted of Johnny, Brice, Josh and Aaron. They dubbed it "Fo' by Fo.'"

"There was so much pride behind that relay," Aaron said.

All the while, Aaron wore a green Tech Memorial sweatshirt he had inherited from his father. Aaron donned the shirt as motivation to surpass his father's athletic success.

A True Leader

As the athletes grew closer, they became a family. And within that family they had not one, but several sets of parents.

The parents of Aaron, Josh, Brice, Johnny and Emmanuel and Peter were there to support them through practices, home and away meets and team dinners.

"They cared for not only the sons they had themselves, but for the ones they inherited," Aaron said.

Josh recalled that, one night during his senior year, he ran into Felicia Overare at a gas station.

Out of sheer kindness, she bought him gum and soda.

The boys had another parent in Joe Sanford. As much as he pushed

his athletes to be their best, he showed how much he cared for them.
"Sanford was a second father," Aaron said.

Peter agreed.

"He's almost like a father figure in terms of, he had the fatherly love and discipline," he said. "He gave you the discipline. He's your biggest fan and your biggest critic. He wasn't afraid to tell you if you were really wrong."

That criticism was never to hurt, but to help.

"When he said something negative, he meant it," Josh said. "And it was to better you, not to bring you down."

Everything, from the hint of gravel in his dignified voice to the way he molded himself to best motivate each individual athlete, made Sanford an exceptional leader.

"He was probably the first person I've ever seen that defined and truly was the definition of a leader," Brice said.

Emmanuel noted that Sanford is a man of Christian faith and great integrity, and that his values bled through everything he did.

"He was driven to win, but not at the cost of selling your soul," Emmanuel said.

Indeed, he inspired others to be better.

"He commands respect, and you need to act a certain way around him," Johnny said.

Sanford's approach was the same whether an athlete was an All-American or a newcomer. There were more than 100 athletes on the boys and girls teams combined, and he knew all of their names. He also took the time to understand what motivated each of them.

"His confidence, his belief in what he said, he made you believe it because he had so much of it," Brice said.

Sanford compiled a coaching staff that was just as dedicated as he was. In addition to the prowess of coaches Gunther and Hoffman, they had superb distance coaches in Becky Glus, Kevin Slagle and Jeremy Boehm. They also benefited from Dan McGahen, a stellar 4x100-meter relay coach, and an outstanding high jump and javelin coach in Doug Stratton. Max Alwens, Christina Bokulich, Kristen Szabat and Jason Pauli held it down as formidable throwing coaches. Sanford and his wife, Cindy, teamed up to be exceptional pole vaulting coaches.

"There were a lot of eyes watching those (athletes) perform," Sanford said. "Not only were there a lot of eyes, but they were very educated eyes. They knew what they were looking for."

49!

With a cast of supportive parents behind them and experienced coaches guiding them, the athletes trained with a paradoxical mixture of patience and urgency.

"You just can't redeem time," Sanford said. "So, I was always wanting our young athletes to be patient, but at the same time be urgent, because we're gonna run out of time."

Practice was only half the battle. The coaching staff designed an intensive weight-lifting program that required immense discipline and dedication.

The athletes bought in wholeheartedly. Several of them stayed later than required.

"They couldn't kick us out," Aaron said.

As always, they melded their silliness with a sense of purpose.

"The weight room was where you could be yourself," Josh said. "You could goof off in there, but we were serious about it."

Tracks like Trillville's "Neva Eva" and Freeway's "Flipside" blasted through the speakers as they got to work. Emmanuel led the charge as the first one to take lifting seriously, as well as the one who put up the most weight.

"He was a savage with it, man," Johnny said.

Gunther stood to the side with his arms crossed, yelling, "Get it!" as they pushed themselves past their limits. They shouted out "49!" as they squatted to declare their goal of sprinting the 4x4 in 49 seconds apiece.

"I lifted harder in track than I did for football," Aaron said.

The similarities between Aaron's drive in the mid-2000s and Stephon's competitiveness 30 years before was not lost on Sanford.

"They accepted nothing less than the best from themselves," Sanford said.

The same could be said about the rest of the Trojans, and their dedication paid off. With each rep, the Trojans became fine-tuned machines of track and field excellence.

"We won those state titles in the weight room," Sanford said.

All these elements — the bonding, the friendly competition, the parental support, the outstanding leadership, and especially, the hard work and discipline — created a recipe for success. Emmanuel and Brice had already qualified for the state meets multiple times, and Chad made a trip to the outdoor state meet as a junior.

The team's confidence and stature were growing. They were

beginning to see what they could accomplish if they continued down the path of drive and dedication. By the time the 2007 indoor season arrived, the athletes had their sights set on the biggest prize of all.

Top of the Podium

It wasn't explicitly stated, but the Trojans wanted the top of the podium.

"We knew it was something we could do," Emmanuel said. "It was just a matter of performing."

While Sanford said the goal of the indoor season was to prepare for the outdoor season, it wasn't long before the PTFCA meet became a focus in itself.

"Once we knew how good we could be, then that kind of took on a life of its own," he said.

The Trojans won meet after meet, but it wasn't until an invitational at Kent State University that everything clicked. The 4x4 relay team of Brice, Johnny, Josh and Aaron excelled against top opposition.

"That 4x4 was just like, 'We are it,'" Brice said.

McDowell was in Class AAA in the outdoor season. However, 359 schools of all classes competed for the PTFCA indoor state title.

Rather than focus on the standings, though, the athletes concentrated on the jobs they had to do.

The results spoke for themselves. Chad won a bronze medal in the shot put with a distance of 57-8.75, while Dan was sixth with a mark of 54-9.5.

Emmanuel earned a silver medal in the triple jump with a measurement of 47-0.25, while Aaron finished sixth in the 400 in 50.37 seconds.

Brice had lost previously that season in the 60-meter hurdles to future NFL wide receiver Toney Clemons, of Valley High School.

"I knew this dude was going to be the one to beat for the state title," Brice said.

The gun was fired, and Brice had tunnel vision as he took off. He could feel Clemons close, but he kept pushing, and when he dipped across the finish line, he knew he had won.

Brice let out a yell and saw Aaron moving through the crowd.

"He was like, 'I see you, boy!'" Brice said.

Aaron and Josh dapped each other up, while Hoffman was ecstatic in the stands.

"You didn't see other schools getting hyped for their athletes like that,"

Johnny said.

Brice took home the gold with a time of eight seconds flat.

The clincher, though, was the 4x4. The foursome of Johnny, Brice, Josh and Aaron combined for a time of 3:24.68 and a fourth-place finish that ensured the Trojans were the 2007 PTFCA state champions.

McDowell placed first with 35 team points, six points ahead of second place Neshaminy.

It was a fitting capstone to an undefeated season. The team was thrilled.

"This (was) three years, four years in the making," Brice said. "So much hard work went into this."

Josh was even happier for his teammates than he was for himself.

"That was the best, to see everybody work hard and get it done," he said. "It truly was a team win."

Several Trojans competed at the Nike Indoor Nationals meet.

Emmanuel placed sixth in the triple jump with a distance of 46-9.5 to be named a Nike All-American.

"There was definitely a lot of pride in continuing a very long and storied tradition in the McDowell jump program," Emmanuel said. "To have my name included with some of the amazing jumpers that came before me and after me is an incredible honor."

"We Takin' Over…"

Sanford wanted his team to have convenient amnesia after winning the title. He didn't want the pressure that came with being indoor champions to seep into the outdoor season.

However, it was well known that only three teams in Pennsylvania high school history had won the indoor and outdoor state championships in the same year.

"Hoffman just said, 'Congratulations, you guys won, but you just put a target on your back,'" Josh recalled.

But the state championship wasn't the sole focus, and it wasn't spoken of.

"Our goal was to individually perform, and do the best that we could do and get better throughout the season," Emmanuel said. "And if the pieces came to be, then that would be great."

Just as they had during the indoor season, the Trojans shot past the competition on their outdoor schedule. They won every dual meet and invitational in which they competed. This included the Baldwin

Invitational, which Sanford considered to be the unofficial Western Pennsylvania final because the best from the west all competed at the invite.

The team adopted a mantra from a hit song that spring, DJ Khaled's posse cut "We Takin' Over." As they went from meet to meet, they'd sing to themselves and each other, "We takin' over...one track meet at a time!"

The Trojans got their first taste of adversity that season when Josh pulled his hamstring just before the District 10 Championships. He reaggravated it at the District 10 meet, and George had to take his place.

George — whose specialty was the 800 — had only run the 4x4 once before, for fun with the other distance runners at the Baldwin Invitational. However, he had experience competing in the 4x800 relay, and quickly gelled with the sprinters.

"I joked around, they joked around, but when it came to our events we knew it meant business," George said.

McDowell dominated the district meet, placing in every event and winning 10 events.

"We were like a well-oiled machine at that point," Johnny said.

The Trojans' tremendous performances set the stage for the biggest meet of their lives.

Before the Meet

Sanford was at home, mowing his pasture on his tractor when he got the call.

It was Hoffman. He asked Sanford whether or not they should take Josh to the PIAA Class AAA state meet, as Josh was hurt.

Sanford said they should. Hoffman agreed.

Josh, though, didn't want to go. He boarded the bus to Shippensburg University with his teammates, but he was despondent.

"I just had so much anger because everything that (I'd) put in work for, for three years was now gone," he said. "I was so mad at myself; I just didn't know what to do."

Because of his injury, Josh was listed as an alternate rather than as an official member of the 4x4.

"It was a weird feeling to not have him on there," Johnny said.

The coaches took the athletes out to dinner the night before the meet. They dressed up and they ate, relaxed and laughed together.

"I wanted them to feel special," Sanford said.

For Emmanuel, who was making his sixth combined trip to a state meet, the dinner had become tradition.

"It was kind of nice to go and do something familiar and take the pressure off, and take your mind off of what's to come," he said.

The team bunked in the Shippensburg University dormitories. The eve of the meet, Sanford went over procedural instructions for the team. The coaches wanted their athletes to outperform their seedings, but were careful not to put pressure on them.

"I can't remember ever saying, 'We've gotta win,'" Sanford said. "It was, 'Do your best, and everything else will take care of itself.'"

Still, the coaches knew that, to win, everyone would have to do their part. Every point mattered. It was a lesson learned at the 2000 outdoor state meet, when the McDowell girls team lost to Harrisburg by one point.

"We always say that every point counts," Sanford said. "I don't care if it's eighth or seventh or whatever it is, every point counts."

Emmanuel, Brice and Chad were the only athletes who had been to an outdoor state meet before, but the Trojans' team chemistry kept them relaxed.

"We all knew what we came here to do, but the friendship kind of helped keep the nerves away," Emmanuel said.

Friday

The coaches were nervous. Very nervous.

"You're on pins and needles, just making sure that everybody who has to qualify, qualifies," Sanford said.

The athletes, however, competed with an edge.

"We weren't expected to win, and we carried that chip on our shoulder, which really helped us out," Emmanuel said. "It gave us that extra motivation."

Emmanuel put McDowell on the board in the triple jump.

After two jumps that he was sure wouldn't earn him a placing, he switched up his strategy. He moved further back behind the line so he could lengthen his strides and finished with a jump of 46-2.25 to place fourth.

"I was a little disappointed with how I finished," Emmanuel said. "But going from not even making the finals, to placing, was a little bit of a load off."

Chad and Dan put up more points for the Trojans in the shot put. Chad placed fourth with a mark of 56-1.75, while Dan was fifth, measuring 55-8.25.

Chad noted how getting early points in the triple jump and shot put bolstered the team's mood.

"Once those points get scored, that word travels fast," he said. "And it spreads, almost like a wildfire of excitement."

Decked out in matching Nike Superbad socks, the 4x4 turned heads in the preliminary race with a time of 3:18.31.

"We had never run that fast," Johnny said. "After we saw that I was like, 'Yo, we got this.'"

The Trojans felt good after a hard day's work, but Sanford didn't want them to rest on their laurels. He took them to a gazebo on campus and calmly told them that the next day would be when they had everything to prove.

There was a mixer on campus that night, which the athletes called "the losers' dance" as it was often attended by those who didn't qualify for Saturday's events.

Not one McDowell athlete went to the dance. They knew what they were there for, and it wasn't dancing or punch bowls.

Johnny and Peter shared a room, just as they had when they were little kids. They laid awake in their beds, overcome by the surreality of the moment.

"It was just too hard to put together, like, how could this actually happen?" Johnny said.

The Finals

The sun rose, and so did the Trojans. George delivered an impassioned speech to his teammates before the day's events.

"I have one more run in me, and I plan to leave it all out on the line," he told his teammates. "Not because I'm ambitious to have a personal best, but because I'm willing to do that for my family. "I'm here because of you, and I'm here with you."

Then, the Trojans hit the track with focus.

Aaron earned points in the 400, sprinting the loop in 49.24 seconds to finish sixth.

George had qualified for the 800-meter final, but the coaches didn't tell him about it until an hour before the race. He was the 12th seed in the 800 and unlikely to earn points.

Sanford had learned many years earlier, when he was the head track coach at Corry High School, the importance of having fresh legs in the 4x4. He'd seen it not only in the '78 Tech Memorial team, but in the strategies of the legendary North East track coach Ted Miller.

Glus told George they had chosen to hold him out of the 800 so he could be fresh for the 4x4.

He agreed.

"I trusted her judgment," he said.

Meanwhile, Josh didn't think he was going to run at all, so he ate a heavy lunch of macaroni and cheese, deep-fried chicken and ice cream.

"I ate so much food," Josh said.

Brice had the heaviest workload. He was slated for the 110-meter hurdles, the 300 hurdles, the 4x100 relay and the 4x4.

He won a silver medal in the 110 hurdles in 14.20 seconds and placed eighth in the 300 hurdles in 40.56 seconds.

He teamed up with Nate, Johnny and Peter in the 4x100, and the foursome finished seventh in 43.34 seconds.

Johnny ran again in the 200, placing fourth in 22.07 seconds.

Sanford found him in the bleachers afterward and asked him if he was up to running in the 4x4.

He told Johnny that if he were to run his personal record or better, they'd win the state title.

"I felt like I didn't have much of an option to decline running at that point," Johnny said.

Fo' by Fo'

Brice, however, was gassed. Between the preliminaries and the finals of multiple races and relays, he had already done so much.

Sanford noted Brice's progression, from leaving the team his freshman year to becoming the most dependable athlete on the squad.

"He was tremendous," Sanford said.

Aaron recalled Brice standing in front of an expectant Hoffman.

"Hoffman's just like, 'Well?' Can you do it?'" Aaron said.

Brice couldn't speak. He shook his head as his eyes welled with tears.

"I looked at it like, something's going on here," Brice said. "I'm losing it mentally; I'm losing it physically.

"We got the guy right here."

Josh was up. His first thought was the lunch he had devoured.

"My biggest fear was the ice cream I had just eaten, because lactic acid is horrible," he said. "Ice cream is the worst thing you can eat before you go run."

Then, the Trojans received a break from above. Rain began to fall, causing a 30-minute delay that allowed Josh's stomach to settle as he stretched out his muscles.

"I felt good, my hamstring was good," Josh said. "I'm like, 'Well, if I get hurt again, I don't care. You can cut my leg off afterwards. I gotta get in the zone. I have to do this for them.'"

Stephon, who had been in the stands, came down to give his son and Josh a pep talk during the delay. He knew just what to say to Aaron. After all, he'd been in an eerily similar situation 29 years earlier when he had led off Tech Memorial's mile relay team. The foursome had needed at least a second-place finish to win the state title.

This time, his son was the anchor, and McDowell needed to finish in at least fifth place to win it all.

"Do what you need to do, Josh, and don't let anybody pass you," Stephon told his son's best friend.

Then, he turned to Aaron.

"It's coming down to the exact same position that I was in," he said. "You ain't got time to be dilly dallying. Just run."

Even though the stakes had never been higher, the bond that had been forged over the years allowed them to stay calm. So calm, in fact, that they dozed off during the break.

When they awoke, Aaron cracked a joke.

"It didn't seem like it was that big of a deal," Johnny said. "We knew the state championship was on the line, we had worked so hard the whole year for it, but it was like, we're with our brothers.

"It's another day, we've done this 100 times. We've come out, run 400s so many times, like, let's just do it."

Eventually, the rain stopped and it was time to run.

"It was as if the clouds had opened up and the sun started coming (out)," Johnny said. "It was really poetic and really symbolic as to, now our opportunity is here."

They huddled up in their blue McDowell warmups as Aaron led them in prayer and they hyped each other up.

"We said, 'It's just us out here,'" Johnny recalled. "'We've been training for this the whole year. Let's do it for ourselves.'"

Johnny led off, and when the gun was fired he was overcome by a sense of calmness. He didn't hear the crowd, and he didn't even feel as though anyone was watching him.

"I didn't feel tight, I didn't feel tired," he said. "It was just like, you felt your heart beating, you heard what was going on around you."

Johnny passed the baton to George with McDowell in first place.

George knew he had to stay in his lane for the first 100 meters until the break line, or his team would be disqualified.

"I watched every single step," he said.

When George came off the break line, he gradually moved over to Lane 1 so he could run the shortest distance around the track. He bumped shoulder to shoulder with Harrisburg High School's Andre Clark.

"He looked up at me, I looked down at him, and we kind of gave each other that, 'It's either you or me' (look)," George said.

Clark turned on the jets and George stayed on his heels as long as he could.

"I kept telling myself, 'This is my last 400, this is the last time I'm gonna put it all on the line for my team,'" he said.

No one else passed George, and the Trojans remained in second place as he passed the baton to Josh.

All of Josh's pent-up frustration over his injury came spilling out onto the track. He loved the chase and was inspired by Harrisburg's Matt Davis running ahead of him.

What worried him were the runners behind him. As he reached the back turn, two runners crept up on him. They grew closer and closer, and Josh veered between lanes 1 and 3 trying to keep them at bay.

Sanford, Gunther and Stratton were standing at the 200-meter mark, while the rest of the coaches were at the finish line, all of them screaming, "Hold 'em off!"

The official, apparently anticipating that Josh was going to get passed, tried to move Aaron into Lane 4. But Aaron had faith in Josh.

"Hold on, hold on, hold on," Aaron told the official.

Josh couldn't feel his arms anymore. About 20 meters from the 100-meter mark, he stopped trying to block the runners off. He knew that if he kept running back and forth, one of them would likely make a move to the inside.

"It was like, 'Welp, I just gotta go,'" Josh said. "And I was like, 'I hope I get there.'"

Josh broke into a dead sprint and the runners fell back.

"Straight guts, that's what took him around that track," Johnny said.

Josh knew they had won with 20 meters to go, when he had about 15 meters on his competitors.

"I couldn't hear them anymore," Josh said. "And as soon as I knew what happened, I just smiled."

Aaron took the baton with the goal in mind to finish strong.

"Josh ran the race of a lifetime," Aaron said. "How do you top that? Well, you run for him."

Aaron hit the turn faster than he ever had in his life and opened up on the final stretch with the silver medal on his mind. However, he was edged out in a photo finish by Cumberland Valley's Josh Shumberger, and the Trojans finished third in 3:18.77.

No matter: They were the state champions.

Aaron looked up in the crowd and found his father looking back. Stephon nodded.

"Everything that we had talked about (with) these types of moments, (how) you gotta just take it all in, just enjoy it and do your best, it all just sank into my heart," Aaron said. "And that was that."

Aaron had done it. He'd run his leg of the relay in 48.37 seconds, beating his father's time of 48.5 seconds.

"It was the happiest day of my life," Stephon said.

McDowell won with 39 team points, beating second place North Penn High School by three points. They did it all without a single first-place finish and placed in nine events.

The North Penn coach greeted Sanford as they descended from the awards stand.

"The coach said to me, 'What you did was amazing,'" Sanford said.

"'No first places, no first places,' and he said, 'The number of events that you placed in was amazing.' And it was."

A reporter came up to Aaron to interview him, but he deferred to Josh, whom he gave a hug.

"That just shows how much we all meant to each other, how much we would all do for each other," Aaron said.

It was, as Peter described it, "pure joy." All those spaghetti dinners, all those repetitions on the track, all the late evenings in the weight room and bus rides back from invitationals, had led to a perfect season and back-to-back state championships.

Sanford was overcome with emotion. Eyes filled with tears, he embraced Josh with a hug.

"I knew you could do it," Sanford told him. "I knew we could do it."

The Legacy of the Platoon Squad

A lot of things have happened since the McDowell boys track and field team stepped off the podium that day in May 2007.

Peter soaked up what he learned that year to become one of the finest sprinters in the state. He and Johnny teamed up with Robert Ward and Alex Schmude to become All-Americans in the 800 medley relay in 2008.

Aaron, Brice, Chad and Dan all went on to have successful collegiate track and field careers.

Brice was a six-time All-American and qualified for the U.S. Olympic team trials.

The boys have become men. They graduated from college. They have wives, fiancées or girlfriends. Aaron is a jumps coach at Chartiers Valley High School, and they all have good jobs in various fields.

"I'm most proud of them (for) where they are today," Sanford said. "That speaks volumes. Listen, they're not competing in the Olympics, but they're great young men, coaching and in business. So, that is more, I don't want to say more gratifying, but that's just as gratifying as winning a state title. Because they're still winning titles today as young adults."

Through it all, they haven't forgotten what's most important: each other.

Aaron, Brice, Josh, Emmanuel, Johnny and Peter are still close friends. They keep in touch regularly. Brice, Aaron, Josh and Peter live in Pittsburgh, and the group, which includes a few others from high school, hangs out when they're all in the city.

Each year, the group, which named themselves "Platoon Squad" in their college years, gets together for a Secret Santa gift exchange. When they're together, track and field is never far from their minds.

"It was just special, in terms of being able to have success," Peter said. "And then just (to) be able to laugh and think about it, and joke about it and reminisce about it."

Their former coaches, too, have stuck with them, not only in their memories but in the lessons they learned.

The values that were instilled in them — humility, perseverance, discipline, work ethic — are ones they carry with them as they continue to grow as young men.

"You gotta keep pushing," Josh said. "You gotta find things to work on, no matter what."

They feel indebted to the coaches, especially Sanford. Though they remember him fondly, they know he is much more than a memory. Now in his seventies, he's shown no signs of slowing down. He still coaches pole vaulters at McDowell and is an assistant to Ned Bailey on the Trojans' freshman football team. He often sees Aaron at track meets, now as fellow coaches. He lives in the country with Cindy, and is an active member of Grace Church, of which his son, Derek, is lead pastor.

Sanford, too, took something of value from that state championship year: the importance of discipline. He said hard work and discipline are two factors that will always pay off.

"It may not pay off with two state titles, like these guys can talk about," Sanford said. "But it's always gonna pay off eventually."

In October 2019, Peter got married. Emmanuel was his best man, and Johnny, Aaron, Brice, Josh and McDowell distance runner Alex Rupert were among his groomsmen.

Their friendships go back to those afternoons spent on the track at Gus Anderson Field.

"It's just a testament to the bond that was created and forged those four years," Emmanuel said.

That bond is not only maintained, but strengthening as time goes on.

"We've been through fights," Brice said. "We've been through ups and downs. We've been through so much, and that just keeps building on what we are today."

As they've grown with each other, they've also grown from knowing one another.

"We all have a piece of each other," Josh said.

They are aware, too, of how uncommon their bond is.

"I'm blessed to have these people in my life, and I wouldn't wish it any other way," Peter said.

That blessing is not just in their presence, but in their dependability.

"What I learned, honestly, was that it's OK to let your guard down and rely and depend on someone else at times," Aaron said.

It's a lesson learned from their days on the track, and one that is ever-present as the years go by.

"As we change and grow and evolve and reach different stages of our lives, I always think back to how we were a team that state championship year," Johnny said. "And it's like, I can rely on these guys because they always had my back at that moment.

"And how ever we change and evolve, that will always remain true that we were there for each other, and will continue to be there for each other."

Photo provided by Veronica Harden and Mark Vatavuk

Sam "The Jet" Jethroe (right) sits with his godson, Kenneth Harden. Jethroe, a longtime Erie resident, became the oldest player in Major League Baseball to be named Rookie of the Year, at age 32 in 1950.

The Jet

By Kevin Cuneo

Kevin Cuneo served as sports editor of the Erie Times-News *for 17 years. He wrote multiple articles about Sam Jethroe in his tenure with the* Times-News. *He is now retired and resides in Erie with his wife, Mary. He has three sons: Dan, who lives in Connecticut, and Sean and Joe, both of whom live in Erie.*

The tap on my shoulder, as I stood on the edge of the playing field at Atlanta's Fulton County Stadium just before the start of the 1995 World Series, startled me. But when I turned around and saw Henry Aaron standing there, I was shocked.

"How is my good friend Sam?" Aaron asked.

He had spotted the name "Erie" on my media credential and immediately thought of Sam Jethroe, former Major League Baseball star and longtime Erie resident.

"Sam's a good guy," Aaron told me. "Always was. When I was a fresh kid from Alabama, Sam took me under his wing. You have no idea how tough it was for us back then. But people like Sam made it easier."

Aaron recalled his first trip to spring training when he was a 17-year-old farmhand for the Boston Braves.

"There were only a few of us in camp," Aaron said, referring to Black players. "Sam knew how to drive, and he had this big car he was motoring around town. I don't know where he got it, but I don't think it was his. He was never the kind of guy who did things for show. Every day after workouts, he would take the other Black players — me, Billy Bruton and Wes Covington — to places in town where he knew we'd be welcome."

Aaron smiled at the memory, and then he said, "If you see Sam, please give him my best."

Almost immediately, I was surrounded by a half-dozen reporters demanding to know what Aaron had said. I shared the story, but most of the guys — young reporters in their 20s and 30s — seemed disappointed. Though George Vescey, a columnist for *The New York*

Times, found the exchange fascinating.

"They never forget," he said. "These men forged such deep bonds decades ago when they went through hell together. Simple kindnesses mattered so much back then."

Several years later, Covington and Orlando Cepeda stopped at Jethroe's tavern in Erie. Cepeda talked about the winters Sam spent playing for a Cuban all-star team.

"I was just a kid bat boy at the time, but I remember how much the Cuban people loved Sam," Cepeda said. "(Fidel Castro) modeled his batting stance after Sam's. When he was young, Fidel was crazy about baseball."

Sam "The Jet" Jethroe, born in East St. Louis, Illinois, in 1918, starred in the Negro Leagues for seven seasons before Branch Rickey, general manager of the Brooklyn Dodgers, bought his contract from the Cleveland Buckeyes for $5,000.

A standout in high school in basketball, football and boxing, Jethroe had a brief trial with the Indianapolis ABCs of the Negro American League in 1938. But he played mostly semipro baseball before signing with the Cleveland Buckeyes in 1942. The Buckeyes were owned by Ernie Wright, whose family ran the Pope Hotel in Erie. The Wrights would arrange for jobs in the offseason for Cleveland players, which is how Sam came to work as a bartender at the hotel.

In 1943, he met the love of his life, Elsie, and settled in Erie. Jethroe also worked at Erie's General Electric plant in those years to earn extra money.

After winning the Negro American League batting title in 1945 with an average of .393, Jethroe was summoned for a tryout — along with Jackie Robinson and Marvin Williams — by the Boston Red Sox. The team had been under pressure to integrate, but Robinson claimed later that the tryout had just been for show. None of the players was ever contacted again by the Red Sox.

Robinson broke the color barrier in 1947 with the Dodgers, and the following year Jethroe began playing for the Montreal Royals, Brooklyn's top farm team.

"I had to take quite a cut in pay — from $700 a month to $400 a month — when I signed with the Dodgers," Jethroe said later. "But it was the right thing to do."

After a season and a half with Montreal, Rickey traded Jethroe to the Boston Braves for several players and $150,000. When Jethroe joined the Braves in April 1950, he became the first Black player in Boston. Only four other MLB teams had integrated — the Dodgers, the New York Giants, the Cleveland Indians and the St. Louis Browns — and

Jethroe became the fifth African American to play in Major League Baseball.

Jethroe, who stood a strapping 6-foot-1 and weighed 178 pounds, was nicknamed "The Jet" for his blazing speed, and made an immediate impact with the Braves. In 1950, at age 32, he batted .273 with 18 home runs and 100 runs scored to become the oldest-ever National League Rookie of the Year. He also led the league with 35 stolen bases, a feat he duplicated the following year.

Don Newcombe, the first outstanding Black pitcher in Major League Baseball and Jethroe's one-time teammate on the Montreal Royals, called Sam "the fastest human being I've ever seen." This kind of basepath prowess was nothing new for Jethroe, who led the International League in 1949 with 89 stolen bases. Buck O'Neil, who played against him in the Negro American League, said that when Sam came to bat the infield would have to come in a few steps, "or you'd never throw him out."

In 1951, Jethroe virtually duplicated his statistics from his award-winning rookie season, but he slumped the following year after undergoing extensive surgery on his leg. In addition to being unable to use his blistering speed or slashing style at the plate, Jethroe also developed eye issues. At the end of the season, the Braves sent him to the minor leagues, where he started to wear glasses for the first time. Recovered from surgery, he also regained his batting stroke and, at age 35, still showed good speed on the basepaths.

A strong season in Toledo, for the Braves' AAA farm team, earned Sam a shot with the Pittsburgh Pirates in 1954. But his return to the big leagues lasted just two games before the Bucs sent him to their top minor league affiliate, the Toronto Maple Leafs, of the International League.

For the next five years, Jethroe starred for the Leafs, becoming a favorite of the Canadian fans.

"I really enjoyed my time in Toronto," Jethroe said in 1994. "I actually made a little more money there than I'd earned in the big leagues, so I was happy about that."

He was such a sensation north of the border that he was ultimately voted into the International League Hall of Fame.

Jethroe retired from professional baseball in 1958 when he was 40 years old. Back in Erie, he joined a team of former Negro League all-stars that competed for years as the Pontiacs, sponsored by a local car dealership, in the semipro Glenwood League. Looking years younger than his actual age, Jethroe was a bona fide star. He played several positions, hitting with power and even occasionally taking a turn on the mound for an inning or two.

In the 1950s, Jethroe opened a popular Erie bar and restaurant, Sam Jethroe's Steakhouse. After more than two decades in business, a local redevelopment authority forced him to move. He eventually opened a smaller tavern on Erie's west side.

Friends would say that in all the years they knew Sam, he rarely uttered a word of complaint, even after his house burned down and he fell into financial difficulty. He did, however, stand up for his rights in a suit against Major League Baseball to get pension money on the grounds that, had MLB not had a color barrier, Jethroe would have been able to play enough years to qualify for a pension. He was conflicted about the suit, saying he participated in it with "a heavy heart." Eventually, club owners agreed to pay Jethroe and other former Negro League players a small monthly stipend.

In December 2020, MLB made a monumental decision to recognize seven leagues from the Negro Leagues — including the Negro American League — as major league organizations. This means that Jethroe's statistics from the Negro American League will be added to MLB's record books, at least somewhat righting a wrong that had been done to Jethroe and generations of other African American players.

Toward the end of his life, Jethroe found that a new generation of baseball fans was taking a serious interest in the former Negro League stars who became Major League pioneers. Jethroe was invited to attend various all-star games and reunions, where he was always a popular presence.

In 1995, when Jerry Uht Park, now UPMC Park, opened in Erie, a bronze plaque dedicated to Jethroe was established at the minor league stadium.

Upon his death in 2001 at the age of 83, Jethroe was mourned in Erie and throughout professional baseball as not only a great player, but also a truly great man.

Photo provided by the Erie SeaWolves

Curtis Granderson (standing) connects with a pitch during a game for the Erie
SeaWolves. Granderson was a favorite of Dr. Brad Fox, who has covered
professional baseball in Erie for nearly 30 years.

My Second Home

By Brad Fox

Brad Fox spent his youth in Jamestown, N.Y., watching the Jamestown Expos and seeing Larry Parrish, Randy Johnson, Andres Gallaraga and Marquis Grissom play. He studied at Cornell University. Upon graduating, he moved to Syracuse to pursue medical school, and then relocated to Erie for his family medicine residency. He has continued to practice in Erie since graduating from residency in 1994. While his wife does not favor baseball, his two sons, Tyler and Adam, have grown up around the SeaWolves and both have worked for the team in one capacity or another.

I've been a team physician for the professional baseball teams in Erie for the past 29 years. In that time, baseball has woven itself into the fabric of who I am. People have asked me how I juggle working my full-time job with being responsible for the health of a minor league baseball team for six months out of the year. The truth is, I have done it for so long that it will be stranger when I no longer do it. Not being involved with professional baseball in Erie would create a huge void in my life.

My story begins in 1992. I was the team doc for the Erie Sailors, who had the distinction of being the first affiliate of the Florida Marlins expansion franchise. Marlins owner Wayne Huizenga flew three jets full of Marlins officials, including Marlins General Manager Dave Dombrowski, to Erie for the first game of the season against the Jamestown Expos. John Lynch took the mound that day to throw the first pitch ever for the Marlins organization. He was considered the club's top prospect at the time, though he never played an inning for the Marlins. He traded in his batting helmet for a football helmet and earned a Super Bowl ring with the Tampa Bay Buccaneers. He's currently the general manager of the San Francisco 49ers.
The Marlins moved on after the 1992 season, and the Texas Rangers took over the affiliation for 1993. The Sailors went unaffiliated in 1994,

but that didn't stop them from winning the Frontier League under the talented scout/manager Mal Fichman.

The Sailors played at Ainsworth Field, a hometown favorite that has been home to the Pastime since 1914. In fact, Ainsworth Field hosted Babe Ruth's All-Stars in 1923. Ruth's team won that game, but that's where facts end and myth has trickled down through the generations. According to legend, the Babe hit a home run that either went into the smokestack of the adjacent Roosevelt Middle School, or flew all the way over the school itself.

Erie built a new stadium in 1995 with one goal in mind: to bring affiliated baseball back to the city. The new, 6,000-seat ballpark built in downtown Erie was complete with a manicured infield and outfield, smooth basepaths and a big, beautiful, electronic scoreboard, all abutting the Civic Center. The stadium took Erie from a park that was like a fully functional, slightly beat-up Yugo to something like a brand-new, polished Ferrari. Like the Jeffersons, professional baseball in Erie was "Movin' On Up."

The new ballpark, known at the time as Jerry Uht Park, achieved its purpose. The Welland Pirates, a Class A ball club affiliated with the Pittsburgh Pirates, moved from Ontario to Erie. They would be known as the SeaWolves, as a Sea Wolf is another name for a Pirate.

Who knew, when I was doing José Guillen's preseason physical for short-season New York Penn League baseball, that he would go on to be the National League Rookie of the Year just two years later? The year after that, Erie was graced with the presence of future MLB All-Star Aramis Ramirez. Guillen and Ramirez were joined in the majors by the likes of J.J. Davis, Kory DeHaan, Yamid Haad and Rob Mackowiak, all of whom played for the 'Wolves during their four-year run in the NY-Penn League. Only one guy, catcher Chance Reynolds, played for both the Sailors and the SeaWolves.

My son, Tyler, frequently accompanied me to SeaWolves games, and was often with me in the locker room. Before one game in 1998, then 3-year-old Tyler and I were in the locker room. As the players walked by him, he'd say, "You're Shaun Skrehot. You're J.J. Davis. You're Keith Maxwell."

The players were amazed as he proceeded to rattle off every position player who approached him. Then, one of the pitchers came over and asked Tyler to identify him. Tyler answered his question with a blank look, which he gave to each and every pitcher who asked Tyler to identify them.

We couldn't figure it out at first. As it turned out, Tyler learned the players' names as they were announced coming to bat, but he identified them by the numbers on their uniforms instead of their faces. Since the pitchers were not announced in the same way, he didn't know who they were.

One summer, a player for the Pirates-affiliated SeaWolves hit a home run that broke a second-story window in the house across from the Uht. The team replaced the window, only to have the same player hit another home run through the very same window later in the season. After that, one of the local painting companies put a billboard over the window as an advertisement. That house is no longer there.

Erie made the jump to Class AA baseball in 1999. The Eastern League awarded two expansion franchises, and the SeaWolves became the AA affiliate of the Anaheim Angels.

The Angels invited me to spring training, where I got to know the team physicians. I also became friendly with many of the major league players including Mo Vaughn, Jim Edmonds, Darren Erstad and Troy Percival, as well as manager Terry Collins and coaches such as Larry Bowa and Rod Carew.

The SeaWolves were managed in '99 by former MLB All-Star Garry Templeton. The '99 team was loaded with prospects and saw 10 pitchers and seven position players break into the majors.

One of them in particular sticks out to me. Shawn Wooten was the opening-day starter at third base for the '99 team. He once took a ball off his face, splitting his lip wide open. Despite a cut lip dripping blood onto his jersey, Shawn did not want to leave the game. I got a call from the doctor covering the game, who did not feel comfortable repairing the injury at the ballpark.

Shawn went to the emergency room, where he spent several hours in the waiting room and then getting stitched up. That, however, did not stop him from suiting up the next night. Shawn knew that getting to the major leagues at third base was going to be difficult and, between the 1999 and the 2000 seasons, he changed positions and became the team's starting catcher. When I talk about gritty players, I always bring up Shawn.

Shawn wasn't the only SeaWolf who exemplified grit. Jumping ahead a bit, Erie's Brandon Douglas was part of a play that, in my opinion, changed the rules of Major League Baseball.

On Sept. 4, 2013, Douglas charged into Harrisburg Senators catcher Brian Jeroloman. Jeroloman dropped the ball and Douglas scored.

Jeroloman spent several days in the hospital with multiple injuries and, while he did return to play baseball, he was never the same. The following season, MLB enacted a rule which outlawed charging the catcher. They called it "The Posey Rule," even though the injury San Francisco Giants catcher Buster Posey sustained in a charging incident happened three years earlier.

To this day, I believe that the rule change occurred because of Dougie's collision.

With AA came a longer season. The SeaWolves play several day games on weekdays during the school year. The bat boys, for the most part, are high school kids — most of whom play ball. Because of this, the team has difficulty finding bat boys for those games. During their first season in AA, the 'Wolves realized they had a problem. I volunteered to work as the bat boy for those games. and have continued to work as bat boy at least once per season every season since — and usually many more.

During one game, I was in uniform as a bat boy and Connor Harrell was at bat. He took a pitch to the face and went down, with blood streaming from his nose. I ran to home plate to check on him, and was surprised and confused when the umpire tried to hand me his helmet and bat. In the moment, I had forgotten that I was in a dual role. Despite the circumstance, we both had to laugh.

The SeaWolves broke from the Angels in 2001 and became the Detroit Tigers' AA affiliate. The team, managed by Luis Pujols, produced 14 major leaguers including Omar Infante, Andres Torres and Fernando Rodney. One day that season, six-year-old Tyler came into the training room with a $5 bill. I asked him where he got it. He told me he had won a bet with Eric Munson. Apparently, Munson had bet Tyler that he, Tyler, could not be quiet for five minutes and Tyler had won. My six-year-old targeted the right player, as Munson had signed a then Tigers-record $3.5 million signing bonus.

In 2004, the Erie SeaWolves were graced with the one player I ever got to know who I consider to be, to use my own term, a "seven-tool player."

We all know that a five-tool player is one who hits for average and power, and can run, throw and field. The two categories I add are articulateness with the media and consideration to the fans. Curtis Granderson is that player.

In 2004, Curtis batted over .300, hit 21 home runs, knocked in 93 runs and stole 14 bases while performing as one of the most graceful center fielders I have ever seen. He also signed autographs both before games and late into the evening. He gave great interviews and did not decline a chance to represent the SeaWolves. He was also extremely charitable, a characteristic that followed him throughout his career in the majors.

In 2006, or maybe 2007, I made a trip to Detroit to catch a game. Before the game, former SeaWolf Justin Verlander was talking to some fans down the right field line. I walked over to say "hi," and he acted as though he had never seen me before. As I was standing there waiting to get Justin's attention, I heard a "Hey, doc!" from the outfield. The call was from Curtis, who ran over to say "hi." He not only asked how I was doing, but how the SeaWolves and the Erie fans were faring.

That wasn't the only time I got a shout-out from an outfielder.

In 2006, I was in Washington D.C. for a convention, and former SeaWolves center fielder Nook Logan left me a pair of tickets to a Nationals game. We had great seats on the third-base line in the upper boxes.

When we got there, I saw Nook running in the outfield and I wanted to say "hi." The usher for the lower box section would not let me go down to the field because I did not have field-level box seats. As I tried to explain that I just wanted to thank Nook for the tickets, a "Hey doc, you made it!" came from the field. Nook was standing at the fence waving to me. The usher let me pass.

The SeaWolves have had some phenomenal pitchers on their rosters over the years, including Verlander and Andrew Miller. Some incredible pitchers also took the mound against the team.

The SeaWolves faced CC Sabathia, Phil Hughs, Luis Severino, and even squared off against Andy Pettitte while he was on a rehab assignment. In 2002, Erie fans got to watch Cliff Lee pitch against the SeaWolves as a Harrisburg Senator and then, a week later, he pitched against them for the Akron Aeros.

Of all those aces, one pitcher's performance stands above the rest. One day in 2005, team trainer Rob Sonnenburg and I were in the dugout and Joel Zumaya was on the mound. He threw a pitch that registered "00" on the radar gun. I had never seen double zeroes on the gun. Rob and I immediately looked over to the radar guns in the stands behind home plate to see if it was true. The guys with the guns nodded.

He threw the next one at "00," and then slipped in an off-speed pitch at 93 miles per hour before reverting to "00" to finish off the batter and end the inning. When Joel got back to the dugout, we told him that he had hit 100 MPH with not one, but three pitches. The excitement was palpable. He went on to throw pitches recorded at 103 and 104 MPH in the majors, but it was amazing to be there the first time he hit a "century."

Even then, I knew Zumaya would make it to the majors. I felt the same way about Granderson, Verlander and Cameron Maybin. I also had high expectations for next-level opposition like Grady Sizemore, Alfonso Soriano, Matt Wieters and Victor Martinez.

And, of course, a kid named Bryce Harper.

The Harrisburg Senators came to Erie in 2011 with Harper in tow. Just like all the other teams in the Eastern League, the SeaWolves limited fan access to him and told their employees they needed to respect Bryce's space. No employee was to ask for an autograph.

Tyler, who was 16 then, and his good friend Chris, also 16, served as the batboys for the entire four-game series. They each worked two games in the home dugout and two in the visiting dugout. When the series was over on Sunday, both boys complained that they were not allowed to get a Bryce Harper autograph despite handling his bat, helmet and batting gloves, as well as talking to him for four days.

I went into the Harrisburg clubhouse after the game and asked the trainer if Bryce would mind signing autographs for Tyler and Chris. He said he wouldn't mind and told me to get two balls. Instead of having the trainer get the autographs, I brought the balls to Bryce and asked if he would sign them for the batboys.

"Of course not," he said with a big smile.

He signed both balls. I thanked him and, as I turned to walk away, he asked me, "Do you want one, doc?"

"No," I said, and I smiled back.

When I met the kids at the car to take them home, they were still complaining. The look on their faces when I handed them each an autographed ball was priceless.

Fans at the ballpark never know which major leaguer they might see or meet. They could on any given day run into legendary former Tigers manager Jim Leyland, World Series hero Kirk Gibson or six-time Detroit All-Star and Hall of Famer Allen Trammel in the stands. Dave Dombrowski — yes, the same Dave Dombrowski from the Marlins — was in Erie at least once a year while he was the Tigers' general manager. Sometimes, fans may run into these big leaguers without even realizing it.

Patrons of the ballpark also have gotten to see several major leaguers on rehab assignment through the years. Those who graced Erie's rosters while healing include Gary DiCarcina, Devi Cruz, Dontrelle Willis, Dmitri Young and Tim Belcher.

Belcher's stint was in 2000, when Tyler was 5. Given my son's loquacious nature, I felt the need to prepare him for his encounter with a major leaguer.

"Tyler, Tim Belcher is a pitcher for the Anaheim Angels who will be with the SeaWolves today to pitch," I told him on the way to the Uht. "You need to treat him differently than the other players. You need to give him more respect."

Tyler nodded his understanding.

We walked into the clubhouse and Tyler belted out, "Which one of you is Belcher?!"

Tim looked at him quizzically, raised his hand and said, "I'm Belcher." Tyler grabbed his hand and shook it, saying, "I'm Tyler, good to meet you, Belcher."

Tim was back in Erie many years later as a roving coach with the Akron Rubber Ducks. I introduced him to a 20-year-old Tyler and reminded him of that first meeting — which he actually remembered.

The 2019 season was a special one for the SeaWolves. The team had the first overall draft pick/No. 1 prospect Casey Mize and No. 2 prospect Matt Manning. They also had top prospect and first-round draft pick Alex Faedo at the top of the pitching order. They finished the regular season with the best record in the Eastern League.

Despite all of this, the 'Wolves did not make the playoffs because of the split-season format that gave preference to the division winners of each half of the season.

More than a win-loss record, the '19 SeaWolves were special because they were a cohesive unit with a great clubhouse atmosphere. One of the team's anchors was catcher Chace Numata, who was new to the organization. I had met him when he played for the Yankees' organization and enjoyed getting to know him during the 2019 season.

He had the best attitude. He kept the clubhouse rocking after a win by blasting music and dancing. On the flip side, he kept his teammates from turning negative after a loss. He was always smiling and made time for fans and friends. He was Hawaiian and he was happy to share that. He was older for AA, but he had some of the best pitchers in baseball throwing to him and he was there to make them better. Early in the morning on August 30, 2019, Chace was riding his motorized skateboard back to his apartment. He fell off the board and suffered a head injury. He arrived in the emergency room in a coma, and he was moved to the intensive care unit.

With Chace still in Erie, the SeaWolves went to Akron to play the final series of the season with the playoffs still in sight. On September 2, the last day of the season, Chace passed away. The 'Wolves defeated the Akron Rubber Ducks, but came off the field to find out that they did not make the playoffs and that their starting catcher, the life of the locker room, was gone.

Chace's family had come in from Hawaii to be with him after his accident, though they did not know anyone in Erie. The family went to Akron to see the SeaWolves play. They did not enter the clubhouse, but, for them, seeing Chace's other family play and win was a silver lining on a very black cloud.

Chace donated his organs. In an early morning ceremony during which the doctors and nurses lined the hallway to the operating room, Chace gave his final gift. Hopefully those who received his organs also received his shining attitude. The Erie community rallied around the family, posting pictures and memories on Twitter with #forNumi attached. A GoFundMe was started for the family, and raised over $50,000.

The SeaWolves created a scholarship for Erie high school seniors who are baseball or softball players pursuing college and who demonstrate the characteristics that Chace did. Honorees will be selected based on their on- and off-field accomplishments, their contributions to improving a team and their positive impact on the lives of others. #LiveLikeNumi is still active today with people posting inspirational images on Twitter.

Throughout 29 seasons, professional baseball in Erie has meant a lot to thousands upon thousands of people in and around the city. For me, it has become an integral part of my life.

As long as I am in Erie, and there is baseball in Erie, the ballpark will be my home away from home.

Photo provided by Gannon University Athletics.

Joe Gaeta (above) was the starting point guard on the Gannon men's basketball team and was a driving force in the Golden Knights' first-ever trip to the NCAA Tournament.

Way Back When

By Joe Gaeta and Joe Mattis

Joe Gaeta was an outstanding basketball player at Gannon College (now Gannon University) from 1958 to 1961. After graduating, he had careers in the U.S. active Army and Army Reserve and in sales at GTE. He is a founding father of the Gannon Golden Knights Booster Club. He was elected to the Metropolitan Erie Chapter of the Pennsylvania Sports Hall of Fame in 2006 and the Gannon University Athletics Hall of Fame in 2011.

Joe Mattis was an award-winning writer at the Erie Morning News *and* Erie Times-News *for parts of three decades. He was elected to the Metropolitan Erie Chapter of the Pennsylvania Sports Hall of Fame in 2009 and the Gannon University Athletics Hall of Fame in 2017. He is currently an assistant coach for Gannon's women's golf team.*

1958 was a big year for sports.

That year, a 28-year-old Arnold Palmer earned the first of his four Masters Tournament victories. Richard Petty finished 17th in his first career NASCAR start in Toronto, Canada. And the New York Yankees beat the Milwaukee Braves in seven games to capture the World Series title.

In Erie, Milt Simon began his third season as the Gannon College men's basketball head coach. Meanwhile, Joe Gaeta, a standout basketball and baseball player at LaSalle Academy in Brooklyn, N.Y., enrolled at Gannon.

This was a leap of faith for Gaeta, who would later be inducted into the LaSalle Academy Sports Hall of Fame. His interest in Gannon was sparked by the positive experience that two Brooklyn basketball players had at the college. Gaeta's former LaSalle teammate Jack Ahearn and Ahearn's twin brother, Jim, who went to St. Augustine High School, were freshmen on Gannon's basketball team when Gaeta was a senior in high school.

Gannon assistant coach George Hesch went to New York to recruit him when he was at LaSalle. At the encouragement of the Ahearns' father, Gaeta made the trip to Erie. Before he left, he was offered a scholarship to suit up as a Golden Knight.

Gaeta's freshman year was just the 15th basketball season for the Golden Knights, and only six times before had they finished with a winning record. While they had previously participated in the National Catholic Invitational Tournament in 1953, they had never been invited to play in the NCAA Tournament.

That would all change in the 1961-62 season, thanks to a passionate coach, strong leadership from upperclassmen and outstanding athleticism from the incoming freshman class. Gaeta's first three seasons were pretty much basketball as usual at Gannon, as the Knights won 30 of 57 games. Simon's contract was not renewed after a 48-49 record across five seasons at the helm.

1961 arrived, and with it, Arnold Palmer captured his first and only Open title with a win in the U.S. Open. Richard Petty won two NASCAR races, bringing his career win total to five. The Yankees bounced back from their 1960 World Series loss to the Pittsburgh Pirates by reclaiming the title with a win in five games over the Cincinnati Reds.

Back in Erie, Farrell High School legend Ed McCluskey was hired to replace Simon and become Gannon's eighth basketball coach as Gaeta began his senior year.

McCluskey never coached a game at Gannon. He had signed a five-year contract, but early in the summer he told Gannon officials that he could not fulfill his contract because of undisclosed personal reasons.

Gannon then turned to Hesch to be the head coach. Hesch had played for the Knights from 1951-54, was the first Knights player to score 1,000 career points and was Gannon's career leading scorer when he graduated. He also was a respected chemistry professor at Gannon. Hesch filled out his staff with assistant coaches Howard "Bud" Elwell, a teammate of his at Gannon, and Dick Fox, a Knights player from 1955-56.

Hesch had a mix of experience and enthusiasm on his side as he took the reins. A set shooter in his day, he told Gaeta to shoot 100 set shots a day and wanted him to shoot more from the outside.

"Our practices were different than we were used to," Gaeta said. "We ran a lot more plays than before. And during the games we really ran the ball quickly up the floor."

Hesch had raw talent in his starting lineup as the season began. Gaeta, nicknamed the "Little General" by Hesch for his rank of cadet first lieutenant in the ROTC program and his team leadership skills, was a 5-foot-11 point guard.

He was joined in the opening lineup by Jerry Lott, a 6-2 senior from Pittsburgh. Gaeta and Lott were the team's co-captains.

"(Lott) was a really tough ballplayer," Gaeta said.

Jack Byrnes, a 6-3 sophomore from Swissvale, was nicknamed "Spaceman" for his jumping ability.

Gaeta remembered him as an "outstanding forward." He also recalled that Byrnes had varicose veins — a condition that causes blood in the veins to pool or flow in the wrong direction — and had to be taken out of some games. Byrnes would sit on the bench with his legs raised until he thought he could go in again.

The biggest difference on the floor that season was the incoming class of freshmen, which included two highly touted freshman recruits of McCluskey: 6-3 guard Willie Alford, of Farrell, and 6-2 forward Al Lawson, of Homestead.

"Getting to know Willie Alford and Al Lawson was amazing," Gaeta said. "They were great kids. I can't remember the number of times one or the other, and sometimes both, scored 20 points or more."

The top players off the bench were freshmen Jerry Bodnar, of Sharon, and Dick Hauck, of Kutztown.

"I was excited to have them coming in," Gaeta said of the freshmen. "Right from the start they all played a big role for our team. With them, we had more quickness than in my previous years at Gannon."

The season began with a 21-point win at Baldwin-Wallace, followed by a 62-55 loss at Mansfield. It would be more than a month later before Gannon would lose again.

The Knights rolled to eight straight wins, which set a school record. They cruised to a 79-58 win over Belmont Abbey — which was coached by the colorful Al McGuire — for the eighth win of the streak. Alford led the way with 20 points, Byrnes scored 19 and Lawson and Lott each added 13 points for Gannon. But McGuire, a former NBA player who had previously coached at Dartmouth, continually entertained the fans with his antics from his seat on the bench. After the game, he had some words about the officiating, but he did say he was very impressed with the Knights.

Gaeta said that, to the team's surprise, their winning streak drew a large crowd.

"The fans really started to pack the (Gannon Auditorium) then," he said.

These fans included priests, who sat in the front rows of Section A. A group of students from Wehrle Hall sat in Section D adorned in robes, thus dubbing themselves the "Robe Club."

The Knights' winning streak ended when Youngstown State, always a nemesis to Gannon, edged the Knights, 62-61, in front of a large, boisterous crowd at the Gannon Auditorium, now known as the Hammermill Center.

The Knights led for most of the way before the Penguins, coached by Dom Rosselli, pulled out the win in the final two minutes. After two more wins, Gannon's record was 11-2.

The Knights had some intense battles that season against the likes of Steubenville and Alliance. Gannon earned its first win over Steubenville in seven years with a 10-point victory in December, but the teams' January matchup proved much more thrilling.

Alford led the Knights with 19 points, while Gaeta came through with two long-range set shots late in the game. He followed those up with a steal that he turned into a three-point play to give the Knights a 50-49 lead with 2:50 left on the clock. The Barons took a 52-50 lead, but another Gaeta steal and layup tied the score with 26 seconds remaining. The game went into overtime, during which Bodnar hit a shot from the side to give the Knights a 56-54 lead they did not relinquish.

Gannon didn't have as much success against Alliance, losing 63-61 and 65-64 in their two matchups that season. The Eagles, under coach Ted Haluch, always played well against the Knights.

Perhaps the most electrifying moment of the season came during Gannon's 94-84 home upset of Tennessee A&I, which was ranked No. 2 by United Press International at the time.

The Tigers were led by All-American guard Porter Meriwether, who lived up to his reputation with a 20-point effort. However, he was overshadowed by Alford and Lawson, who played like seasoned veterans to score 28 points each. Byrnes and Bodar each added 15 points, while Gaeta had six points and dished out 12 assists.

Gannon led 41-38 at the half, but scored 53 points in the second half against the hyped-up Tennessee team.

The crowd, estimated at 3,000, was by far the largest of the season. The fans stormed the Audi floor at the end of the game, but they did not leave immediately. After the Gannon players emerged from the locker room, the fans formed two lines through the front lobby of the Audi that carried across Peach Street to Perry Square. They didn't stop there as they surged through the streets of downtown Erie.

This upset, as well as the Knights' 16-7 record, caught the eye of

NCAA officials. Gannon earned its first-ever berth in the College Division (now Division II) Tournament. The four-team field in the Mideast Regional, which was played in Akron, Ohio, also included undefeated Florida A&M (25-0), defending national champ Wittenberg (19-4) and Youngstown State (15-11).

However, there was a problem for the Knights. Gannon had applied for NCAA membership in the fall, and just days before the playoff teams were selected, the application was approved. Although freshmen could play during the regular season because Gannon was an NAIA team, the NCAA did not allow freshmen to compete.

That decimated the Knights' roster, as starters Alford and Lawson and top reserves Bodnar and Hauck had to sit out the playoffs. Gannon had little time to put together a revamped lineup. The Knights lost to a powerful Wittenberg team, the defending national champion, 69-43 in the opening round.

Gannon rebounded with a spirited performance against Youngstown State in the consolation game, but lost 58-52. That was the third time the Penguins topped Gannon that season.

The decades since that memorable season have seen legends come and go.

Arnold Palmer finished his career with seven major golf championships, which is tied for seventh all-time in the PGA. Richard Petty set NASCAR records with 200 career wins and seven championships before applying the brakes for the last time. The Yankees went on to win eight more World Series, bringing their franchise total to a league-leading 27.

The 1961-62 Golden Knights basketball team, meanwhile, was inducted into the Gannon University Athletics Hall of Fame.

Four players from that team — Alford, Byrnes, Gaeta and Lawson — also were inducted into the Hall of Fame. They were joined by Hesch and Elwell, who went on to be a long-time athletic director at the university.

Hesch coached just one more season after the 1961-62 season. The Knights finished with a 13-12 record in 1962-63.

Following Hesch's resignation, McGuire was interviewed for the position. However, Gannon hired Jim Harding. It proved to be a good move as the Knights went 57-14 in Harding's three seasons at Gannon, including records of 20-4 and 20-3 in his last two seasons.

McGuire was hired at Marquette in 1964 and had a successful

13-year career there. His 1970 team won the NIT championship, and his 1977 team was the NCAA champion — after winning a final in which he became the first coach to be ejected in an NCAA championship game.

After the 1961-62 season, the Knights didn't return to the NCAA Tournament until 1972.

Between that time, they made four appearances in the NAIA playoffs. Gannon has had a number of great teams and players over the years, from Erie City Councilman Mel Witherspoon to former Erie BayHawks player Kyle Goldcamp.

And yet, nearly 60 years later, the fact remains: The 1961-62 Golden Knights were the ones who started it all.

Photo provided by Mercyhurst University Athletics.

Meghan Agosta (above) handles the puck during a Mercyhurst women's hockey game. Agosta led the nation in scoring and was instrumental in the Lakers' Frozen Four championship game appearance in the 2008-09 season.

Team on the Hill

By Joe Cuneo

Joe Cuneo is an Erie native and a lifelong sports fan. He served as the sports editor for the Gannon Knight, *the student newspaper of Gannon University, where he graduated with a major in journalism communications in 2013. He also was a part-time sports correspondent for the* Erie Times-News, *where he compiled box scores, wrote stories and garnered numerous bylines while covering games. He is currently a marketing communications consultant at Erie Insurance.*

The formation of the Mercyhurst women's hockey team garnered just a four-paragraph brief in the February 4, 1999 issue of the school's weekly student newspaper, *The Merciad.* Far from a snub, such a modest mention was somewhat on-brand for a team that lacked a coach and players to fill its roster, but was still to take the ice that fall. It wasn't until Mercyhurst athletic director Pete Russo tabbed men's associate head coach Mike Sisti to lead the upstart women's team in March '99 that the foundation was in place for an unlikely ascent into the sport's elite stratosphere.

"I decided to do it, and I thought we had a great opportunity to build something," Sisti said about transitioning to the women's game. "We knew we had a challenge, though, because we didn't start recruiting until March or April to field a team by September."

Mercyhurst's foray into women's hockey was part of a bigger movement. Following the U.S. Olympic team's gold medal in the 1998 Nagano Games, women's hockey was surging in popularity. Mercyhurst was swept up in the wave, becoming the 40th college in total and the 11th since the Olympics to add a team.

In the early years — once the Lakers put a team together — Mercyhurst cut its teeth by playing the nation's best programs on the terms of its opponents. This meant the Lakers took to the road more often than not. The team began scoring road upsets against the nation's elite squads and racked up three of the first four titles in the three-team Great Lakes Women's Hockey Association.

It wasn't long before the Lakers gained national prominence. Entering their fourth season, they had even higher aspirations.

While Mercyhurst had become among the nation's strongest teams and were now recruiting at a consistently high level, the team had yet to reach the postseason hockey crown jewel, the NCAA tournament. The 2004-05 season presented the Lakers with an opportunity to remedy this problem, as the NCAA expanded its postseason tournament from four teams to eight.

"We have something left to accomplish, and I think that's what we have to accomplish this year," senior forward Sara McDonald told the *Erie Times-News* before the season started.

Such a desire was clear during a dominant run that saw the Lakers outscore their opponents 44-3 over their last eight games, including a 4-1 win over Niagara in the College Hockey America title game (Mercyhurst was a charter member of the CHA when it formed in 2002.)

The win put the Lakers in the tournament for the first time ever. They were pitted against Harvard, one of the previous year's national finalists. The matchup provided Mercyhurst a chance to make its presence known on the national stage.

The Lakers made the most of the opportunity by pushing Harvard to three overtimes. But the Crimson ended it when they finally got one past goaltender Desi Clark, who was Mercyhurst's first-ever All-American. She racked up a remarkable 78 saves— still an NCAA record— in the longest tournament game in women's history.

"That was one of the best games I can remember being a part of," Sisti said.

Despite the result, the game still retains significance in the annals of Mercyhurst hockey. While many considered it merely a feel-good story about that year's underdog, the game proved to foreshadow the golden age of Mercyhurst women's hockey.

"Most people thought 'Well, this Mercyhurst team, yeah, it's a nice story and they've come a long way, but they're in for a wakeup call and are going to be exposed as not ready for primetime,'" Sisti said.

If there were indeed doubters, Mercyhurst quickly proved them wrong by reaching the tournament in each of the next three seasons. However, each appearance ended in a similar heartbreak in the quarterfinal round.

In 2006, the Lakers took eventual champion Wisconsin to two overtimes before losing, 2-1. The following year, they amassed a program-best 32-3-3 record to enter as a second seed and earn a home game in the first round. But Minnesota-Duluth scored the upset after the Lakers blew a two-goal lead and fell, 3-2, again in overtime. In 2008, the Bulldogs pulled off a similar feat on their home ice, bouncing Mercyhurst 5-4 in the opening round.

Yet, as the Lakers consistently finished in the national top 10 and racked up conference championships — they won every CHA title through 2011 — success begat another type of victory: wins on the recruiting trail.

Sisti had long been successful at selling Mercyhurst's scenic campus and small community to prospects, but the team's lack of a name brand that other power programs enjoyed prevented the Lakers from joining the elite. It was something only consistent winning could cure.

"My thinking was we always went after the best players, but that didn't always mean we would get them," Sisti said. "Once we started winning and we were more recognizable, players started to pay more attention to us. And when we got them on campus, it really started to resonate with them what we were building, and they would see the support we had here and the crowds we had and they decided they wanted to be a part of it."

Soon, Mercyhurst's triumphs on the ice translated to its biggest wins in ink.

Meghan Agosta, a 19-year-old from Ruthven, Ontario, was fresh off an Olympic gold medal as part of Team Canada in the 2006 Turin Games when she signed her letter of intent to Mercyhurst in June '06. Not only would Agosta tilt the rink in the Lakers' direction, she also paved the way for other elite recruits to arrive on the hill.

Mercyhurst's 2006-07 NCAA Tournament season was one to remember. The Lakers reached the No. 1 national ranking and garnered feature stories in *The New York Times* and *USA Today*. Agosta finished as a finalist for the Patty Kazmaier Award, which is bestowed upon the nation's best player. Unsurprisingly, the team landed another blue-chip recruit in fellow Ontario native Vicki Bendus. The subsequent recruiting class further loaded Mercyhurst with elite talent. The signing of players such as goaltender Hillary Pattenden, Jess Jones, Bailey Bram and Kelley Steadman portended a truly special period for the Lakers.

That this group was building a powerhouse on a sleepy campus tucked in between the hockey hotbeds of New England and the upper Midwest provided the team with even more motivation to build its own legacy.

"It was cool to be from a school that no one had really heard about," said Steadman, who played professionally and now serves as an assistant coach for the Lakers. "I'd meet people from camps who would say 'Hey, you're good, where do you go?' and I'd tell them and they'd say, 'I've never heard of it.'"

If there was ever a time for the Lakers to make a run at a national championship, the 2008-09 season seemed like a prime opportunity. And the Lakers knew it.

"Our goal is to not just win the CHA but to win everything," sophomore forward Jesse Scanzano told the *Erie Times-News* before the season. "Another year we didn't make it to the Frozen Four is constant disappointment."

Though Mercyhurst was laden with talent, the team was particularly young. Fifteen of its 21 players were either freshmen or sophomores. This fact became apparent when Agosta went down early in the season with a knee sprain, coinciding with a four-game losing streak that gave the Lakers a 3-4 record to end October.

"We knew we had a talented team, but I think they were a little overconfident, so I told them, 'The way you guys are playing, you might not win another game,'" Sisti said. "To their credit, they had that pride level, and they really took it personally and had the mindset like, 'Screw you, we're going to win every game.'"

The players nearly made good on their pledge to their coach, winning all but one game for the rest of the regular season en route to another CHA title. In the process, the Lakers dominated in style. They won all but three games by multiple goals, all while Travis Tritt's "It's a Great Day to Be Alive" blared from the team locker room after every victory.

Agosta led the country in scoring and became a top-three finalist for the Kazmaier Award for the third straight year. But the individual accolades meant little as Mercyhurst tried to exorcise its postseason demons while hosting St. Lawrence in the first round of the NCAAs. And if the nearly 1,200 fans that crammed into the Mercyhurst Ice Center had any say about it, they would will the Lakers into the Frozen Four.

"I had never seen the rink so packed," Steadman said. "People were crazy. They were standing on the boards, and I could barely hear anything."

Despite the advantage of having a raucous crowd on its side, the Lakers started off slowly. They fell behind after failing to score in the first period. But Steadman put the Lakers on the board, and Agosta gave them the lead for good in the second. Jones added another goal in the third, and Mercyhurst was bound for the Frozen Four.

The final, 3-1 score somewhat belied the dominant win for the Lakers, who outshot St. Lawrence, 44-13. But all eyes were on the road ahead. Nothing could constrict the enthusiasm on the Mercyhurst campus and in the Erie community as the Lakers set out for Boston to take on Minnesota in the national semifinals.

"It was cool to experience that," Steadman said of the support. "And I feel like everybody on campus was supporting us as we achieved more and more success."

The Merciad — in contrast to its short mention of the team's inception a decade earlier — splashed a huge photo of the Lakers mobbing Pattenden in goal across its front page with the headline, "Women's hockey bound for Boston." For Bendus, the excitement was palpable. "You could feel it every moment you were on campus, whether it was in class, in the gym or at the rink," she said.

Waiting in the wings, however, were the second-seeded Golden Gophers, who had won national championships in 2004 and 2005 and were again favorites over the Lakers at Boston University's Agganis Arena.

But in the Friday nightcap of the two-game semifinal doubleheader — Wisconsin dropped Minnesota-Duluth 5-1 in the first game — Mercyhurst stunned anyone not familiar with the team by jumping to a 5-1 lead to enter the third period.

The Lakers had ripped off five unanswered goals and seemed destined for a chance at the title when Minnesota answered. The Gophers rallied in the final period by netting three straight goals of their own. A pair were scored on power plays, the second of which came on a 6-3 skating advantage and cut Mercyhurst's lead to a single goal with 1:17 left. But Pattenden, the staid freshman stalwart in goal, stayed strong by standing on her head as the remaining time evaporated.

Mercyhurst's 5-4 win in the national semifinals didn't just catapult the Lakers into the Frozen Four championship game. It also sent a message to the college hockey community as to who was the new powerhouse in town.

"(Minnesota) had so much firepower in their lineup that I'm not sure anyone, including ourselves, expected we had a shot at winning," Bendus said. "But we dumped our guts out that game, every single player."

Mercyhurst had defied the odds and would play for a championship. But the exuberance the Lakers felt in the moment couldn't compensate for the energy they had expended before heading into the title game with Wisconsin less than two days later.

"The final game, though, I'm not sure we had much left in the tank," Bendus said.

Though Mercyhurst stood its ground by battling the Badgers to a scoreless tie in the first period, Wisconsin wore down the Lakers with three goals in the second en route to a 5-0 win. The victory marked the Badgers' second championship in three years.

Mercyhurst seemed primed for vengeance in 2009-10, despite Agosta deferring her senior season to participate in the Vancouver Games for gold-medal-winning Canada. The Lakers held the nation's top ranking for much of the season as they blew past their competition. They tied a program-record 32 wins before entering the NCAAs as the top seed. Along the way, they dominated opponents. They lost just once in conference play as Bendus, Bram and Scanzano were finalists for the Kazmaier Award.

In the first round of the NCAA tourney, the Lakers had little trouble dispatching Boston University, 4-1 at home.

Yet, they were stunned in the semifinals when fifth-seeded Cornell pulled off a 3-2 upset in overtime.

The next day, Bendus won the Kazmaier Award, but the moment was bittersweet.

"The loss to Cornell in the semifinals was devastating," she said. "It was such an emotional rollercoaster the entire weekend."

The following season held just as much promise, as the team's core remained intact. That included Agosta, who returned for her senior year. Adding to the Lakers' motivation for finishing the deal was their role as host of the Frozen Four, which would come to the Louis J. Tullio Arena. Mercyhurst even scheduled three games at the Tullio Arena during the season to prepare the team for March.

But the Lakers unexpectedly drew a road game against Boston University in the tournament's first round and struggled in a 4-2 loss. The shock of the defeat left lasting scars on the Lakers who concluded their collegiate careers.

"There was so much build-up to it during the season, not only on campus but across the city," Bendus said "The loss to BU in the final eight was heartbreaking. We felt like we had let the entire school and community down. For our senior class especially, finishing our careers like that was extremely tough."

Bendus went on to play professionally for several years and now serves as a performance coach at Brock University in St. Catharines, Ontario.

Agosta, who left Mercyhurst as the NCAA all-time leader in points and goals, earned another gold medal in the 2014 Sochi Games and added a silver in 2018 in Pyeongchang, where she was joined by Bram. She now serves as an officer in the Vancouver Police Department.

The loss to BU wasn't the final game for many of Mercyhurst's graduating stars, who played professionally and in international competition. But it did mark the end of an era for a group that captured the imagination of a city and made Mercyhurst hockey synonymous with winning.

While the players were gone, the reputation remained.

"Those years put Mercyhurst on the map and made us a hockey school," Steadman said.

It's a distinction that continues to endure for the Lakers, who are now entrenched among the nation's elite and returned to the national semifinals in 2013 and 2014. These days, there's only one thing Sisti considers missing on his resume: a national championship.

"We've arguably had more success than any other team, other than just three others, when you look at winning," he said. "I really think that's the one thing that we haven't accomplished yet."

Should the Lakers again summon a run at a national championship, Sisti knows who to thank.

"One of the things that I always say is, 'I hope every past and present player is smiling because they helped us,'" he said. "All players and coaches and everyone else around the program have played a big part in building the program."

Photo provided by Kelly Patterson

(From left) Michael Conner, Kelly Patterson, James Conner, Richard Conner and Glen Conner Jr. pose for a family photo together. Kelly raised her four boys to become upstanding citizens and outstanding athletes.

Momma

By Aaron McKrell

Conner Strong.

It's become a mantra. A way of life. It's the concept that fear is a choice, and that quality of life depends on how one deals with inevitable adversity.

Many people know the story of James Conner, the Pitt star-turned-cancer survivor-turned-Pro Bowl running back for the Pittsburgh Steelers. Fewer people know of his older brothers, who also are athletically gifted and who helped pave the way for James' success.

However, even fewer people are aware of the critical role played by their mother.

Ironically, the woman who helped birth the concept of Conner Strong is not named Conner at all.

Kelly Patterson is the backbone of her family. She overcame enormous adversity to raise four strong young men: Glen Jr., Richard, Michael and James. All of them have found success on the basketball court or football field, and more importantly, in life.

She set an example for them on how to deal with hardship, something she learned to do at a young age.

When Kelly was a child, her mother worked odd hours. This left Kelly to play by herself without complaint for hours at a time.

Marital issues between her parents meant constant moves within Erie, from living above a bar at one point, to living in a refurbished garage at another. Kelly went to five different elementary schools.

"I never thought about it as a bad childhood as I was going through it, but as I got older, I realized how hard it really was," Kelly said.

Hard times sharpened her survival skills. She began dating Glen Conner Sr. as a teenager, and became pregnant at age 16. She got her own place and had Glen Jr. in March 1989, during Easter break of her junior year in high school. Glen Sr. was there every day and provided financial support.

Kelly graduated from Strong Vincent High School in 1990, and had her second child, Richard, in August of that year.

She completed a nine-month certification program and internship while pregnant with her third son, Michael, who was born in December 1991. A few months later, she began secretarial work at what was then the Human Services Support Corporation.

Glen Sr. worked as a cook at various restaurants during this time. They married in April 1992 and moved into a house on the east side of town.

She was 20, with three young boys and a new job, and she was still growing up herself.

"Half the time, I felt like a glorified babysitter," Kelly said. "There was never really, 'OK, let's sit down and let's read a bedtime story, boys.' It was just all I could do to keep them fed and bathed and get them to daycare, get myself to school or work or whatever, (and) get on the bus until I had a car."

No matter how much she struggled, Kelly was driven by the desire to break the cycle of teen pregnancy in her family (her mother had had her at age 16) and to prove any doubters wrong.

"It just kind of clicked with me that I'm creating people," she said. "This is important work."

This meant providing her sons with activities which could help them grow as individuals. The four Conner brothers played football, basketball and even wrestled.

"I wanted to start something to keep them out of trouble," Kelly said. "Being involved with sports, you have rules you have to follow. There's discipline. There's teamwork."

The boys took to sports naturally, especially Glen Jr., who was tall for his age.

James, who favored basketball, wanted to quit football after playing in his fifth grade year. Kelly, however, signed him up for another go-round, and changed the trajectory of his life in the process.

"James playing with older brothers and older kids helped him a lot (to) get better early, at a younger age," Kelly said.

Both Kelly and Glen Sr. worked long hours while co-owning a restaurant. During her break from her day job, Kelly would dash to the restaurant to work the lunch hour. They were still young, and the stress and strain of their schedules took its toll on their marriage. They divorced in the summer of 1998.

Soon after, Kelly began dating, and she and her boys moved into a house with her boyfriend in Millcreek in 2000. They married in 2003. Kelly was careful about when and where she let her boys go, so they spent much of their time together. This led to an extraordinary bond that continues to this day.

"How do you not develop unbreakable relationships when you're on top of somebody all day, every day?" Michael said.

The boys were rambunctious. They wrestled, they played. But they always knew who ran the show.

Kelly is 5-foot-5. Her sons, all of whom are over 6-0, were tall for their respective ages as children.

"They had to know who was in charge, even though they were big, strong kids," Kelly said. "It wasn't really a fear (thing), but it was more of a respect thing."

She had a lieutenant of sorts in Glen Jr. Kelly said he showed her the utmost respect, and that he expected the same treatment of her from his little brothers.

"He was my protector," she said. "He was my right hand. He did everything to help me."

More than anything, the boys knew that their "Momma," as they call her, would always have their backs.

"She was just always there," Glen Jr. said. "The most consistent figure in our life, hands down."

That support translated to their athletic experiences, as Richard and James played football for McDowell High School and Glen Jr. and Michael were starters on the Trojans' basketball team. Whether it was driving them to and from practices, attending games, paying participation fees, working concession stands, participating in fundraisers and booster club activities or providing emotional and vocal support, Kelly did it all.

"It didn't matter if I scored two points or 20 points, my mom (was) gonna have the same reaction," Michael said. "'Baby, you did so good out there. I'm so proud of you.' My mom, her love was watching her babies being out there and having fun, and doing something they were good at."

Michael saw playing time as a sophomore for the 2008 McDowell squad that won the District 10 and Region 7 titles, and was much more involved when the Trojans repeated as region champions in 2009.

More than winning championships, though, Kelly made sure her sons valued themselves.

"(I was) trying just to make sure that they loved who they were and didn't feel some kind of way, because they love who they are," she said.

Her positive reinforcement bolstered their growth both on and off the field or court.

"That's really all it takes for people, is to realize that you have people who believe in them," James said. "She really was it. It was nothing but praise from her."

Kelly certainly had faith in her sons, and knew James had immense talent on the football field. He broke McDowell's single-season sack record as a junior despite only playing at defensive end for part of the season.

However, a lifetime's worth of hardship taught her to be skeptical of things that seemed too good to be true. The best she allowed herself to hope for was a scholarship to a Division II university for James.

"I just felt like, my life has been so hard from always that, is something this great really gonna happen to us?" Kelly said.

As always, Kelly did whatever she could to provide support. Though she was often under financial strain, she did creative things such as selling wreaths and crafts made by her and her mother to come up with money for football camps.

James excelled at those camps, earning MVP status at the VTO Sports Elite 100 Showcase as a junior. His outstanding performance at the University of Pittsburgh's camp earned him an on-the-spot scholarship offer, which he accepted.

He became McDowell's star running back in his senior year and made the leap to the Panthers' backfield. He broke out with a star turn — 226 yards and one touchdown on 26 carries — to be the 2013 Little Caesars Bowl MVP as a freshman. He was named the 2014 Atlantic Coast Conference Player of the Year and ACC Offensive Player of the Year — beating out Heisman Trophy-winner Jameis Winston — after a gargantuan sophomore season.

Kelly got divorced a second time that year. She continued to support her sons; she and the rest of the family were there to cheer James on, with Richard teaching Kelly the finer points of football as they went.

Adversity struck in September 2015 when James tore his MCL during Pitt's season opener.

"It's a setback, and I just knew he was putting (in) his whole heart and soul and it was football or nothing," Kelly said. "He had everything riding on it, so I just felt so heartbroken for him."

As the family put it, though, the injury turned out to be a blessing in disguise. It was cause for medical appointments that allowed doctors to catch something much more serious.

Kelly got the call on Thanksgiving. Her youngest son told her he might have cancer.

She got off the phone and broke down.

"I'm like, 'My kid does not have cancer,'" she said. "'Stop it. This can't be real life.'"

As quickly as she fell apart, she put herself back together for the sake of her sons. The following Monday, James' diagnosis of Hodgkin's Lymphoma was confirmed.

"After that Monday appointment, it was like, 'OK, momma bear mode,'" Kelly said. "'It's time to kick cancer's ass.'"

She took time off work to be there for every one of James' chemotherapy treatments. She'd get up at 5 a.m. for the two-hour drive to Pittsburgh. She'd be at his apartment by 7 a.m. so they could be there for the all-day treatment starting at 8 a.m.

Kelly was hyper-vigilant throughout the process, whether she was lecturing nurses on the proper application of numbing cream or jumping every time James dry heaved.

"It's just like, 'I just want to fix it, I just want to take it away,'" Kelly said. "'I want to do whatever I can do.'"

When it was over, she'd spend the evening with him at his apartment until he was feeling better and she felt comfortable enough to leave him. Then, she'd drive back to Erie so she could go to work the next day.

It was during this time that James developed the mantra of "Conner Strong," driven by the concept that fear is a choice.

"Fear is all in the mind, and in the mind, you always have a choice of how you're gonna react to something," James said. "Sometimes fear is made up. Every day we have decisions to make."

James primarily drew from two people for this mindset. One was NFL safety Eric Berry, who beat Hodgkin's Lymphoma and went on to earn Pro Bowl honors. The other was his mother. James pointed to Kelly's early life as a young mother, and how she overcame the fear of the unknown to excel in womanhood.

"(My brothers and I) realized she was the first one to really struggle, and probably struggled the most out of all of us," James said. "She set the tone."

On May 23, 2016, it was confirmed that James' cancer was in remission.

"(I was) just so thankful to God, just so glad it was over," Kelly said. "I knew he was gonna be OK, but just to finally hear it and it to be confirmed, I was so happy about that."

Her other sons were hardly sitting on the sidelines. Rather, they were making moves to better themselves, with their mother backing them all the way.

For a time, Glen Jr., Richard and Michael were without a higher education or career path. Kelly was concerned, but had faith in their ability to figure it out.

It was her willingness to let her sons make her own choices — and fight their battles beside them rather than in front of them or behind them — that helped them grow into independent, strong men.

"That was huge," Michael said. "It lets you think as a man. It lets you make your own decisions." The decisions they've made have proven largely successful.

Glen Jr. entered the human services field while keeping his focus on family. He married his wife, Sabrina, in 2017, and they had a son, Giulio, in 2019 and a daughter, Gia, in 2021.

That same year, he was nominated for a child healthcare services award for his work at Harborcreek Youth Services. He currently attends Edinboro University, where he is off to a strong start as he pursues a degree in the health and fitness field.

Kelly is proud of him for not only his professional strides, but his commitment to his family.

"He has overwhelmed me with what kind of father and husband he is," she said.

In turn, Glen Jr. credits his mother with showing him how he should treat Sabrina.

"To me, it's not hard to make a woman happy," he said. "They don't want a lot of things. It's simple. Follow the rules of marriage and be a good husband. And you'll be a good husband by being a good man. A good, Christian man."

Richard became the first of the four Conner brothers to earn a bachelor's degree when he graduated from California University of Pennsylvania in 2019. He followed that up by earning his master's degree in sports management from the same university in December 2020.

"I'm in awe of his drive and work ethic, and all that he's accomplished," Kelly said.

Richard's dream is to become an NFL agent. Kelly, who dubbed him "the great debater," believes he has the skill set for such a high-stakes position.

"You can't get anything over on Richard," she said. "He's gonna debate it to the end."

Still, Richard values humility, which was taught to him at a young age by Glen Sr. His father once told him, "You ain't better than nobody, and nobody's better than you."

"That stood out to me," Richard said.

Through all the studying and test taking, all the long drives from Pittsburgh to California, Pa., Richard has received love and support from Kelly.

"(She) always lets me know that I make her proud in that sense,"

Richard said. "Honestly, just whatever I have needed, (she's) just always there to provide positive reinforcement and encouragement."

Glen Jr. and Richard played on the Erie Express semipro football team for several years. Glen Jr. is a multi-winner of the team's Defensive Player of the Week award and was named to the 2019 Gridiron Developmental Football League All-Pro team. Richard was part of an offensive line that earned Offensive Player of the Week honors. Both were instrumental in helping the Express to multiple 10-win seasons and playoff appearances.

Just as she's there for James, Kelly was in the stands at the Express games, cheering on her oldest boys.

"It means a lot," Richard said. "It's equal love."

Michael had a successful career as a staff sergeant in the United States Air Force, during which Kelly would often visit him where he was stationed in Florida. He currently works for Otis Elevator Company. He and his wife, Kayla, have two sons: Michael Jr. and Maceo.

Kelly called Michael a loving and devoted father and husband. She also described him as a comedian, the one who is always singing and dancing and is the life of the party.

"He's something else," she said.

But, more than his vibrant soul, he learned from his mother to have a loving heart.

"The biggest thing my mother has taught me about is how to provide unconditional love," Michael said. "Even if you don't have (anything) — you could be the brokest people in the world, lights shut off, but my mom was always just so loving."

James went on to have a strong senior season at Pitt and was chosen in the third round of the 2017 NFL Draft by the Pittsburgh Steelers. He earned Pro Bowl honors in his second season after racking up 13 touchdowns and 1,470 yards from scrimmage. He recently wrapped up his fourth season with the Steelers, during which he played as the starting running back.

He continues to work hard, a value that Glen Sr. impressed upon him in his youth.

"For 40-plus years, hours on hours, so that was his way of helping us and showing us that a man's got to work hard or he isn't gonna have anything," James said. "So, he definitely instilled a work ethic in all of us."

James' battle with cancer touched him with compassion for other cancer patients, and he spends some of his free time doing volunteer work at cancer treatment centers.

"Even though he's been through what he's been through — he's been through a lot — he's just so appreciative for what he does have," Kelly said. "And, the opportunity to even play, to get a college scholarship, and then to be in the NFL, he just thanks God for everything and just wants to pay it forward."

Kelly left her position as an administrative assistant at Harborcreek Youth Services in 2019. She lives in a home in Fairview Township — bought for her by James — along with Richard, Michael and Kayla and their children.

Kelly continues to play a supportive role in the lives of her sons, a fact that is not lost on Glen Sr.

"God blessed us both with four great boys," he said. "She's an awesome lady. Although we split, we did what we had to do to make sure that they were well taken care of."

When her sons look back on their childhoods, they remember a strong, selfless woman who was their rock of stability.

"She put us above her," Richard said. "And she always did what she thought was right and in our best interests."

Conner Strong.

It's a mantra.

The woman who inspired it?

Her name is Patterson.

Photo provided by Greg Hoffman

Greg Hoffman (middle) holds the PIAA Class AAAA District 10 boys basketball trophy while surrounded by his friends, loved ones and teammates of the McDowell boys basketball team.

Calmness and Courage

By Joe Mattis

During nearly one quarter of a century covering thousands of sporting events for the Erie newspapers, I've witnessed many memorable moments. However, two things accomplished by high school athletes will forever be etched in my mind.

What makes those moments different from everything else I have written about? In a word: uniqueness. In each case, there were unforeseen circumstances that had to be overcome for success. One involved the calmness of a basketball player in the face of an extremely tense moment with the game on the line. The other time, a football player showed great courage beyond what you would expect of a teenager. He continued to play in a close game while filled with emotion following a health scare concerning his father.

Let's set the stage for the display of calmness.

During the 2001-02 basketball season, the Cathedral Prep Ramblers and McDowell Trojans split their two regular season games. Prep won the first game by four points, while the Trojans evened things up with an overtime victory later in the season. The third matchup came on February 28 in the District 10 Class AAAA championship game in front of a reported 3,300 fans at Edinboro University's McComb Fieldhouse.

Typical of Prep-McDowell games, neither team could get a big lead. The score was tied 16-16 after the first quarter before the Ramblers held a 28-26 margin at halftime. At the end of three quarters, it was McDowell with a 42-41 advantage.

Prep eventually forged a 51-48 lead into the final minute of the fourth quarter. The Trojans were working to tie the game with time running down when McDowell senior Greg Hoffman attempted a contested 3-point shot. The clock showed no time left and, at first, it appeared the Ramblers were the winners. But, it was determined Hoffman was fouled just before the buzzer sounded. He would shoot three free throws. If he missed any of them, the Ramblers would walk away with the win and the championship. If he made all three, the game would move into overtime.

"Actually, we ran two plays to get Matt Miller open for the shot, but they took it away," Hoffman said of the final seconds. "I went around a screen and was supposed to drive and kick it out. But (Prep's) Andy Kubinski hedged on the screen for a second, I dropped back and shot and was fouled by Joe Jones."

You might think Hoffman was shaking in his sneakers as he walked to the free-throw line with the boisterous crowd in a frenzy. He stood there almost alone, with just the referees joining him on the court. But it was something that his coach, Tom Hansen, told Hoffman before he attempted his free throws, that dispelled any nervousness.

"He called me over and said, 'Find your sister (Megan) in the crowd and make them for her,'" Hoffman said. "I couldn't find Megan in the stands, but I knew she was there. That took my mind off the moment. I blocked everything out and made all three of them."

The overtime was all Trojans as they rolled to a 64-59 win and the D-10 title. Hoffman had scored nine of his 23 points in the fourth quarter, and five more in overtime. He also was a perfect 10 from the free-throw line.

"I was in a zone that game," Hoffman recalled some 18 years later. "I scored the most points of my high school career at the most important game."

A strange thing happened after the championship game. Cathedral Prep head coach Andy Sisinni was talking to fans in McComb Fieldhouse. When he finally went to the parking lot, he discovered the Prep bus had already departed for Erie. The parent of one Rambler player was still in the lot, but his minivan was filled. So, Sisinni was searching for a way to get home.

In stepped Bobby Hoffman, Greg's father and a friend of the Prep coach. He quickly offered a ride to Sisinni, who just as quickly accepted. Bobby Hoffman saved the day for the Rambler coach after his son Greg had just ruined it on the court.

Unfortunately for the Trojans, their season came to an end one game later — and it came in another overtime scenario. Gateway derailed the Trojans 50-48 in a PIAA first-round inter-district matchup.

Ironically, Greg Hoffman had been accepted to and was planning on attending Cathedral Prep for his high school years. However, he played in a summer league with Trojan players before that happened, which led to a change of heart and enrollment at McDowell. As things would happen, he would be celebrating with his Trojan teammates several years later in the most memorable game of his high school career.

Photo provided by Matt Glass

(From left) Brothers Matt Glass and Phil Glass Jr. and their father, Phil Glass Sr., coach together at an Iroquois High School football game in 2005. Matt Glass excelled on both sides of the ball while playing for his father in the 2000s.

Four years before Hoffman's show of calmness, Matt Glass displayed outstanding courage in a 1998 Friday night Erie County League football game at Fairview High School. The Tigers, who had a 1-2 record, hosted an Iroquois team that had won two of its first three games.

Fairview scored on its opening possession. Quarterback Jason Wallace, who was sidelined for the Tigers' first three games with an ankle injury, ran for an 11-yard touchdown. The score was 7-0 after Drew Macko kicked the extra point.

Iroquois finally reached pay-dirt midway through the third quarter when Matt Cadden bulled his way into the end zone from the 1-yard line. But the PAT kick by Matt Glass was wide, and Fairview held on to a one-point lead, 7-6.

Later in the quarter, the Tigers had the ball deep in Iroquois territory when everyone's attention turned to the Braves' bench. Play was stopped at the 3:39 mark as Iroquois coach Phil Glass was attended to after experiencing chest pains. After a delay, he was taken to Saint Vincent Hospital. Iroquois assistant coach Matt Shesman — who had been the head coach at North East prior to coming to Iroquois — took over for the Braves.

"I thought he was having a heart attack," Matt Glass said of his father. "My mother wanted me to go to the hospital. But coach Shesman, who was like a second father to me, and my brother Phil talked me into staying. They said there was nothing I could do to help (my dad) at the hospital."

After that, Glass — and his teammates — played with a fury. When Fairview's drive finally resumed, it was stopped at the 4-yard line. Matt Glass remembers that moment as if he were still playing in his linebacker position.

"The game was like in slow motion, but I was in full speed." he said in early 2020. "It was fourth (down) and nine (yards to go). I read the play and made a tackle about a yard short of the first down."

Back at quarterback, Glass helped Iroquois march downfield into Fairview territory in the fourth quarter. That drive ended when Fairview's Steve Pettis recovered a fumble at the 20-yard line.

The Braves held their ground for three plays and forced the Tigers to punt. Fairview coach Buster Wellek didn't want the ball punted to Glass, but the Iroquois leader fielded it anyway.

Glass came across the field and grabbed the ball on his own 41-yard line. He bolted toward the left sideline and was finally stopped after a 41-yard return to the Iroquois 18-yard line.

It was now do-or-die time for the Braves, and a determined Glass knew what he wanted to do.

"In the huddle I told my teammates to give me the ball," Glass said. Five plays later — with just 26 seconds left in the game — he rolled out from the 5-yard line and raced to the end zone for the go-ahead touchdown. Glass then threw a 2-point pass to Kevin Loftus as the Braves prevailed, 14-6.

After the game, Glass spoke to reporters through tears. He was exhausted, both physically and emotionally, but had just received word that his father's blood pressure had dropped and that the coach would be OK.

"I blew the extra point, and I knew I had to get back down the field and score," he said. "I know (my father) wanted me to be out here to lead the team. And with coach Shesman calling the offense, it was fine."

As it turned out, Phil Glass was hospitalized overnight and returned to practice the next week.

There were multiple coaches who spoke about the courageous performance that Matt Glass, still a junior, displayed after his father was stricken.

"What Matt Glass did was one for the record books," Wellek said. "People will be talking for a long time about the character of that kid."

Shesman also had words of praise, not only for Glass, but for his teammates as well.

"I have to give great credit to our entire football team to the way they responded, especially Matt Glass for the most courageous performance I ever saw an athlete make on a football field," he said.

Matt Glass vividly remembers what Wellek and legendary former Fairview coach Jack Bestwick did after the game ended.

"Buster gave me a hug, and Bestwick said, 'Great game kid. I hope your father is okay,'" Glass said.

Where did Matt Glass, a two-time All-Erie County League selection, get the courage to keep playing while his father was in the hospital?

"I did it for him," Matt said of his father. "He made me the athlete that I was."

Photo provided by Quentin Orlando

Strong Vincent head football coach Joe Bufalino (right) awards a plaque to Vincent running back Quentin Orlando following the Colonel's 1991 PIAA Class AAA District 10 title win. The Colonels went on to win the state championship that year, a victory that cemented Vincent as the first school in Erie County history to win a football state title.

The Little Things

By Aaron McKrell

"It's the little things, gentlemen."

Those five words sum up Joe Bufalino's philosophy as much as any other phrase or sentence ever could. The legendary Erie football coach took the game — and life — one bird-dog-lovin' step at a time. And he drilled this mantra into the mind, heart and body of any brave soul who dared step across the white line onto the football field with him.

Bufalino's intensity was such that not everyone joined him at the finish line. But those who did were better for it in nearly every conceivable way.

The most rugged testament to the success of Bufalino's approach is the 1991 Strong Vincent High School football team. Never did a finer group of bay rats emerge from the lower west side of Erie, and they proved that by becoming the first football team from Erie County to win a state championship.

More importantly, the bonds formed and lessons learned from long, brutal evenings on Strong Vincent's rock-strewn practice field turned a group of scrappy kids into successful men who value family and friendship above all else.

And to think, it all started from a butcher shop window.

The Butcher's Son

Joseph Patrick Bufalino was many things: a top-shelf cook, a dedicated gardener, a butcher, an innovator and a family man. To his son, Joe, he also set the standard for hard work.

Joseph, a first-generation Sicilian American, ran Bufalino's Meat Market at a spot just south of West 29th Street and Peach Street. He lived with his wife, Alvina, and their three children in a home above the store.

From seven in the morning until 10 at night, Joseph poured his energy into the market. Alvina ran the cash register, while Joe, the oldest child, stocked shelves and bagged groceries. According to Joe, his dad was the first Erie store owner to have rotisserie chicken displayed in the window. This taught Joe the importance of taking a chance. More importantly, he watched and learned from his parents' tireless work ethic.

"There was not an ounce of quit in that man," Joe said. "Today, he would work me under the table."

But Joseph was not unreasonable. He knew his son loved sports and didn't keep him tied down to the store. On Saturdays, Joe and his friends rushed to Tech Memorial Field early just to get a spot on one of the day's pickup teams.

"We played everything at the drop of a hat," Joe said.

He took a special interest in football, especially after his father bought him a helmet and shoulder pads to play in.

"I had my gear, and I just fell in love with the game," Joe said.

The game loved him back. Joe was quick and excelled as a halfback and defensive back at Cathedral Preparatory School from 1962-66. He played under Tom Duff, a hard-nosed, old-school football coach who wasn't above corporal punishment to motivate his players.

"It was nothing to get smacked in the helmet," Joe said.

Joe would be involved in football for more than 40 years in one form or another, but he never experienced practices tougher than the ones at Prep.

"You were all out any time you were on that field," he said.

He graduated from Prep and went to nearby Edinboro University, but initially didn't go out for the football team. His moratorium on cleats didn't last long, though. He realized that he didn't just *want* to play football. He *had* to play.

Earning a Rep

Bufalino joined the Fighting Scots' football team and was a three-year starter in the defensive backfield. He earned his undergraduate degree from Edinboro in 1970 and joined Fighting Scots head coach Bill McDonald's staff while he earned his master's degree from the Boro.

After getting his master's, Bufalino immediately jumped into teaching high school math and coaching junior varsity football at Academy High School in Erie. One of his players was Tom Cacchione, who, along with his brothers, became an assistant to Bufalino at Strong Vincent. He later succeeded Bufalino as the Colonels' head football coach.

As tough as Bufalino was, the teenagers who played for him actually received a dialed-down version of what he had experienced as a student-athlete. He quickly realized that the extent to which his coaches screamed, swore at and name-called their players would not go over well with his own teams.

"Where we took it as a discipline, they took it as an insult," Bufalino said. "And that wasn't gonna happen, so you better change quickly."

After a few years at Academy, Bufalino was laid off by the school district and, for a time, was out of both teaching and coaching. He returned to the sidelines as an assistant at East High School, and took the reigns as the head coach of the Warriors in 1978.

Even then, the values and reputation that Bufalino would become renowned for were in place. Keith Latzo, who played quarterback and inside linebacker at East, described Bufalino as strict, intense and passionate, but also loyal and caring.

"As soon as you crossed the white-chalk sideline and you were on the field — whether it was practice or game — it was nothing but football," Latzo said.

Bufalino was influenced not only by the coaches he had played for, but also by East High's then principal, Viola Andrews.

Andrews loved athletics but prioritized academics, and instilled in her educators the need to be efficient and focused in the classroom. Bufalino took this "time on task" approach from the blackboard in math class to the chalkboard in the locker room.

It worked: Bufalino turned around East's once struggling football program, and in 1981 led the Warriors to their last winning season until Leonard Ford's East team posted a 5-4 record in 2009.

Following that season, Bufalino made the jump to the college level. He joined Tony DeMeo's staff at Mercyhurst College (now Mercyhurst University), a move which Bufalino later called the "best decision I made in my life."

Bufalino built on the lessons he learned from Andrews as an assistant for the Lakers. DeMeo was all about budgeting time efficiently to get the most out of practice.

"These are things that you had to go out and learn, so for me it was a great learning tool," Bufalino said.

After two seasons, Bufalino left Mercyhurst to be the offensive coordinator at Erie's Tech Memorial High School. There, he learned the concept of the Wing T offense and helped the team to a Metro League title. He returned to Mercyhurst for a stint as a running backs coach, but it wasn't long before he'd once again take the mantle of a program.

The Missing Piece

Jon Cacchione was an Erie guy, through and through. He played football and baseball at Academy High School, and continued his tenure on the diamond for a few years at Gannon University. By the time he graduated from Gannon, he had already begun his football coaching career as a JV coach and varsity assistant at Strong Vincent.

Cacchione coached under Pete Donatucci, who in 1985 had agreed to take over Vincent's football program after the previous coach had been fired. Donatucci brought a considerable amount of enthusiasm to the role, which was crucial in the Colonels' time of transition.

"Pete saved the program," Bufalino said.

Donatucci brought along a formidable group of assistants, including Jon Cacchione, Jon's brother Tim Cacchione, John Popoff and Ed Dalton. Together, the staff quickly began to move the Colonels in the right direction.

"We were on our way back," Jon Cacchione said. "But we were missing something."

They needed an established, battle-tested leader. Someone who knew the game of football inside and out.

Jon Cacchione was told by Norm Kuhn, a Vincent booster club parent whose son was an incoming freshman, that Bufalino was interested in coming to Vincent. Cacchione and Bufalino met, and Bufalino confirmed his interest.

There was only one catch: He would only do it if he could be the head coach.

Cacchione knew of Bufalino by reputation. He was aware of his success at East and Tech Memorial, and knew he'd been a valuable assistant at Mercyhurst College.

This was the guy they needed, Cacchione told Donatucci. Gracefully and selflessly, Donatucci agreed to the transition.

Bufalino was all in. He wanted to run a program his way, and he already had a good relationship with then Strong Vincent principal Ray Fiorelli, whom he had known from his time at East.

Bufalino took over as the Colonels' offensive coordinator in 1987 and implemented the Wing T, an old, seldom-seen, direct-snap offense that loads the backfield and incorporates the midline option. Even though Bufalino was the assistant, he essentially ran the show, and a smooth transition was assured for when he became the head coach in '88.

Donatucci stayed on as the defensive line coach, while Jon

Cacchione coached the wide receivers and defensive backs; Tim Cacchione coached the offensive backfield and linebackers; Dave Grack and Mike Burke coached the offensive line; and Bufalino took care of special teams and quarterbacks. Mark Williams took charge of the scout team and was involved with the JV squad. Tom Cacchione, while not officially on staff until 1992, contributed in a voluntary capacity. Another Cacchione brother, Dr. Joe Cacchione, was the team physician. While a few assistants left when Bufalino took the helm, the core that remained was willing to learn and hungry for victory. They'd find kindred spirits in the incoming freshman class.

Neighborhood Kids

There was no such thing as "school of choice" in Erie in the '80s. Where a kid lived determined where they would go to school and play sports. While this rule limited the talent pool, it also created chemistry through closeness.

Vincent's 1988 freshman football class was made up of lower-middle-class kids from an area between West Third and Liberty streets and West 40th Street and Greengarden Boulevard. Like Bufalino and his friends before them, they spent their days on the ball fields and playgrounds of the city's west side.

Some of them, like Dan Olson, Tim Romanski and Greg Baney, went to Roosevelt Middle School. Others, like Tony Robie and Quentin Orlando, went to Catholic schools.

Whether public or parochial, these neighborhood kids had one thing in common: They were tougher than a two-dollar steak. They were scrappy — the kind of boys who weren't afraid to throw hands over a pickup game on Saturday afternoon, and fold those same hands in prayer at Sunday morning mass.

"We had a lot of guys that had that mindset that you weren't afraid to throw down if you had to throw down," Robie said.

While they loved pickup games, they also played organized sports. Several of them played in Erie's Bay City Youth Football Association, and they also played basketball and baseball together.

By the time they were in eighth grade, Bufalino was already the offensive coordinator at Vincent.

He and Jon Cacchione visited middle schools including Roosevelt, St. Andrew and Blessed Sacrament to talk to kids about playing football. Cacchione, who coached basketball at Blessed Sacrament School and had led the team to a state championship, already had a stronghold with the eighth graders there.

All of the students they spoke to were in Vincent's district, so there were no ethical or legal concerns about their recruiting pitches. However, that didn't mean the staff's ransacking of parochial middle schools didn't ruffle some feathers. A disgruntled Cathedral Prep headmaster, Monsignor John Hagerty, complained to Cacchione about it.

"We were recruiting our asses off," Cacchione said.

Their zeal left an indelible impression on the middle schoolers.

Robie's first reaction to meeting Bufalino? Fear.

"He was definitely an intimidating guy, to say the least," Robie said.

Baney wanted to go to Prep with some of his friends, but his parents had other ideas. Vincent it was, and Baney convinced Romanski, who had reservations about playing football, to join the team with him.

Orlando, who went to Blessed Sacrament and whose older brother had played for Bufalino, knew very well of Bufalino's stalwart reputation.

But, as Olson put it, "Nothing could prepare you for the intensity of Joe Bufalino on our football team."

The White Line

It has been written that the meek shall inherit the earth, but they had no place on Joe Bufalino's practice field.

"It was a whole different world going out there on the field," Romanski said.

Bufalino's mantra was simple: "You play like you practice."

"If you didn't win in practice, you weren't gonna win on game day," he said.

Stepping over the white line onto the practice field was like transferring into an alternate reality, one in which taking off your helmet was permitted only during water breaks or if otherwise told to do so.

As for sitting down?

It wasn't an option.

Ever.

No one, healthy or injured, was allowed on the field if they couldn't stand for the duration of practice.

"If you dared make that mistake, believe me, you would never make it again," Jon Cacchione said.

No one, from a scout-team freshman to an All-Metro senior, was above the rules. Robie, who grew to be a star halfback, learned this the hard way. He described himself as "hard-headed" and said he and Bufalino would sometimes butt heads.

"I have a lot of respect for the fact that he really held me to a standard, and it didn't matter how good I was or how much I contributed to the team," Robie said. "If I didn't get in line, or I didn't do it his way, I wouldn't have played."

A poor week in practice would get a player yanked from Friday night's starting lineup, no exceptions. But the players respected Bufalino, in part because they always knew where they stood with him.

Bufalino was not afraid to take a jab at the pride of a player, or even an assistant. But it was all in the name of progress.

"You better not listen to how he says it, but rather you better listen to what he says," Jon Cacchione said.

Yet, Bufalino said he worded his criticism differently than the coaches he had played for. He didn't identify them by their mistakes. He wouldn't say, "You are…," but rather, "You're playing like…."

"It was (about positive reinforcement), but yet they had to know that if their commitment wasn't up to par, that I had to let them know about it," Bufalino said. "To the point where they could accept it."

He found creative ways to do this. There were several players and coaches of Italian heritage on Vincent's roster, and they were proud of their roots. So if one of Bufalino's Italian American players wasn't playing up to snuff, he'd discipline them by taking the vowel from the end of their last name.

"You're not Johnny Pirrello anymore," he told one player. "You're Johnny Pirrell."

Bufalino said that, while the starting guard's teammates laughed, Pirrello was sparked to perform in a way that left no doubt about his ties to the old country.

Even though Bufalino sprinkled in humor, the main course of the day was always intensity.

Players kept their mouths shut and ears open when he talked.

"Coach Buf was really good at grabbing your facemask and pulling you close, and making sure that you knew he was talking to you," Baney said.

The players' parents trusted Bufalino — even if they didn't always agree with him — in large part because some of them had played football with him at Prep. Their support allowed Bufalino and his staff to be extremely intense, though both Jon Cacchione and Romanski asserted that the Vincent coaches' style would be too abrasive for today's climate.

Even in '88, some couldn't handle it. A few found themselves ditching the high demands of three-a-day practices at Camp Sherwin in Girard one year in favor of a hike down Route 5.

But those who survived prevailed, and even more players caught on once they saw that Bufalino's style translated into marks in the "W" column.

"The players at Strong Vincent were the hungriest kids I've ever coached in my life," Jon Cacchione said. "They wanted to win and they wanted to be coached, so they embraced Joe well."

Motivated by Bufalino's goals, the players personalized them for themselves and their teammates. No one wanted to make a mistake, because they knew they'd hear about it later in the locker room.

"(Bufalino) used fear, and it worked," Romanski said.

And if a player had a bad game on Friday, he'd be walking on eggshells heading into the following film session. One poor soul was relegated by Bufalino to stand outside in the weeds for 20 minutes.

Sometimes, Bufalino would intentionally make practice chaotic to simulate the tension and pressure of a Friday-night fourth quarter. Players would get amped up, throw down their helmets and get kicked off the field. But they always came back, humbled and ready to work.

"They knew what the goals (were), and, God bless 'em, they wanted it as much as I did," Bufalino said.

Olson reflected that Bufalino's approach was very strategic. The Wing T required precision, and Bufalino's purpose was the pursuit of perfection. He stressed again and again the importance of doing the little things right as they "bird dogged" every play, step by step. Even if practice went longer than three hours, the Colonels did it until they did it right.

It was in Bufalino's nature as a math teacher to be so thorough. He reflected on why math and science teachers, such as himself, Jon Cacchione and Erie County legends Jack Bestwick and Joe Shesman, have had success coaching football. He believes it's because of their ability to find the right answer.

"We see a challenge in solving the problem," Bufalino said. "And we won't stop until it's solved."

Olson's take on Bufalino's extensive preparation?

"We're all human, and he was kind of cyborg-like," he said.

Everyone — from the starters to the scout team — had an essential role to play. They were building something, and all the pieces mattered.

"The difference between ordinary and extraordinary is that little bit extra," he'd say, while other times he'd tell them, "You're ate up like a soup sandwich."

Bufalino brought Mercyhurst's all-consuming college football schedule with him to Vincent. The coaches worked seven days a week, intensively analyzing film and never leaving the film room until they had a plan on paper that would beat whatever their opponent could throw at them.

"I never asked them to do anything I didn't do," Bufalino said of his assistants.

Jon Cacchione soaked up Bufalino's knowledge and lessons like a sponge, and the two bonded over their shared Sicilian heritage. Cacchione would tell him, "The only Sicilian I know who is more intense than you is my mother."

Bufalino, Jon Cacchione and Grack were fiery, while Burke and Tim Cacchione counterbalanced them with a more laid-back approach. In turn, the coaching staff gelled well with the players. Even though Bufalino rarely showed a crack in his veneer, he fed off their tight-knit, neighborhood bond to instill undying loyalty both on and off the field.

"You dance with who brung ya," Bufalino would tell them.

The message was clear: They were marching down the steps of Erie Veterans Memorial Stadium together, and they'd stick together no matter what.

"You were going into battle with him," Olson said. "And he was leading the charge."

Winning was imminent. Bufalino's first season at the helm, in 1988, saw the Colonels go 6-4 for their first winning record since 1971. The following year, Vincent went 9-2 before losing to eventual District 10-champion Reynolds High School in the D-10 playoffs.

No matter; the Colonels were just getting started.

"Cooch"

Kareem Carson wasn't a neighborhood kid. At least, not in the sense that Vincent's band of bay rats were. Carson was from the east side, and his only connection to Strong Vincent was his older cousin, Sonny Carson.

Through Sonny, Kareem became a waterboy for the Colonels when he was in middle school. As he fetched water for the players, he'd see Bufalino, as he put it, "go crazy" on the sidelines.

"I thought he was really mean," Carson said.

But Sonny Carson did well at Vincent, and Kareem wanted to suit up in the red and black.

"I knew I didn't want to go to high school with my friends, because there ain't no telling where I'd be right now," Carson said.

He moved in with his uncle, who lived in Vincent's district. A change in addresses didn't make Carson one of the guys, though. While there was mutual respect between him and his teammates, he initially struggled to adapt.

The Vincent kids weren't ritzy, but they had gear that Carson couldn't afford. And while his teammates' parents cheered them on from the stands, Carson had never met his father, and wouldn't until well after he graduated from Strong Vincent.

"I never thought I would fit in with those kids," he said.

Without knowing a soul, Carson had a thirst to prove himself. As a freshman at training camp in 1990, Carson paid dues as a scout team running back with tenacity and a tireless work ethic.

"I didn't want an opportunity to pass me by," he said.

It wasn't long before the upperclassmen took notice of not only his toughness, but his talent as well.

"(Carson was) very athletic, very skilled," Orlando said. "(He had) soft hands, could absolutely run and was a great player for us."

Carson became closer to his teammates during camp in his sophomore season, and learned from Romanski, Robie and Orlando as he fought for and won a spot on varsity.

"Once you see those guys play (you realize), they're down to earth, they're just like me, and that's what brought us closer together," Carson said.

His friends on the team even gave him a nickname: "Cooch."

Carson became the most versatile player on the team, learning every position in the backfield, starting at cornerback and running kicks back on special teams. He also grew to love and respect Bufalino.

Comparing Bufalino to the great New England Patriots coach Bill Belichick, Carson said he considered his coach a mentor, teacher and father figure all rolled into one. Bufalino made sure Carson got home from practice every day, and that he ate every day.

"He was my guy," Carson said.

As Carson developed in his freshman year, Vincent went 8-4 and beat Harborcreek High School to reach the District 10 title game. There, the Colonels faced an onslaught of late hits and trash talk from Sharon High School.

A bench-clearing brawl that nearly ended the game broke out amidst the fog and rain. After play resumed, the Colonels were bested by the Tigers, who went on to be the Class AAA state runners-up.

1991 was a good year for payback.

Steamrollers

The late, great, Erie sports radio personality Jim LeCorchick used to put out a magazine each year previewing area high school football. LeCorchick was a walking encyclopedia of Erie sports facts both past and present, and his gauge on the scene was as good as anyone's. So, when the cover of his magazine featured Tony Robie and Tim Romanski sitting on a steamroller, it couldn't have been any clearer that those in the know expected excellence from Strong Vincent football in 1991.

Bufalino, not wanting distractions or too much pressure put on his players, didn't feed much into the coverage.

"Jimmy LeCorchick, I had to tone him down," Bufalino recalled.

Still, the Colonels knew what they had.

"The expectations were there," Bufalino said. "The kids knew it, I knew it, we all wanted it."

"It" was the holy grail of Pennsylvania high school football: a state championship. The advent of the Pennsylvania Interscholastic Athletic Association state playoffs had occurred in 1988, and only one team from Erie County — Cathedral Prep — had made it to the playoffs. No team from Erie had been to a state title game yet, let alone won it.

That didn't mean it wasn't seen as a possibility. Each year at training camp, Vincent's players would write down their goals for the season on an index card. Both Robie and Romanski penciled in a state championship.

Robie, though, said the Colonels lived in a "fish bowl," and weren't familiar with teams on the east side of the state, or even the teams from Pittsburgh.

Even if they had been, it wouldn't have been talked about.

"We weren't even allowed to look off into the horizon," Olson said.

Instead, the Colonels focused on performing to the best of their abilities and letting the rest take care of itself.

"Joe knew how tough they were, so he probably coached harder that year (and) was even harder on the kids because he knew they could take it," Jon Cacchione said.

The Colonels were not only tough, but also talented and smart. Far from the misguided stereotype of the "dumb jock," the team finished the season with a cumulative grade-point average of 3.2. And what they lacked in numbers — they finished the season with a little more than 30 players from grades 9-12 on their roster — they made up for in grit and resourcefulness.

"(The coaches) molded us well," Olson said. "Every single one of those guys had a role to play."

They proactively cross-trained athletes to know multiple positions, so if someone went down another could step up. Carson's versatility paid off in a major way. In addition to starting at cornerback, he filled in for injured players, such as when Tim Romanski was hurt for the Academy game.

"He was excellent," Bufalino said of Carson.

Bufalino and his staff continued to drill each play, step by step, into the players until Vincent's X's and O's were ingrained in not only their cerebellums, but muscle memories. And they did it all by balancing attention to detail with efficiency.

"Strong Vincent!" Bufalino would bellow. "What's your enemy?"

"Time!" the players would roar back.

Olson was the field general; he matched his skills with his wits as the team's quarterback. The Wing T was all about timing, and Olson ensured he and his teammates had it down pat.

"It was almost like coach Buf saw what Danny had, and knew he had it from day one," Baney said.

In turn, Olson learned from Bufalino how to lead his teammates, and how to pick them up when they were down.

"If you can't learn to be a leader from Joe Bufalino, you can't learn it from anybody," Olson said.

It was fortunate Olson remained healthy, because Vincent didn't have another true throwing QB on its roster.

Behind Olson was Orlando at fullback, while Robie and Romanski were halfbacks. Craig Bennetti spread out at wide receiver, while Baney lined up at tight end and Vincent bookended its offensive line with two dominant tackles: Jamal Crawford and Malik Martin.

The tackles were big, tall, quick and athletic. Crawford, who carried the greatest size of anyone on the team, later became the lone '91 Colonel to play Division I football when he earned a scholarship to suit up for Michigan State University.

"Jamal was a beast," Baney said.

Martin, meanwhile, joined the team as a junior and rapidly progressed to become one of the most essential elements of the Colonels' success by his senior year.

Baney recalled Martin's gigantic hands, and how his size and quickness enabled him to get past offensive linemen.

"If he got a hold of you, you were at his mercy," Baney said.

The Vincent coaches were ahead of their time in stressing weight lifting, and Crawford, Martin and Romanski embodied the "Bigger, Faster, Stronger" slogan that was on the wall of the room where the

Colonels pumped iron.

"(The coaches) almost started to create a different atmosphere for all of us in the weight room, and then it became a competition," Baney said.

Most players played both ways out of necessity, so starters rarely left the field aside from special teams. Even there, Bufalino found specialists; his cousin on his mother's side, Jamie Potosnak, was a soccer player recruited by Bufalino to be a part-time member as the placekicker. As time went on, Potosnak chose football over soccer and was essential for both point-after attempts and field goals.

Jeremy Roach, meanwhile, later proved important in the playoffs as the starting punter when an injury prevented Romanski from carrying out his punting duties.

Vincent ran a 4-4-3 defense, but rotated its secondary for a two-deep look. Even so, they weren't exactly setting records in the 40-yard dash.

"We could time our 40s with the calendar," Jon Cacchione joked. Exceptions were Romanski, whose speed was utilized to cover the pass, and junior Jason Kleps, who emerged as a leader in the secondary.

The players were close off the field and could often be seen hanging out together. In addition to dubbing Carson "Cooch," they gave each other nicknames: Tony Robie was "Tone Loc" (as in the '90s rapper, of "Wild Thing" fame), Quentin Orlando was "Q," Greg Baney was "G Bags," Malik Martin was "Motown" and Tim Romanski was (NBA player) "T.R. Dunn." Dan Olson and Jamal Crawford, were, well, Danny and Jamal.

Their camaraderie off the field bled into their chemistry on it. They were selfless and did whatever they were asked to do. They didn't care about who rushed for the most yards, and took as much delight in pancaking a defender for each other as they did in scoring touchdowns.

"We played as a team as much as any team that I've been a part of," Robie said.

Crucially, they played with a chip on their shoulders.

"There was no fear," Robie said. "At no point were we ever afraid of anybody in the course of the season."

This included undefeated Cathedral Prep, which was the area's Class AAAA powerhouse. The Colonels were the region's top dogs in Triple A, and the regular season meeting between the two teams was predictably hard fought.

A few turnovers made the difference, and the Ramblers edged the

Colonels, 7-0.

"'Remember,'" Olson recalled Bufalino telling them. "'They didn't beat us. We beat ourselves.'"

Carson was more frank.

"We should have beat their ass," he said.

The loss, though, proved to be a blessing in disguise. It simultaneously humbled and provided confidence for the Colonels, who now knew they could hang with anyone as long as they took care of the little things.

"If we don't lose to Prep, we don't win state," Olson said.

Hungrier than ever, Vincent won out in the regular season.

"We wanted to beat you not just on the scoreboard, but we wanted to beat you mentally and physically, too," Orlando said.

They'd need that mentality heading into the playoffs, where a grudge match awaited.

Payback

There was no way around it: Vincent didn't like Sharon, and Sharon didn't like Vincent. Bufalino called them a "nasty team." So when the Colonels again reached the District 10 Championship game to face the Tigers, they knew what they had to do.

"We don't teach nasty," Bufalino said. "But when you play a nasty team, you have to be nasty." Bufalino reminded his players of the year before, when Sharon littered the field with insults and late hits and a fight had broken out. That was all the motivation the Colonels needed, and in the first quarter of the game, Vincent defensive end Steve Ulrich laid out a Sharon running back when he was out of bounds.

The Colonels were flagged for a 15-yard personal foul, but the message was sent.

"We set the tone that we were not going to be intimidated," Bufalino said.

Though Vincent trailed at halftime for the first time all year, the game was a back-and-forth affair that came down to a few crucial plays. Late in the game, the Colonels found themselves on third down with nine yards to go. Orlando took the ball off tackle to the left. He got hit, but spun and made it seven yards upfield running backwards before turning and falling forward for the first down.

Then, a delightful mistake. The play call was for Baney to run a flag route, but he ran an in route instead. He ended up wide open, and

Olson hit him with a beautiful pass that brought the Colonels inside Sharon's 10-yard line.

Baney didn't even realize he had run the wrong route until after the game was over, and the coaches ended up adding that particular in route to the playbook.

"Sometimes I say, 'I'd rather be lucky than good,'" Baney said. "So I was lucky on that one."

Bufalino called timeout, and then Robie ran off tackle to punch the ball in for the 14-10 lead. The Tigers' last hopes were dashed when Vincent intercepted them on their final drive, and a fight was started.

As the playoffs went deeper into November, Vincent's practice field got dark earlier and earlier each day. The parents joined in, sitting in their cars with their headlights shining on the field so their boys could keep practicing.

When they weren't at practice, the coaches buried themselves in game film to get an edge on their opponents.

All the while, Jon Cacchione recalled, Bufalino insisted that they hadn't come this far to be the best Strong Vincent team ever.

"'We've done what we've done to be the best team this area has ever seen,'" Cacchione recalled Bufalino saying.

First up for Vincent in the state playoffs was Brookville High School, a school near Clarion. The Colonels blew out the Blue Raiders, 41-0.

Then, Vincent hosted a playoff game at Vets. But home field advantage only went so far, as visiting Lock Haven brought 15 busloads of fans to match Vincent's crowd.

The Bobcats had only lost one game, and Jon Cacchione described them as "tough country kids and good athletes." They were led by three-sport athlete and all-state quarterback Joe Caruso, who was later selected by the Kansas City Royals in the 1997 MLB Draft.

Vincent jumped ahead to a 14-0 lead, but Lock Haven battled back to make the score 14-12. The Bobcats went for a two-point try following their second score, but the Colonels stopped them short to seal the win. As Olson reflected, the simulated chaos of Vincent's practices proved crucial in preparing them for high-pressure situations such as that one.

The only thing standing between Vincent and the state final was Blackhawk High School, a Beaver County team from the Western Pennsylvania Interscholastic Athletic League. The prevailing wisdom of the day was that teams from the WPIAL were superior to Erie County teams, and some people thought Vincent didn't stand a chance.

The Colonels, though, weren't having it.

"Why are these guys better than us?" Robie mused. "Because they're from Pittsburgh? That doesn't add up to me."

It was November in Erie, so naturally there was an onslaught of snow. Mercyhurst College opened up its facility to allow the Colonels to practice indoors, but they weren't able to work on special teams.

The game was played at Sharon High School, and the Tigers were forced to open up their home locker room to a group of guys they had just come to blows with a few weeks earlier. Bufalino's point of emphasis on preparation was proven when Blackhawk ran back the opening kick for a touchdown. But, as they had all year, the Colonels responded to a score with one of their own.

Bolstered by a stunning performance by Quentin Orlando, who ended the day with four touchdowns, the Colonels went into the half up by three scores.

Blackhawk battled back in the second half, and Vincent clung to a one-point lead on its way to victory.

A win, as they say, is a win. The Colonels were on their way to the PIAA Class AAA Football Championship game.

The Smile

Not one, but two Metro League teams were to play for a state title on December 14, 1991. Vincent was squaring off against Conestoga Valley High School, of Lancaster, while still-undefeated Cathedral Prep was to play Central Bucks West for the AAAA crown.

Back then each class fought for a title in a different town, so while Prep was playing in Altoona, Vincent settled up in Moosic, just south of Scranton.

When the Erie kids stepped off the bus and headed into the hotel where they'd be staying, it hit them: They were there. Playing for the state championship.

Maybe it was the excitement, or maybe it was the surreality of it all. Whatever the reason, when the Colonels arrived at Lackawanna County Stadium to practice on the eve of the game, they did so having forgotten to bring footballs with them.

Media outlets were there to cover the practice and Conestoga Valley was also there, just having finished a practice of its own.

Bufalino, not wanting to show any weakness, had the Colonels go through practice without a ball as if it were part of their normal routine. Conestoga Valley and media members watched as they went through a tip drill with no football.

"Either they think that we're the most innovative team in America, or that we're really stupid," Bufalino said.

Practicing without a ball in no way lessened Bufalino's intensity. He said that, after he scolded a player for not going for the "ball" during a drill, his players knew: Their coach had lost it.

Eventually, Tom Cacchione went back to the hotel to retrieve the footballs.

A practice mishap aside, the players were loose the night before because they had been so well prepared. They were assigned rooms by their positions, which was another fine-tooth detail organized by Bufalino to create cohesion.

Strong Vincent fans also made the trip to Moosic and stayed overnight on the eve of the big game.

The players kept a loose, casual vibe rolling into game day, but also had a business-like mindset. Bufalino changed tack during their pregame meeting. He wasn't the intense, fiery coach they had grown to know and love over the course of four years. Barely raising his voice, he instilled the final bit of confidence his players needed to reach their goal.

Olson described it as "almost eerie."

"He just seemed to be one of the guys for the first time," Olson said.

Ten thousand fans packed into Lackawanna County Stadium to watch the state championship game.

The Conestoga Valley Buckskins, or "Bucks," were electric. They ran an uptempo, no-huddle, pass-heavy offense that was akin to the University of Miami football teams in their 1980s-early '90s heyday. It was an attack the Colonels weren't used to, but adapted to by signaling in their defensive play calls.

"It was rough, but we were prepared," Carson said.

Vincent defended the pass well in the first half; Romanski intercepted a pair of passes while Kleps picked off another. But Valley caught the Colonels by surprise with a secret weapon: the option pitch. All three of the Bucks' touchdowns came on the ground, including rushes from three yards out and 17 yards out — the latter on the option pitch — by running back Brady Myers.

The Colonels responded with touchdown runs of two yards and three yards by Orlando, but Valley quarterback Tyler Demmy punched it in from one yard out to give the Bucks a 20-15 halftime lead.

The players waited in the locker room at halftime, thinking they were going to get chewed out for being behind.

Instead, Bufalino calmly walked in and addressed his team very briefly.

"Good job, gentlemen, take a seat," he told his players. "We'll be back in a moment. Talk amongst yourselves."

The coaches left, leaving the players to sit in stunned disbelief for half a minute. They were quiet as church mice.

When the coaches returned, they talked to the players as equals.

"It wasn't coach to player," Olson said. "It was teammate to teammate, it was comrade to comrade, and that just gave us the utmost confidence to go out in the second half."

The Colonels didn't fret about Valley's option pitch. They widened out their linebackers, brought in another cornerback and threw some blitzes in their scheme to confuse Demmy. The effects were undeniable; in the first half, Myers had rushed 15 times for 97 yards. In the second, he gained just three yards on two carries.

Maybe it was because the Bucks knew Vincent would adjust to the option pitch, but for whatever reason, the Colonels didn't see that play in the second half.

"(They) should have at least given it a shot," Bufalino said. "I'm glad they didn't."

Meanwhile, the Colonels strategically ate up clock to keep the Bucks' offense off the field. Then, in the third quarter, Vincent had the ball at its own 16-yard line on 2nd and 9. The play called was Liz Fade 958, which lined up three players on the right side of the field for go routes. Vincent had run the play successfully before, but had never gained even 10 yards at one time on it.

Olson set Robie in motion, left to right, and Valley's outside linebacker bumped out to cover Robie. The insider backer, though, didn't budge. It could have been the backer's own mistake, or a flaw in Valley's scheme. Or, it could have been because he was trained on the fullback, as the Colonels had audibled Robie earlier in the game and had run the ball with Orlando.

It was a fatal error; the linebacker had left Romanski, one of Vincent's fastest players, wide open.

Romanski looked up and saw a clear path ahead of him.

Oh my God, he thought. *They're leaving that open.*   .

Olson looked at his childhood best friend. Romanski returned the look with a grin. Then, Olson took the snap, released the ball almost instantly and hit Romanski about four yards upfield. With lead blocker Bennetti running ahead of him, and Olson pumping his arms and running behind him, Romanski was off to the races and left all comers in the dust for an 84-yard touchdown.

It was, as Olson said, "magical," and the culmination of four years of tireless repetition.

"We had done that so many times, we knew that's exactly what our role was," Olson said. "It was like taking candy from a baby. It was a beautiful thing."

The Colonels never trailed after that, and sealed the win on a one-yard touchdown run by Robie on 4th and goal. Robie had to reach the ball over the goal line to get it in. To Jon Cacchione, Robie's grit on that play was true to form.

"(He is) pound for pound the toughest kid I ever coached in my life," Cacchione said.

The Colonels led, 29-20, as time wound down. Bufalino, though, didn't breathe easy until after a clock mixup late in the game. The time-of-day clock and the game clock were on the same board, and both were digital. So, Bufalino thought there were four minutes left, when it in fact was 4 p.m. Once an assistant coach in the press box told him he was looking at the day clock and there was 1:20 left, Bufalino knew the game was theirs.

And so it was: Carson tallied Vincent's fifth and final interception with 16 seconds left, and when the clock hit zero, the Colonels were the state champions.

The first thing the Colonels wanted to know was whether their Erie brethren, the Cathedral Prep Ramblers, had won.

They hadn't; Prep fell to Central Bucks West, 26-14. Though the Colonels had wanted to see the Ramblers win, nothing could dampen their spirits as they celebrated their victory in what Bufalino described as "absolute jubilation."

You would have thought they were back playing pickup as grade school kids on the west side, the way they ecstatically ran around the field, looking for another player to jump on and hug.

Baney quipped, "I'm going to Disneyland!" a few steps back from a TV camera. Then, Martin jumped in front of him and shouted, "Disney World, baby!"

"Motown, that's my line!" Baney exclaimed.

But it was all love. Martin and Crawford grabbed a bucket of Gatorade and doused Bufalino. He jumped up, shiny red Vincent jacket on, his hair just a touch of gray, and threw his fist in the air and turned.

"It was like everything came out of him," Robie said. "Joy, excitement, pride."

And he did something his players had only seen him do a handful of times: He smiled.

"He was always business, he was always focused," Romanski said. "And when he was relaxed enough to smile, you knew things were going good on the team, or that he was satisfied."

A classic Erie blizzard kept the Colonels from receiving a police-and-fire escort when they returned home that night, but they were later recognized by Erie City Councilman Mario Bagnoni at a city council meeting and by Mayor Joyce Savocchio at a Strong Vincent basketball game.

But trophies, medals and recognition didn't matter much to the Colonels. It wasn't about going 15-1, or the fact that Robie, Romanski and Orlando each finished the year with more than 1,000 yards rushing. It was about the guys they'd shed blood with on the gridiron.

"To go to war with your buddies and come out on top, and realize that you're the best team in the state at your level, and we were a bunch of kids from the neighborhood," Orlando said. "There's something to be said about that."

It was a ride they simply didn't want to end. They approached their coaches and asked them if they could play a state champion from Ohio or West Virginia. The coaches just laughed.

Forever the First

It's been a long time since the boys in red and black became men on Strong Vincent's practice field. So long, in fact, that there is no Strong Vincent High School anymore. Vincent and East became middle schools, while the building that housed Tech Memorial (later Central Tech) became Erie High School, the result of a merger of the city's three public high schools.

And yet, the legacy of the 1991 Strong Vincent football team remains, not only as the first football team from Erie County to win a state championship, but in the outstanding accomplishments of the members of that team.

Bufalino coached Vincent through 1997 before taking a year off to watch his son, General McLane football standout Lincoln Bufalino, play in his senior year. He said that going with his family to watch his son play football remains one of the best parts of his life.

He returned to the sidelines in 1999, this time as an assistant to Jon Cacchione, who took over as the head coach of McDowell's program. With Bufalino by his side, Cacchione coached the Trojans to a cumulative record of 40-27, while winning two District 10 titles and making two state playoff appearances.

Cacchione said he couldn't have had the success he had as a head coach without the influence of Bufalino, and carried on many of his mentor's lessons in his own program.

"Practice has to be game-like," Cacchione said.

Cacchione retired after the 2004 season to spend more time with his family, and Bufalino, after more than three decades in coaching, hung up his whistle.

Lincoln Bufalino had an excellent football career at Edinboro University, and was a special education teacher at Northwest Intermediate Unit while pursuing his master's degree in secondary counseling at Edinboro. He died at the age of 29 in July 2010, just one course short of earning his master's.

The university posthumously awarded him the degree, and the Bufalino family set up the Lincoln Daniel Bufalino Foundation as a memorial for him and as a way to give scholarships to General McLane and Edinboro University students.

Years later, Bufalino is still grateful to have people come up to him and share positive stories about his son.

"I was proud of (Lincoln) on the way he conducted himself as an educator," Bufalino said. "He was a compassionate kid and he cared about people, and he was a team player."

Bufalino retired from his position as a guidance counselor at Strong Vincent in 2011. Nowadays, he spends much of his time remodeling his Edinboro home and property with his wife, Sherry, whom he called "tough" and "very competitive."

He also said her willingness to pull "double duty" in their family while he was coaching enabled him to be successful..

"She (was) 100 percent on board with what (I was) doing," Bufalino said.

She suffered a subdural hematoma in December 2019, and Bufalino has been helping her along in her recovery. He said she's been "recovering marvelously." They also enjoy spending time with their grade-school-aged granddaughters, who live in Edinboro.

Bufalino hosts former players from his East High days on his pontoon boat once every few months. Among them is Latzo, who went on to become a family man and a football coach at Saint Luke Catholic School in Erie. Whether during his long career as a middle market underwriter at Erie Insurance, or when utilizing the Wing T to lead Saint Luke to a parochial league championship in 2001, Latzo has lived by what Bufalino taught him.

"We never laid down and we never quit," Latzo said. "I still carry that in life."

Bufalino still sees the Cacchiones occasionally, though he's no longer plugged into the Erie sports scene. But he still dreams about X's and O's in his sleep. And, though he's not quite sure why, he's still drawing up plays and preparing his next offense. He said he wants to get rid of big linemen in favor of athletic players who can run.

"I'm turning the game into rugby," he said.

Every now and again he gets the itch to coach, but has no plans to do so in the near future.

"(Sherry has) been so loyal to me all these years, it's time to help her out," he said.

It's a decision not lost on his former players.

"He has shown such patience with Sherry, and such compassion," Olson said. "He's still teaching us things to this day."

It's a remarkable notion, considering all Bufalino has already taught them, and how they have applied those lessons in their lives after high school.

A few of them went on to play college football, and Olson joined Bufalino and, later, Tom Cacchione, on the sidelines as an assistant at Vincent. Carson also had a long career as an assistant, and coached his son, Kareem Jr., to state championships at Cathedral Prep in 2017 and '18. In doing so, he became the only person ever to win a football state title on an Erie County team as both a player and a coach.

Just as Cacchione did at McDowell, Carson took lessons he learned from Bufalino and instilled them in the players he coached at Prep. He taught them to have self-confidence and to never give up.

"Buf's big thing was, 'Believe in yourself,'" Carson said. "'Take an approach, hold yourself accountable, believe in yourself.'"

Outside of football, the alumni of the '91 Vincent team have gone on to remarkable things. Now in their 40s, many of them have wives and children. Olson became a podiatrist, Orlando a cardiologist, Romanski a firefighter, Baney the deputy chief of the Erie Police Department and Carson a child care behavioral specialist.

Robie, meanwhile, went on to become an All-American wrestler at Edinboro University. He is the head coach of Virginia Tech's wrestling program, and twice has been named the Atlantic Coast Conference Coach of the Year.

Still, when Robie visits Erie, he is remembered by old acquaintances more for Vincent's state title than anything he has accomplished in wrestling. And through it all, Robie hasn't forgotten Bufalino.

"The guy had a huge impact on my life," he said. "And if I hadn't had the opportunity to play at Strong Vincent and play for him, I don't know if I would have ever went on to do what I did at the college level and be where I am today."

Every five years, coaches and players from the '91 title team get together for a reunion. The players recite Bufalino's many sayings, reminisce and laugh about old times and harass each other as if they were still kids on the west side.

"It mattered about winning, it mattered about being on a team, but what really mattered was being friends," Baney said. "That was the big thing, and to this day it proves that friendship is inevitably gonna keep you going very well."

They reflect on what Bufalino and his coaching staff taught them: responsibility, commitment, dedication, loyalty. And, of course, obsessive attention to detail.

"It's ingrained in you to pay attention to detail," Romanski said. "My kids might not like it."

And sometimes, neither did the Colonels when they went through it.

"It wasn't for everybody, as far as assistants and even some players," Jon Cacchione said. "But those that endured, they prevailed, and they had the formula to be successful in anything or everything that they were going to do for the rest of their lives.

"And that was Joe."

Cathedral Prep became the second Erie County team to win a football state championship by exacting revenge against Central Bucks West in 2000. The Ramblers have won several state titles since.

General McLane also won a state championship, capturing Triple A hardware in 2006.

But Strong Vincent will always be the first.

"That's the good thing about the state playoffs," Bufalino said. "It gave our kids recognition that they could play."

In the summer of 2020, some of the Vincent alumni — including Robie, Orlando and Baney — went camping together. It was a way to get away from the pressures of life and spend time with old friends.

"It's not (about) cars, houses, or anything like that," Orlando said. "When we're talking about state championships, it's the feeling. It wasn't really winning the state championship that matters to me, it was the journey we took together and the people we did it with."

And sometimes, it's good to commemorate that journey by sitting around a campfire, throwing back some cold ones with your buddies and laughing about stories of days gone by.

It's the little things.

Photo provided by Edinboro University Athletics

Tony Robie (above) is recognized as the winner of a match during his tenure as a wrestler at Edinboro University. Robie was one of the driving forces of Edinboro wrestling's rejuvenation in the 1990s.

Boro Built

By John Dudley

John Dudley spent nearly 19 years as a sportswriter and columnist for the Erie Times-News, *where his beats included the NFL, college and high school wrestling, the Erie BayHawks and the Erie SeaWolves. He was a three-time finalist in the Associated Press Sports Editors contest for project reporting and feature writing, the winner of 13 Keystone Press Awards for column writing and features and a Western Pennsylvania Press Club Golden Quill Award finalist for investigative reporting on steroids use in sports. He now lives with his wife, Ellen, in South Florida, where he serves as national media relations manager for the University of South Florida, one of the nation's largest public research universities.*

Adapted from Dudley's book, The Fighting Scots of Edinboro: One Small School's Rise to Prominence Among College Wrestling's Heavyweights (Reedy Press, 2008)

Edinboro University's wrestling program was in flux when Tony Robie arrived in 1992. Robie had been a standout among a group of standout athletes at Strong Vincent High School, finishing with two District 10 championships and two PIAA third-place finishes as a wrestler. He also was a two-time All-Metro League running back, and was instrumental in the Colonels' 1991 state-championship run.
He was accustomed to the kind of success Edinboro had enjoyed several years earlier, when the program posted multiple top-10 NCAA finishes. But that's not where the Fighting Scots were when Robie got there. Not even close.
Mike DeAnna, the coach who had led Edinboro's ascension from the Division II level and coached the program's first Division I champ — Sean O'Day, in 1989 — was gone. A mediocre 1989 recruiting class and the graduation of several top wrestlers contributed to three straight finishes out of the NCAA top 25.
Head coach Bruce Baumgartner, an Olympic freestyle wrestling hero

and DeAnna's former assistant, needed to change the culture in the wrestling room. Robie was part of a new wave of talent that also included assistant coach Tim Flynn and another top recruit from Pennsylvania, Jason Robison. The transformation that those three helped to lead was as much about attitude as ability.

Robie, as he later said, wrestled at a high school where wrestling was not a priority and where the Colonels never produced a complete lineup. Numerous forfeits were commonplace in their matches. Robie said that as such, he didn't reach his potential as a high school wrestler, and was not a blue-chip recruit for big-time wrestling schools. But Robie had talent, and, more importantly, grit. He possessed the mental toughness and physical style that could almost immediately change the trajectory of Edinboro's future.

Building on an idea DeAnna and Baumgartner had used to some success, Baumgartner and Flynn sold recruits on the notion of coming to Edinboro and becoming a big fish in a small pond. The two coaches came right out and told kids that, sure, if they picked a Big Ten or Big 12 school, they might enjoy some of the trappings that came with major college sports in towns with more nightlife or more culture than Edinboro had to offer. But when it came time to make headlines or enjoy campus-wide recognition, there would be no comparison.

"We played pretty heavily on that," Baumgartner recalled years later. "Let's face it, if you go to Ohio State to wrestle and Ohio State has a great NCAA tournament, you get some positive ink for a day or two, but as soon as the men's basketball team plays a game — whether it does well or it does poorly — that will overshadow all of the positive wrestling stories you can find. I know that frustrates guys like (former University of Minnesota wrestling coach) J Robinson, who has had phenomenal success. They can win a national championship, which they've done, and everybody at the school is more worried about the fact that the new football coach is struggling."

Robie, who chose to stay local in part because Edinboro was the only Division I program offering him a scholarship, soon learned that Baumgartner's sales pitch was legit.

"Wrestling mattered," Robie said. "It was a big deal. It was something that we took pride in, (and) our coaching staff took pride in."

Inside of a year, the new coaching staff landed two wrestlers whose work ethic and relentless training would become the stuff of legend in Edinboro's practice room and help define the program's next era of greatness. In Robie — a craggy, hard-nosed, square-jawed middleweight from a tough and talented inner-city school — Baumgartner saw potential that had barely been tapped when he got to Edinboro in the fall of 1992.

Robison, a PIAA champion from Allison Park, outside Pittsburgh, followed the next season. Away from the mat, he wore glasses that made him look a little like an Algebra teacher, and he had been so intrigued by the notion of wrestling under Baumgartner that Edinboro was the only school he had seriously considered.

But success didn't happen overnight. The afternoon of his first official college practice, Robie walked into a wrestling room he described as very much in transition. There was undeniable talent, including lightweight Lou Rosselli, who was winding down a brilliant, 136-win career; Tom Shifflet, who would become a three-time All-American; and a few somewhat lesser-known names such as Ken Bauer, a workhorse who won 94 career matches without reaching the NCAA medal stand.

There also were what Robie described as a handful of wrestlers who were simply hanging on, providing little in the way of competition or motivation. Through their actions and, in some cases, inaction, they generally served as distractions to those wrestlers who were training seriously to become national champions.

Part of the reason was that Baumgartner had been traveling heavily for international competitions in preparation for the 1992 Olympic Games, and before Flynn's arrival he had been forced to get by with more volunteer assistant coaching help than usual thanks to a budget crunch brought on by statewide educational cutbacks. Flynn called the atmosphere when he arrived "generally negative." He recalls several times when he questioned whether he would even want to stay beyond that first, difficult 1992–93 season, which ended with a 6-7 dual-meet record and a sixth-place finish in the Eastern Wrestling League.

After Edinboro lost at West Virginia, 21–14, late in the season, Flynn stormed off the floor of the West Virginia University Coliseum in Morgantown and slammed his fist against the wall in what he described years later as an angry, tearful outburst.

"I came from Penn State and our mindset was, you womp West Virginia, and here we were losing to them," Flynn recalled. "We just never sucked that bad at Penn State, and I remember thinking that we legitimately sucked. We had Lou and we had Shifflet, but really not much else. I thought, things are going to change or Timmy's not gonna be around much longer."

The Scots did manage a 15th-place finish at that year's NCAA tournament, but that was on the strength of top-six finishes by Rosselli and Shifflet, two of the few wrestlers who, in Flynn's mind, didn't suck.

Robie, meanwhile, was still getting acclimated to the culture of college wrestling. He had never been to a college wrestling match before arriving at Edinboro. He spent his freshman year around teammates who didn't share his aspirations, which included winning a national title.

"It wasn't good," Robie said of the overall atmosphere in the practice room during his first winter at Edinboro. "You had guys who were there to work, and you had guys who seemed like they were there to do just about everything but work. It took a little time, but we weeded them out and we got a great bunch of guys in the room."

Robie evaluated his priorities and improved his mental fortitude heading into his sophomore year. His emergence as a leader and Robison's arrival the following spring provided a huge lift for the Scots. Robison was cut from the same cloth as Robie, a relentless trainer who tolerated zero shenanigans. The two, along with Shifflet, quickly took roles front and center in Edinboro's room after Rosselli finished up in 1993 and began to train for international competition while staying on as a volunteer assistant.

"I did my business," Robie said. "I tried to lead by example."

While Robie said Robison had on blinders for wrestling, Robie's own relatability helped ease the culture shift. He would pound wrestlers on the mat all week, but he wasn't above pounding a beer or two with the guys on a Saturday night.

Robie, along with Shifflet and Robison, led the kind of no-nonsense practices Robie had become accustomed to while playing for legendary Strong Vincent football coach Joe Bufalino.

"(Bufalino) always used to say, 'You play like you practice,'" Robie said. "And you look back, and you look at some of the things that he said and the standard that he held you to. And there was no question that that spilled over into my mindset when I got to Edinboro and I started to have success in wrestling."

Bufalino lit the competitive flame in Robie, and Baumgartner, Flynn and Rosselli stoked it into a fire that burned within Robie and helped create the ferocious competitor he became. With the team's discipline tightened, Flynn practically bouncing off the walls and preaching to them to share his through-the-roof expectations, and Baumgartner on a more regular, post-Olympics schedule, the improvement was rapid and dramatic.

It also was a different-looking training room, in many ways, from those of a few years earlier.

O'Day's finesse and explosiveness had enabled him to deliver the program's first NCAA Division I championship, but under Baumgartner and Flynn, this next wave of great Edinboro wrestlers would be fronted by brutishly strong, physically dominating bullies like Robie and Robison. While DeAnna and Baumgartner carefully picked their spots for O'Day to go hard in live action during practices, the coaches simply turned Robie and Robison loose on each other and on anyone else who happened to be nearby and let them whale away.

"The tide started to turn with Robie," Flynn later recalled. "He provided fight in the room. Robie was just this tough kid from Erie, and some of the guys on the team weren't one-tenth as tough."

It was a toughness born and bred on Erie's lower west side, when a young Robie played pickup football games with his friends. Oftentimes, the games turned to fisticuffs.

"You weren't afraid to fight, and we fought a lot," Robie said.

Robie and Robison didn't just beat opponents; they broke them mentally and, sometimes, physically. Their styles were established long before they got to Edinboro, but their time in the college wrestling room, when they were able to feed off of one another's intensity every day, made them meaner and even more unflinching in their willingness to go hard all the time. And that rubbed off on their teammates.

"Tony needed the battle," Baumgartner recalled of Robie. "If he came out of the practice room and didn't spend at least an hour pounding on somebody, he didn't feel like he'd gotten anything done."

Robie went on to have a 126-win career. He achieved a runner-up finish in the 158-pound weight class at the 1997 nationals, losing to Iowa's Joe Williams. Robison placed second the following year after taking a 45–0 record and a No. 1 national ranking into the title bout, where he lost 6–4 in overtime to Minnesota's Tim Hartung. He graduated as the school's all-time wins leader, with 145 career victories.

As much as any of the program's early D-I stars, Robie and Robison helped to shape Edinboro's profile as a place where blue-chip recruits — and even those who weren't quite as sought after — could find coaches capable of fully developing their talent and helping them bloom into national title contenders.

The year before Robie's runner-up finish, the early Baumgartner-Flynn recruiting classes had finally culminated in a season that set the bar for the future. Edinboro went 14–0 in dual meets — including a 27–13 spanking of West Virginia and wins over Ohio State, Pittsburgh, Arizona State and Oregon State — and finished sixth at nationals, then the highest NCAA Division I finish in the program's history. Shifflet was third that year, while Robie and Robison, who had begun to come into their own, finished fifth and seventh, respectively. That year's nationals, in the shadow of Gable's great Hawkeyes program in Cedar Falls, Iowa, would be the last for Baumgartner and Flynn together. After the season, Baumgartner, who was preparing to make one last run at an Olympic gold medal in 1996, became Edinboro's athletic director. Jim McDonald, whose temper and persistence had helped elevate the program to the Division I level 12 years earlier, retired to pursue overseas missionary work, in which he remains deeply involved. Flynn, the bundle of energy who had inexplicably struck McDonald as a preacher five years earlier, would take his place, and Rosselli would be his assistant.

McDonald's retirement and Baumgartner's resignation represented yet another massive transition, but one eased by the building blocks already in place. Baumgartner would still be around, his presence felt not only as a recruiting aid but as a resource to the young coaches. The atmosphere in the practice room had long since been established and cultivated. O'Day recalled later that the early years established a tenacious sense of competition at practices and even during conditioning workouts. Every running session became a race, and wrestlers would push one another into ditches in an attempt to win. In subsequent years, Robie, Robison and Josh Koscheck helped add toughness and attitude. Even with DeAnna and McDonald gone and Baumgartner stepping aside, the recipe remained for Flynn and Rosselli — and later Flynn and Cliff Moore—to brew up more national champions.

In 2014, Flynn was named the NCWA NCAA Division I Coach of the Year after coaching Edinboro to a then program-best fifth-place finish at the national tournament. A year later, Flynn and the Scots topped themselves with a monumental third-place finish at nationals. Flynn left the program in 2017 for the head coaching position at West Virginia University.

Robie, meanwhile, also went on to have an illustrious coaching career. After stops at Edinboro, West Virginia and Michigan as an assistant and Binghamton as head coach, he joined the staff at Virginia Tech as associate head coach in 2006. He helped build the Hokies into a national power before taking over as head coach just before the ACC Tournament in 2017. He led the Hokies to their first conference title in three years, and shared ACC Coach of the Year honors with his predecessor, Kevin Dresser.

In 2018-19, Robie coached Mekhi Lewis to the program's first national title. The meet was close to home in Pittsburgh, where Virginia Tech finished in the top 11 at the NCAAs for the eighth straight season and had three All-Americans. Robie again was named ACC Coach of the Year.

His continued success can be traced to his days in the wrestling room beneath McComb Fieldhouse.

"There's work ethic, and then there's the kind of work ethic it takes to accomplish something that's extraordinary," Robie said. "The one thing Edinboro helped to instill in me was the kind of work ethic and commitment and discipline it takes to work toward a goal. And (Flynn) was definitely a huge part of that."

Photo provided by Bob Shreve

(From left) Billy Kalbaugh, former Mercyhurst College athletics department employee Joe Hepfinger and Tony Demeo pose together for a photo. Kalbaugh, who coached Mercyhurst men's basketball, and Demeo, who coached Lakers football, are two of several coaches who stand out as longtime collegiate sports information director Bob Shreve recalls his career.

View From the Scorer's Table

By Bob Shreve

Bob Shreve served as the sports information director at Edinboro for 22 years, along with nine-plus seasons at Gannon. All told, he was an SID for 38 years, along with serving as the general manager of the Erie Orioles (NY-Penn League) for two years. He was inducted into the Metropolitan Erie Chapter of the Pennsylvania Sports Hall of Fame in 2018 and was the recipient of the Eastern College Athletics Conference's prestigious Irving T. Marsh Award in 2016.

A sports information director doesn't lead a very glamorous life. And that's just fine by me. I like being behind the scenes, making sure coaches and student-athletes receive the recognition.

One thing that strikes me as I reflect on my nearly 40 years of working in athletics is that I have been very fortunate to deal with some great coaches. Many of whom you haven't heard about, who were on the Division II and III levels, but they were outstanding in their own right. They left an indelible mark on me, particularly as a youngster in my formative years.

I have served as the sports information director at five universities — Frostburg State, Mercyhurst, West Chester, Gannon and Edinboro. I also was the softball and baseball coach for a year at Mercyhurst. Enough said. No need to go scurrying through those record books! I also served as the general manager for the Erie Orioles of the NY-Penn League for two years. There's a whole other chapter.

There are so many good coaches I've had the pleasure of working with over the years that I couldn't cover them all here, including people like Doug Zimmerman and Bob Dukiet (Gannon), and Gary Kagiavas (Edinboro).

While at Mercyhurst, I had the opportunity to work with two outstanding coaches in Tony DeMeo and Billy Kalbaugh. Both came to the Hurst from the Division I level, but their similarities ended there. Tony coached the Mercyhurst football team for eight years and ended with a 41-21-2 record while guiding a fledgling football program from its infancy. Tony was P.T. Barnum, always looking for a promotion or gimmick.

My favorite stunt of his was having Scott Gorring, a lightning-fast wide receiver, race a horse. That's right — a horse! In fact, I took Scott out to practice at Commodore Downs. It didn't go well. If you've ever walked on a race track, you know it's about two inches of loose dirt. Great for horses, but not for a wide receiver. Kind of like walking in the sand. The media, however, loved it.

Tony wasn't afraid to challenge anyone. Just a few years into football, Tony challenged Edinboro, the long-established program in the area, to a game. The first meeting in 1982 saw Edinboro win, 38-8. The next year, Edinboro head coach Denny Creehan wasn't quite as kind, hammering the Lakers, 74-13. The series did not resume until 1999.

One night, Tony and I were working late. I stopped by his office and he was on the phone with Bob Reade, the head coach at Augustana College in Illinois. At that time, Augustana was what Mount Union is today. They won four straight Division III national championships. Tony was trying to persuade Reade to have Augustana play Mercyhurst. When Reade asked him why they should, Tony responded, "Because you're the crowned champion and we're the uncrowned champion." It didn't work, and Augustana and Mercyhurst never met.

But make no mistake, Tony could coach. Through the years he has maintained a presence as a guru of the triple-gun attack. He would go on to coach at Temple, Delaware, Washburn and Charleston (West Virginia).

One other memory in particular sticks out to me about Tony. Mercyhurst was playing at Widener, another one of the top Division III programs in the nation. The specialists came out to warm up, and several older gentlemen were sitting in front of the press box. They were talking about Mercyhurst as a women's school, which at one point it was, and then talked about how small the players were. Of course, they were looking at the specialist and skill position players. Then the linemen came out. Mercyhurst had a huge team physically, particularly for a Division III team. You could hear these same gentlemen give a collected gasp. To make a long story short, with James Sherrod and the rest of the defense abusing the Widener offense, Mercyhurst won 17-7. Tony DeMeo could put together a team.

Billy Kalbaugh was best known for being the point guard on the St. Bonaventure team that made it to the Final Four in 1970, only to see Bob Lanier blow out his knee. Billy eschewed the limelight and was a devoted family man.

Billy was a lot of fun to be around, and I loved to sit around and listen to his stories. He also was as shrewd as they came and knew his way around. His days as an assistant coach on the recruiting trail at St. Bonaventure served him well.

He posted a 102-87 record in seven seasons as the Mercyhurst men's basketball coach, including a 21-7 record in 1985-86. It was the best record at Mercyhurst since 1977-78, and the Lakers would not record more wins in a single season until the 2015-16 team won 22 games. Many more people would have realized just how good of a coach Billy Kalbaugh was, but he had the misfortune of coaching at the same time as Tom Chapman at Gannon.

Once, four of us Mercyhurst staff members flew into New York City for a pair of games, with the rest of the team busing it. We needed to go to Long Island, and cab fare was going to be astronomical. Billy told us to wait out front, and he went around the corner and found us a "scab" cabby who charged us about a third of what it would have cost. Billy knew his way around the Big Apple.

I loved to watch Billy's practices. He believed in having teams that played with toughness. He may not have looked the part, but he knew you had to be tougher than the guy you were guarding. I recall a practice one day after a "soft" performance the night before. Billy ran a drill in which the players had to dribble one-on-one full court. There was no such thing as a foul, and he made it a point to pair up players who didn't necessarily get along with each other. Plenty of elbows that day!

When I first started in the early '80s, there weren't that many female head coaches at the collegiate level. To the substantial benefit of sports, that has changed greatly over the years. At Gannon, I worked with Jodi Kest. Kest took over as the women's basketball coach in 1996-97. After a slow start, Jodi caught fire over her last four years, winning 81 games. Unfortunately, I only worked with her during her first two seasons.

Jodi didn't enjoy as much success those two seasons, but I credit her with setting the tone for a Gannon women's basketball program that has enjoyed great success since then. Jodi's biggest contribution was her fight for equality with the men's program. She battled for equal wages, equal scholarships, etc., and it's obvious she succeeded. Jodi went on to serve as the head coach at the University of Akron for 12 years, and is the program's all-time winningest coach.

Gerry Burbules coached volleyball at Gannon, while Lynn Theehs was her counterpart at Edinboro. Oddly enough, Burbules is an Edinboro graduate and a member of the Edinboro University Athletics Hall of Fame. Theehs coached Edinboro for 10 seasons and posted 20 wins in eight of them, with four trips to the Elite Eight.

The two coaches faced each other just one year, 1994, before Burbules stepped down at Gannon. But to me, they share a stark similarity that would have made their battles a real joy to watch. Both brought toughness to the bench. They also placed high expectations on their players, both on the court and in the classroom.

When Jerry Slocum took over as the head coach at Gannon in 1996-97, he already had 402 career wins. Jerry went on to win 179 games in nine years at Gannon before moving on to Youngstown State. All nine teams won at least 16 games, with the last six reaching the NCAA Tournament. He ended his coaching career with 723 career victories!

Jerry was a regimented, close-to-the-vest coach who brought winning basketball back to a starved fanbase at Gannon. Sadly, I'm not sure he was ever accepted to the extent he should have been. He immersed himself into his basketball team, and was self-professed to have little use for the media and, generally, people who weren't in his basketball circle.

That included me at times. It wasn't the easiest thing to handle, but I learned a long time ago there's no place for an ego as a sports information director. I remember one time I was doing radio for road games and had to get a pregame interview the day before a game. It was not one of Jerry's favorite duties. I probably would have been smart to say "to hell with the interview," because Jerry avoided it throughout the day. I didn't, and finally Jerry told me I was a media "wannabe."

I was furious, because I knew what that meant to Jerry. He meant no disrespect, really. He just didn't feel like doing the interview. The only person he really enjoyed doing the pre- and postgame interviews with was Chris "Red" Hughes. Even back then, Red was a real pro and Jerry knew it.

That being said, when I decided after nine-plus years to leave Gannon, one group of people took me out to lunch before I left for Edinboro — Jerry and his basketball staff. I was fortunate enough to watch Jerry coach at Youngstown State several times. I wish I could have worked many more years with him.

Lou Tepper was a gentleman's gentleman. He arrived at Edinboro to be the head football coach in 2000, replacing a highly successful coach in Tom Hollman. I was in just my second year at Edinboro when Lou arrived with an incredible resume. He had served as the head coach at the University of Illinois for five years, leading the Big Ten squad to a pair of bowl games.

Lou was many things — classy, a fundamentalist, a disciplinarian, and as he proved before long, a winner. He sent a message right away as to who was the boss. He held his first team meeting at 6:30 a.m. before classes. At 6:25 a.m., the doors were locked. A number of players were "late." To this day we still call it Tepper Time. If you weren't 5-10 minutes early, you were late.

There was nothing fancy about football under Tepper. He was old school — run the ball and play great defense. After a couple of years to install his system, Edinboro ran off nine wins, nine wins and eight wins from 2003-05. Under Tepper, the Fighting Scots won three PSAC West co-championships and twice qualified for the NCAA playoffs. Lou left for IUP after the 2005 season, where he served as the head coach for five more seasons.

My journey to Edinboro provided me with an opportunity to work with two more basketball coaches who won over 500 games: Stan Swank and Greg Walcavich. They were about as different as night and day, but when it was all said and done, Swank won 581 games in 31 seasons, and Walcavich won 584 in 31 seasons, including 430 at Edinboro.

Stan coached the women's team. He departed as the all-time winningest coach in PSAC basketball history, including both men's and women's basketball. What amazed me about Stan was that he was like a fine wine that got better over time. His last eight teams all won 20-or-more games, with three PSAC championships. The last eight teams won 193 total games, an average of 24 wins a season. All told, Stan led the Fighting Scots to two NCAA Elite Eights, five PSAC titles and 11 NCAA Tournament appearances.

So, what made Stan so successful those last few years? I believe there were several factors. For one, he got better players. Pretty simple. But I think he believed in those players and overlooked their mistakes. And one of his best players, Callie Iorfido — now Callie Wheeler — joined him as an assistant coach. The two made each other better.

Greg Walcavich, meanwhile, led the men's basketball team for 24 seasons until retiring after the 2012-13 campaign. Under Walcavich, Edinboro won three PSAC championships and qualified for the PSAC Tournament 17 times in 24 seasons. With PSAC championships in 2004-05 and 2005-06, Walcavich became the first coach to lead a PSAC team to back-to-back titles since the legendary John Chaney guided Cheyney to PSAC championships from 1976-80. Walcavich's teams won 20-or-more games 10 times.

Greg was one of those people who was very smart, but would tell you he wasn't. He was sly as a fox and he was brilliant on the bench. He would tell his teams to just keep it close until the final four minutes and he would find a way to win.

Every year we sat down and did a season preview. Most of those years, Greg would tell me that the team he had in November wouldn't be the team he had in January. What he meant was that his teams made vast improvements during the year. That was a tribute to his ability to coach 'em up.

I also can never thank Greg enough for his assistance in my acquisition of the Edinboro job. I spoke with him one day prior to interviewing, and he asked, "Do you want this job?" When I told him I did, he gave me some pointers that proved extremely beneficial. He certainly didn't need to do that for a Gannon guy. Thanks, Greg!

When Stan Swank retired, Callie Wheeler took over as Edinboro's head coach in the 2018-19 season. I always considered Callie to be pound-for-pound the best player I ever saw at Edinboro. The mark of a true great player is the ability to make those around them better. Without question, that described Callie as a player.

As a coach, Callie exhibits those same qualities. She has the ability to bring out the best in her players. While still young as a head coach, I predict great things ahead for Callie Wheeler.

Photo by Rob Frank of R. Frank Photography (provided by the Erie Bayhawks)

Ivan Johnson (above) shoots a jumper for the Erie Bayhawks. Johnson later played for the Atlanta Hawks in the NBA. He was one of several exciting players who helped professional basketball become a mainstay in Erie.

The Surprise Rise

By Duane Rankin

Duane Rankin covers the Phoenix Suns and NBA for The Arizona Republic. *A sports reporter for 25-plus years, Rankin covered the Erie BayHawks' first four full seasons. The Huntington, West Virginia, native has won numerous national and state journalism awards and also produces videos and documentaries.*

They've had different NBA affiliates, coaches and players, but they're still flying in Erie.

I was there when the Erie BayHawks landed and had their inaugural 2008-09 season in the NBA Development League as an expansion team. Covered their first five seasons for the *Erie Times-News*.

Still remember Cleveland Cavaliers general manager Danny Ferry attending one of the team's early press conferences along with Ron Sertz, the BayHawks' first president, who wasn't wearing any socks.

I'm like, this is Erie. Cold nine months out of the year. Who in the hell goes sockless here?

Then I remembered Sertz owned the Erie Otters.

Dude was used to that brisk breeze coming off the lake.

Who would've thought at that time the BayHawks would become a staple in Erie and deliver the city's highest level of basketball with future NBA players and coaches?

There's Jay Larranaga, who led Erie to back-to-back playoff appearances before becoming an NBA assistant with the Boston Celtics.

He may wind up becoming a head coach in the league one day and match wits with Nick Nurse.

Yes, the same Nick Nurse who coached Kawhi Leonard and the Toronto Raptors to the 2019 NBA title. He was the Iowa Energy's head coach and had some great battles with Larranaga's BayHawks.

Got Seth Curry — the younger brother of two-time NBA MVP Stephen Curry — who lit it up in Erie before sticking in the NBA.

Then there's Jeremy Lin, whose one and only game with the BayHawks in 2012 launched Linsanity.

Lin went nuts in New York. Giving Kobe Bryant and the Lakers buckets. Next thing you knew, the BayHawks were selling Lin's BayHawks jerseys at games.

Can't leave out Ivan Johnson, perhaps the most polarizing BayHawks player ever.

Passionate. Aggressive. Physical. Played with rage and intensity. Dunked on people.

You could see why he was banned from leagues overseas — and why he made the NBA, too.

The city didn't see all that coming — and understandably so.

They watched the Erie Wave fizzle out in the World Basketball League for players 6-foot-5 and under within three years in the early 1990s (1990-92).

Financial losses crushed the Wave and later doomed the WBL, a summer league that lasted only five seasons.

So, there was reason to doubt the BayHawks. Plus, Erie was a high school and college basketball town.

Pro ball was 90 minutes west in Cleveland, but having the Cavaliers be one of Erie's two NBA affiliates along with the Philadelphia 76ers piqued people's interest.

The Cavs had that kid from Akron who became a four-time NBA MVP — LeBron James.

He actually did a promo the BayHawks used during their pregame that used to get the fans going.

The BayHawks' majority owner, Cleveland businessman Steve Demetriou, had courtside seats to Cavs games at Quicken Loans Arena.

Like right beside the Cavs bench courtside seats.

You had Owen McCormick as the lead local investor with that hair slicked back. Oh, McCormick and Demetriou were styling, profiling and making things happen.

McCormick was a little more stylish with those sport coats from Tom Karle and Son, though.

And a young Matt Bresee was getting his feet wet, learning the ropes, and is now the team president.

They had all the key elements in place.

Tullio Arena. A stat crew nearby that Edinboro University sports information director Bob Shreve put together. Complementary color combo of red, black and gold.

The BayHawks partnered up with LECOM for training and medical needs. See, the D-League has always been a testing market for the NBA.

While some fans didn't like seeing a sponsor on the front of the jersey, guess who's doing it now?

Yes, the NBA.

Erie had a mascot — Clutch. Whoever was in that buffed-out, red-and-black costume used to do some crazy stuff. Like flying onto the court by a rope.

Can't forget Donnell Jordan, aka BubbaLuv, who transformed into a super fan wearing a cape like Superman and crazy big glasses — and built a following.

Like commercials with Erie General Electric Federal Credit Union.

He had halftime performances with dancers at the games and everything.

Oh, the memories that started with that first season.

I remember guys showing up at the tryouts thinking they really had a shot despite being way out of shape. Then the real players showed up.

Erik Daniels out of Kentucky. He was the BayHawks' first-ever draft pick.

Had Ivan Harris out of Ohio State. McDonald's All-American.

Maureece Rice, who broke Wilt Chamberlain's all-time high school scoring record in Philadelphia, was on the team. But Jackie Manuel became the fan favorite.

Manuel was part of North Carolina's 2005 national championship team. Every time he scored, they'd play "Jackie Blue," a 1975 song by the Ozark Mountain Daredevils.

Carolina Blue. Jackie Manuel.

It stuck.

Erie had a roster that was ever changing that first year — and every year after that.

See, there was a saying in the D-League that everybody wants in and then wants out, meaning this was a path to the NBA. Scouts could see you play, but the players didn't make much money.

Average salary was between $19,000 and $26,000. The BayHawks players were staying in the Avalon Hotel right down the street from Subway, which wound up being their go-to place to eat.

Oh man, those dudes were working for that 10-day contract that actually paid more than a full season's salary, but those weren't easy to land. So, they'd either go overseas for more money or just hang it up.

Head coach John Treloar and assistant Ben McDonald were constantly adjusting to the player carousel.

It never took long to see who'd stick it out — like John Bryant and Cliff

Clinkscales — and who wouldn't.

Then when Cleveland assigned Darnell Jackson to Erie for a couple of games back in 2008-09, Treloar and McDonald had to feature him and keep everyone else involved, too. Those were always big games because fans could see an NBA player. That was a big deal.

Through all the changes, the BayHawks somehow formed into one of the D-League's best teams and made the playoffs in their first year. They became legit in Erie.

Then Mike Gansey shows up that second season after a trade and fans fall in love with him. He first played college at St. Bonaventure, which is about 90 minutes from Erie, and later led WVU to the Elite 8 in the 2005 NCAA Tournament. His following grew in Erie.

Hard-nosed player. Gritty. Blue collar.

Gansey fit right into Erie's mentality as a city. He's now an assistant general manager for the Cavs.

Former Georgetown star Mike Sweetney, a first-round pick in the 2003 NBA Draft, was on that second Erie team, too. He stretched his BayHawks way too far out with his size. Bro was super swollen.

When Treloar left to become director of player personnel for the Phoenix Suns in 2010, that added to the credibility of the BayHawks, but then they had to hire a coach to replace him.

Enter Larranaga.

He was more known by his last game than anything else at that time. His dad, Jim, was a great college coach. Jim led George Mason to the 2006 Final Four.

However, the son made his mark in Erie by leading the BayHawks to consecutive playoff appearances (2011, 2012). Those teams had some talent.

Johnson. Daniels. Garrett Temple, who has played in 11 NBA seasons.

Blake Ahearn was a sharpshooter. Cedric Jackson, headband and all, was a go-getter.

Add bruiser Kyle Goldcamp, who starred at Gannon, and Erie had a local connection to go along with NBA talent. That led to success, bigger crowds and a first-ever home playoff game.

The atmosphere was bananas, but the drama going into it made it even more bananas.

See, Eric Musselman was Reno's head coach. Before that, he was the youngest head coach in the NBA when he took over for the Golden State Warriors in 2002 at age 37.

Hot head. Hyperactive, but a good coach.

The D-League allowed the top three seeds to pick their opponent.

Musselman said they drew Erie's name out of a hat after a lengthy debate with players and coaches. He spun it as if it was too tough to choose one because they were all so good and he had respect for all of them.

Larranaga, who wasn't one to stir the pot, did just that in reaction. Not believing Musselman's story, Larranaga came out and said the BayHawks were chosen because Reno believed it could beat them.

Oh, it was on.

The energy inside Tullio Arena was high and kept rising all game. The Bighorns wound up winning, and I can still see Musselman screaming at the crowd that was unmercifully booing him.

Man, that was playoff basketball right there — and unlike anything the city had seen at that level.

Those were the early steps of what has become a signature and survivor in Erie. The franchise has lost NBA affiliates only to find new ones.

The arena underwent renovations that led to more than a name change — Erie Insurance Arena. It served as a necessary investment to keep pro basketball in the city.

This was after Erie had to once cancel a game because the floor was too slippery. Changes had to be made — and they were for the better, but how long the BayHawks keep flying in Erie remains to be seen.

The G League is thriving and continues to produce NBA talent.

McCormick continues to make moves to keep the franchise afloat, and Bresee knows more about the league than nearly anyone in his position on a G League team.

Whether it ends in a year or 20, the BayHawks did more than legitimize pro ball in Erie.

They developed a loyal fan base. They got kids excited to come see them play.

They developed future NBA players.

Curry. Johnson. Donald Sloan. Henry Sims.

They were a landing spot for future NBA coaches/managers.

Treloar. Larranaga. Gansey.

Gene Cross, Erie's third head coach, is now a scout with the Sacramento Kings.

Danny Green knocked down shots for the BayHawks for a couple of games while in Cleveland before winning three NBA titles, with the second one coming in Toronto — playing for Nurse.

Linsanity made its initial ascent with the BayHawks.

They just keep flying high in Erie, years after no one saw them coming.

Photo by Matt Mead of Matt Mead Photography LLC (provided by the Erie Otters)

The Erie Otters (above) pose for a photo on the ice at Erie Insurance Arena following their Ontario Hockey League Championship win over the Mississauga Steelheads in 2017.

Power Play

By Victor Fernandes

Victor Fernandes covered the Erie Otters from 2003-19 as a beat reporter for the Erie Times-News. *He teamed with longtime colleague Ed Pallatella to win a first-place award from the Pennsylvania AP Managing Editors Association in 2015 for Best Sports Story for their coverage of the franchise's financial struggles and subsequent sale. He now resides in Berlin, Maryland, with his wife, Shelly, and sons Anthony, Nicholas and Zachary. He works as a certified personal trainer after spending 26 years as a sports reporter.*

The tweet was meant as a seemingly innocent and amusing jab at one of the singularly defining periods in Erie Otters history.
I don't recall the exact date of my post, or if it came before or after current owner James Waters purchased the franchise on July 17, 2015, and provided long-awaited stability for a franchise that for several years before the sale seemed destined to leave Erie.
But, there was a bus with the name "Hamilton Bulldogs" emblazoned on the side that was parked behind Erie Insurance Arena, with a tongue-in-cheek question in my tweet as to why that bus was there when the Bulldogs weren't.
Part of me wanted to get a rise out of the Otters' devoted fans, because you should have some fun during a season that at times feels like a grind. But the tweet struck a nerve, which proved to me that nearly losing their Ontario Hockey League franchise in the midst of a historic run from 2013-17 — a run that ended with Erie's second OHL championship — featured equal parts of pain and pride.
It was an intriguing dynamic not often seen at any level of sport. The Otters arguably were the best club in the Canadian Hockey League during that highly impressive stretch, which included a CHL-record four consecutive 50-win seasons.
On one side of the glass, there was Dave Brown, first as director of hockey operations and now as general manager, and then head coach Kris Knoblauch, who molded a roster that produced superstar Connor McDavid and nearly a dozen other current National Hockey

League players. The journey ended with 240 combined regular season and playoff wins, three division, two conference and two league regular season titles, four trips to the conference finals, two berths in the OHL finals and the championship night no Otters fan will ever forget — May 12, 2017.

On the other side, there was a growing fan base that feared all the success wouldn't be enough to save their team. Otters fans know where they were on the night the Otters finally reclaimed the OHL championship. But, where would these fans be if the pieces hadn't fallen into place the way they did? What if the rumors and speculation, lawsuits, bankruptcy and the many twists and turns produced an agreement to sell the franchise to an Edmonton Oilers subsidiary and move it to Hamilton, Ontario? These days, fans choose to remember the good times.

"It may sound strange, but I think the one thing that sticks out to me about that period of the Otters is simply the hockey," said public-address announcer Dean Pepicello. "Despite the cloud of financial issues (surrounding) Sherry Bassin, the potential move to Hamilton, and all the things that go on off the ice to draw fans, it was the actual product on the ice that really mattered to anyone."

Fans have forgiven past indiscretions now that the Otters are firmly entrenched in Erie for the next decade thanks to a 10-year arena lease signed in September 2019. But they haven't forgotten.

"In thinking about the possible relocation, one item that immediately came to mind is when the rumors started," longtime fan David Hahn said. "(Then owner and general manager) Sherry Bassin kept talking about a one-year lease agreement between the Otters and ECCCA (Erie County Convention Center Authority). That never felt great, because it seemed as if Bassin was negotiating with Hamilton at the time and had a few hoops to jump through in order to make it happen."

Rumors of a move surfaced early in 2012, with the Otters mired in the worst season in franchise history. Ten wins, that's all they mustered in 68 games, which made the uncertainty swirling around the Otters seem like a tornado ready to sweep it all away.

Yet there were moments, some more obvious than others, that set the stage for a team few at that time imagined they would see.

As losses mounted, fans eagerly awaited the arrival of 15-year-old phenom McDavid in April 2012. But the path to historic success began a month later in western Canada, and in quieter fashion, when Knoblauch was fired by the Kootenay Ice — a year after leading the club to a Western Hockey League title — for interviewing with his alma mater, University of Alberta, without permission.

That opened the door for Knoblauch to become the seventh head coach in Otters history two months into the 2012-13 season.

A generational talent like McDavid alone didn't spark the record-setting turnaround. It took a change in culture for a club known for losing before Knoblauch arrived, with five non-playoff finishes and one playoff series win in the nine seasons prior to his first full year at the helm. Suddenly, players who knew only losing before Knoblauch learned how to win because of him.

"I could never put my finger on what exactly made him so successful or how he could always get the most from seemingly every player," Greg Parker said.

In his position as part-time practice goaltender, Parker had an inside look few fans have enjoyed, but had a similar sentiment players often shared about an approach that uniquely blended being a teacher, disciplinarian and mentor.

"I don't really know what he's thinking all the time," then rookie center Brett Neumann told me in March 2016. "But he's got a reason behind everything he does. Our guys really trust him, and really like him. Our success has a lot to do with that."

The wins kept on coming, yet speculation surrounding a potential move to Hamilton often shared the spotlight.

Speculation evolved into facts in November 2014, as a lawsuit filed in the U.S. District Court in Erie outlined the deal in place that, if carried out, would have cemented the Otters' fate. According to reports in the *Erie Times-News*, there were $4.2 million in loans from an Oilers' subsidiary that were supposed to be the precursor to a sale and move, and an auction to sell the franchise that may have taken place if current owner James Waters and former team president and chief executive officer Roy Mlakar hadn't rescued it.

Until that sale to Waters' JAW Hockey Enterprises LP for $7.225 million became official, fans feared the worst, and understandably so.

"Without good hockey (from) the OHL in Erie, Pa., this town would have nothing to support," fan Chris Janulewski said. "What fans needed to do was come down to (the arena) and support this franchise (to keep it) from relocating to Hamilton, Ontario."

And through it all they did, as the club averaged 4,300 fans or more per game for all four seasons that culminated in the title run, even as the thought of losing the franchise remained real until the sale to Waters was finalized and rumors finally were laid to rest.

"Traditionally, when the talent has been there and the team has won, the city was enamored and came out in droves no matter what,"

Pepicello said. "When they've lost, it's been more of the traditional long-time hockey fans that tend to show up. It felt at that time like this team would never lose and could score at will. ... With this team, even the casual hockey fan was there to watch the game, the incredible talent assembled, and (they) cared about the outcome."

Devoted and casual fans alike were treated to a memorable experience in Game 5 of the OHL Finals against the Mississauga Steelheads. Anthony Cirelli scored 2 minutes, 41 seconds into overtime to secure an OHL title they waited 15 years to celebrate.

"When Cirelli put that puck in to win the championship, I was tending to another player's skate," then equipment manager Steve Tuholski said. "I remember I was cleaning up the edges and the crowd went crazy and I looked up at (assistant coach) Wes Wolfe and said, 'Did we just win?' And he said, 'Yeah, Stevie baby!' and shook hands with the coaches. But coach Kris (Knoblauch) shook my hand, hugged me and said, 'Congratulations, you just became an OHL champion!'"

These days, fans talk about when the Otters will return to the top of the OHL. It's solely about what's happening on the ice. Complaints about head coach Chris Hartsburg and the team's struggles in recent years have been replaced with talk of the hopeful start to the pandemic-delayed, long-awaited 2020-21 season.

But talk of the club being sold and moving has faded away, which has made fans very happy. Their memories are unforgettable for much better reasons.

"I could probably go on and on and on," Parker said. "These times were some of the best memories of my life."

Photo provided by Fred Biletnikoff

(From left) Bob Biletnikoff, Ken Biletnikoff, Mel Laskoff and Fred Biletnikoff pose for a photo on German Street in Erie. Fred Biletnikoff went on to an illustrious football career that culminated in an induction into the Pro Football Hall of Fame.

Freddie From the Neighborhood House

By Bob Jarzomski

Bob Jarzomski was a versatile sportswriter for the Erie Times-News *for nearly 40 years before retiring in November 2015. He spent the first two decades of his career assembling popular stories and headlines for the daily sport pages. He covered every high school sport, local college basketball, semipro hockey and professional golf, including the 1994 U.S. Open and the 1998 Masters Tournament. He won a Professional Bowlers Association writing award in 2000 for his coverage of the PBA, and even covered pigeon racing, in which his late father, Frank Jarzomski, competed. Jarzomski once interviewed Raiders QB/kicker George Blanda, and attended a surprise party for Biletnikoff in 2010. The party, which was organized by Valahovic and included Biletnikoff's childhood friends from his youth sports days, was filled with jokes, laughter and was a good time had by all.*

Fred Biletnikoff sat on his childhood buddy Rich Valahovic's deck in Erie on a summer night a couple of years ago in a reflective mood, a very content man in his twilight years.

"You know Val, I am so lucky. I can't believe I'm in the (Pro Football) Hall of Fame," Biletnikoff said. "Tens of thousands of players have played the game, and somehow I'm one of the select few to get into the Hall of Fame. I'm truly blessed."

And talented.

He truly deserved to be a Hall of Fame member of both college and pro football.

That truth is well documented.

Born February 23, 1943, Biletnikoff rose from a stellar high school athlete to one of the greatest receivers in NFL history. He attended Erie's Technical Memorial High School, starring in football, basketball, baseball and track and field, was an All-American wide receiver at Florida State University, and went on to have a storied NFL career with the Oakland Raiders.

His zenith in college was in Florida State's first bowl victory, a 36-19, Gator Bowl romp over Oklahoma to end his collegiate career after the

1964 season. He combined with lanky quarterback Steve Tensi for 192 receiving yards and four touchdowns on 13 catches. Not done yet, he got married to his first of three wives under the goal posts after the game.

"That was a mistake of immaturity," Biletnikoff said.

In January of 1977, "Freddie B" — covered in his trademark pine tar-like Stickum — caught four passes from close friend and roommate Kenny "The Snake" Stabler to set up three scores as the Raiders won their first Super Bowl by thumping the Minnesota Vikings, 32-14. Biletnikoff was named the Super Bowl MVP, nine years after he and the Raiders were defeated by the Green Bay Packers in Super Bowl II.

Inducted into the Pro Football Hall of Fame in Canton, Ohio in 1988, Biletnikoff's genesis in athletics began at the Russian Neighborhood House across from the Russian Orthodox Church on Erie's East Bayfront. Biletnikoff grew up not far from there at 109 German Street. He was one of three sons born to Ephriam "Snooky Brill" and Natalie Karuba Biletnikoff. His older brother Kenny and younger brother Bobby were also tremendous athletes. Natalie died when Fred was just 18, and Ephriam and his second wife gave birth to another son, "Tiger."

"I met Freddie at the Neighborhood House, and as young kids the first thing we learned was how to tumble," said Valahovic, 79, a good athlete in his own right who retired in 2019 after working as an electrical engineer for 55 years at Erie Strayer Co. "After we learned how to tumble, then we were allowed to begin other sports." Biletnikoff recalls those days fondly.

"All the kids in that area had fun there, then at the Boys Club on 7th Street, then we played a lot of sandlot baseball and football at 2nd and Wallace," he said. "I learned to compete against older kids who hung out there, and it was great if they picked you for their team because nobody wants to be picked last."

Biletnikoff likely always went in the early rounds on the sandlots. The area between State Street and Parade Street, Front Street to East 6th, was very diverse. From this neighborhood came Russian American Mel "The Master" Laskoff, who starred at East High School in the early 1950s. Valahovic recalled watching Biletnikoff in the Gator Bowl with Laskoff.

The neighborhood was a melting pot of Americans from Irish, Polish, Slovak, German and African descent. Among them was Fred's late friend Earl "Elmer" Woodard, a well-known Erieite, Academy High School graduate and an active member of Shiloh Baptist Church.

Biletnikoff attended Jones Elementary School on 8th and Holland, and then went to junior high at East. He was certainly talented enough in football to be a running back, but the Warriors had a stable of backs and their offense was predicated on run, run, run.

"I wanted to be a receiver," Biletnikoff said. "Al Calabrese, who had a lot of influence on my life, coached at Tech and they would pass the ball. Al wanted me, but said I had to get permission from my father, who agreed to let me transfer."

Biletnikoff said his father, whose boxing moniker was Snooky Brill, was a disciplinarian but was fair to his children.

"I think all of the good fathers then were disciplinarians, but the kids learned respect of others which benefited their own lives," Biletnikoff said.

Biletnikoff himself is a father of five. He lives in the Sacramento suburb of Roseville, California, with his wife, Angela, whom he married in 1991.

Biletnikoff would play in the final season of Tech High — on 10th and Sassafras — in 1960, and then the first year in 1961 at Tech Memorial on 32nd and Cherry. The building now houses the conglomerate of East, Strong Vincent and Central Tech — the latter was the combination of Academy and Tech in 1992 — known as Erie High School.

Biletnikoff could do it all for the Centaurs, catching passes — including ones thrown by his brother Bobby in his senior year — running as a halfback, and kicking extra points for Calabrese and successor Walt Strosser. He starred in hoops for Calabrese — the Al Calabrese Gymnasium remains at Erie High — was a standout jumper in track and field, and was a strong hitter and pitcher on the baseball diamond. Though, it was Bobby who went on to be a New York Yankees prospect after playing QB at the University of Miami.

Ray Dombrowski, who coached football and track and field, was also a teacher and a guiding light for Biletnikoff.

"Ray not only coached me, but he taught me so much about life, and when it was time to go to college, he set me up with (Erie's) Ken Meyer — who was an assistant at Florida State — and I got a scholarship," Biletnikoff said. "Bill Peterson was the head coach and ran a pro-style offense, which was perfect for me."

So perfect that Biletnikoff, a wide receiver at a position once known as "split end" or "flanker," lent his name to the Biletnikoff Award, created in 1994 by the Tallahassee Quarterback Club and given to the best receiver in college football each season.

"I am honored to have such a beautiful trophy given to a young man who is bigger and faster than I ever was," Biletnikoff said with a laugh. Biletnikoff was drafted by the Detroit Lions in the second round of the 1965 NFL Draft, and by the Raiders in the third round of the American Football League Draft that same year. He signed with the Raiders in the pass-happy league that merged with the NFL in 1970.

"I was fortunate to play with great quarterbacks, starting with Daryl Lamonica, then (1970 NFL MVP) George Blanda who was in his 40s yet still could compete, and of course Kenny Stabler, one of the most accurate quarterbacks and (a) great leader," Biletnikoff said.

It was said that Biletnikoff was like a caged lion before games, so nervous that he would vomit, but when he got on the field he made defensive backs ill.

Wearing No. 25 for the silver and black, Biletnikoff was known more for shifty quickness and running precision routes than for breakaway speed, His stringy blond hair flying, he latched on to 589 passes for 8,974 yards and 76 touchdowns in 14 regular seasons (1965-1978). He added 70 catches, 1,167 yards and 10 TDs in 19 postseason games.

"There are so many stories and memories, so many characters and so many victories because everybody just wanted to play Raiders football for (team owner) Al Davis," Biletnikoff said. "I still see friends like (safety) George Atkinson and (running back Pete) Banaszak and other guys I played with when I go to Raiders games, and we always reminisce."

After his playing days were over, Biletnikoff coached at every level of organized football and was a Raiders receivers coach for 18 years. However, he experienced a life-changing event in February 1999 when his 20-year-old daughter Tracey was murdered by her drug-influenced boyfriend in Redwood City, outside of San Francisco. The tragedy prompted Biletnikoff and Angela to form the Biletnikoff Foundation, which funds Tracey's Place of Hope, a rehabilitation center in San Mateo, Calif. for girls who have suffered substance, alcohol and domestic abuse.

"Angela and I are still shaken by Tracey's death, but it's gratifying to see these girls learning and working so hard to turn around their lives," Biletnikoff said. "Their stories are unbelievable, heartbreaking, so we're elated to see them take advantage of their opportunity here." The Biletnikoffs are immersed in the foundation. They host an annual golf tournament and an annual crab fest where former teammates and celebrities attend to help raise funds for the foundation.

"Those events are fantastic, and my son and I try to make it every year," Valahovic said.

In 1989, a football field at 400 W. 32nd St., by what is now Erie High, was named the Fred Biletnikoff Athletic Field in the Erie legend's honor. The original sign on the Peach Street side of the field, which bore the field's name and Biletnikoff's image, saw substantial wear and tear as if it was covered in Stickum and took hits from NFL safeties and linebackers.

Valahovic, Save Our Native Species vice president Eddie Kissell and Save-An-Eye football game coordinator Doug White raised funds for a new sign, as well as improvements to the field. The new sign was put up in 2020.

"Freddie and the school deserve that," Valahovic said.

Jim Zbach, a 1981 Tech Memorial grad and president of the Great Lakes Raiders Boosters Club, designed the sign. His design incorporated the colors of the Raiders' silver and black and the Erie High Royals' purple and gold.

Biletnikoff makes occasional trips to Erie to visit his friends from his youth, many of whom were successful athletes in their own right. When he comes home, he always has one priority.

"My wife Diane always has to bake city chicken for Fred," Valahovic said.

"City chicken" is a Polish dish that is not actually chicken, but cubes of meat placed on a skewer.

"It's delicious, just like the city chicken my mother used to make," Biletnikoff said.

And just like a tasty dinner he would enjoy before and after roaming the sandlots on Erie's lower east side, his first steps to the Pro Football Hall of Fame.

Photo provided by Jovon Johnson

Jovon Johnson (left) hangs out with his close friend Levonne Rowan in Erie during their high school years. Johnson excelled in football at Mercyhurst Preparatory School before starring at the University of Iowa, playing for the Pittsburgh Steelers of the NFL and enjoying a long career in the CFL.

Standing Tall

By Aaron McKrell

Jovon Johnson is no stranger to struggle.

From the Harbor Homes to Heinz Field, the Erie native has worked for everything he's gotten through blood, sweat and a burning desire to prove others wrong.

At 5-foot-9, he might be easy to overlook, and certainly was by NFL scouts and coaches. But Jovon, lightning-quick with an ability to jump out of the gym, made the most of his stature with an outstanding career in the Canadian Football League.

He did so with a personal philosophy that your trials don't define you; it's how you respond to them that matters.

"There's more to life than the struggles that one has to endure to find out who they really are," Jovon said.

It's a lesson he learned early while growing up in the Harbor Homes, project housing on East 18th Street in Erie. Jovon lived with his mother, Sandra Jordan, younger brother, Daquan Crosby, and three younger cousins. Jovon said his mother worked hard to provide for her family, but when the checks rolled in, it wasn't enough.

"Every day was a struggle, but we found a way to make it work," he said.

When Jovon was five years old, his grandmother died, and his teenage uncles, Derick Jordan and Erick Jordan, came to live with them. Still in high school themselves, they acted as father figures to Jovon and the other children.

"I didn't have (a father figure), so I wanted to make sure they took the positive route," Derick said.

A basketball player for the East High Warriors, Derick shared his love of sports with his nephew. Jovon went to his uncle's games and they watched Sunday Night Football together.

"Growing up where we grew up, there wasn't too much positive around me, if you know what I mean," Derick said. "Sports was the only outlet we had."

It was a necessary outlet, as Sandra said drugs were prevalent in the Harbor Homes. She said she wanted her children to focus on school and sports.

"I was just gonna make sure — they were coming out (of) the projects, they had to at least bring me a diploma," she said.

Jovon also benefited from the support of his stepfather, Benny Crosby, who he credits with helping to raise him.

Jovon took to sports quickly, playing basketball with Levonne Rowan and his brother, Dywon Rowan, at the John F. Kennedy Center on East 20th Street.

He played in youth basketball, football and baseball leagues. By the time he was 12, he was dominating the competition. After racking up 30 points by halftime of a youth basketball game and blocking a shot over a fence, he was bumped up to the 15-and-older league.

"I kind of knew at that point that I was different," Jovon said.

Just as he was prematurely running with the big boys, a 12-year-old Jovon found himself stepping into a role meant for a man. Derick and Erick had moved out, and Jovon stepped up to become the man of the house.

He made sure his brother and cousins woke up on time, got dressed and left for school in a timely fashion. He also made sure they ate dinner after school.

"I was doing things that a normal 10-, 11-, 12-year-old kid probably never had the responsibility of doing," Jovon said. "So I kind of grew up fast, but at the end of the day I learned a lot about myself and I learned a lot about life."

Though basketball was initially Jovon's sport of choice, by the time he was a freshman at East High School he was established as a standout in football, too. However, he saw in his teammates a lack of discipline, and wanted to be around more like-minded individuals.

"It was more to me than just being fun at that point," he said.

Jovon didn't have money for private school. However, on a scholarship granted to him by Erie native and Tae Bo creator Billy Blanks, he transferred to Mercyhurst Preparatory School for his sophomore year, along with the Rowan brothers. He said transferring to Cathedral Preparatory School had crossed his mind, but he knew it wasn't financially viable.

As soon as he stepped onto the field at Mercyhurst Prep, Jovon knew he had made the right decision.

"Everybody was on the same page," he said. "Everybody had the same goal in mind."

Jovon played quarterback and defensive back. In his junior year, the Lakers posted a 5-4 regular season record. He approached his senior season with laser focus and decided he couldn't juggle his athletic schedule and school load with being the man of the house.

"It was hard to focus, because I was put in a role where I had to be more of an adult than an athlete," he said.

He spent some of the year living with Mercyhurst Prep head basketball coach Pat Flaherty, and also roomed with the Rowans. Sandra said she didn't have a problem with Jovon's decision to move out.

"He had to become a man to get out there on his own one day," she said. "I just hope I did a good enough job that when he got out there he always maintained, kept his head up (and) always put God first."

Dywon said that time living with each other formed an extraordinary bond.

"Once you break bread with each other, go to sleep with each other, wake up with each other, train with each other and do homework with each other, it makes you so much closer," he said.

In turn, Levonne said that closeness made their on-field chemistry "dynamic."

Jovon remained just a phone call away if his family needed him, and he visited them on the weekends. But he focused on school and football, and no longer had to make the sacrifices in caring for others that kept him from fully experiencing his childhood.

"That took a toll on me," Jovon said. "It formulated my mentality that whatever I did, I was gonna put my all into it. And everybody was gonna feel the pain that I was feeling, because I didn't get to do everything that I wanted to do as a kid."

Football, which Jovon called a "controlled violence atmosphere," was the perfect outlet for his pain.

"Seeing other people feel the pain that I was feeling — guys getting up slow, crawling off the ground — I lived for that," he said. "That was like an adrenaline rush for me, because I lived with that every day."

Those who underestimated him because of his size only motivated him more.

"I had a chip on my shoulder my whole life," he said. "Anytime anybody said something about my height, in my mind I would just think, 'Oh, you think I'm too small? I'm gonna prove you wrong.'"

As aggressive as he was in between the hash marks, that's how compassionate he was outside of them. Dywon said Jovon was always willing to help him with his homework, while Levonne called him a "role model."

"He stayed focused," Levonne said. "We all pushed each other."

The results were undeniable. The Lakers went a perfect 9-0 in the regular season, recording three shutouts and outscoring their opponents by an average of about 37 points.

However, Mercyhurst Prep suffered what Jovon called a "heartbreaking" 14-7 loss to Sharon High School in the first round of the playoffs. Jovon scored four touchdowns, but three were called back because of penalties.

"It was the craziest officiated game I've ever been a part of," he said. His career, though, was far from over.

University of Iowa defensive coordinator Norm Parker and defensive backs coach Phil Parker came to Mercyhurst Prep to recruit Levonne. Jovon was in the coaches' office with them and told them, "If you're looking for a DB, (Levonne's) got a teammate who can make some things happen."

After he showed them his highlight film, they had him dunk a basketball. The next day, they offered him a scholarship.

While the Rowan brothers ended up signing with the University of Wisconsin, Jovon had some familiar faces with him in Iowa. Former Cathedral Prep standouts Bob Sanders and Ed Hinkle were also with the Hawkeyes.

"I knew they wouldn't let me fail," Jovon said. "They wouldn't let me be distracted by all the different things going on."

Jovon made an impression on his team his very first day of training camp. After one of his older teammates grabbed his facemask and slammed him to the ground, they got into a fight.

"That Erie mentality came out real quick," he said.

The entire Iowa defense had his back. In another instance, one of Iowa's tight ends caught a pass in a no-pads practice and Jovon leveled him. He was cussed out and kicked off the field, but back in the meeting room, Phil Parker was ecstatic about the play.

"That's where I started to make a name for myself, because with my size I wasn't backing down and I wanted to inflict pain on other guys to make them feel the pain that I was feeling," Jovon said.

It was the perfect mentality to have in Big Ten football, which was played in a smash-mouth style and often was in front of more than 100,000 fans.

"The Big Ten, every game is like a college football playoff game," Jovon said.

Jovon rose to the challenge, starting at cornerback as a freshman and coming up with three interceptions in his first three games.

Iowa faced the University of Southern California in the Orange Bowl that season, and the Trojans boasted a roster that included future NFL stars Carson Palmer, Mike Williams and Troy Polamalu.

"That (USC) team, they looked like an NFL team in college," Jovon said.

Iowa lost, 38-17. Jovon upped his game in his sophomore season, picking off six passes, which was tied for 13th in NCAA Division I. The Hawkeyes dominated the University of Florida, 37-17 in the Outback Bowl.

"Florida came out thinking that they were the almighty SEC, but we put a whooping on them," Jovon said.

The same thing happened the next year, when Iowa faced Louisiana State University in the Capital One Bowl.

"We were just like, 'We've been here before, we're the giant killers and we're gonna put a whooping on them,'" Jovon said.

The Hawkeyes edged the Tigers, 30-25.

During this time Jovon kept his Erie ties strong. He occasionally visited the Rowans in Wisconsin and invited his family to his games. Derick, who had introduced Jovon to football so many years before, was overjoyed to see his nephew excel on the big stage.

"Going to the college games (were) some of the best times of my life," Derick said.

As he continued to excel, Jovon began to see a professional football career as a real possibility.

Even though Florida avenged their loss with a 31-24 victory over Iowa in an Outback Bowl rematch, Jovon's senior season was still strong. He was named first-team All-Big Ten, and finished his college career with 17 interceptions. His career total is just one behind Nile Kinnick's school record of 18.

Despite his success at Iowa, there were doubts about his size and speed, and he wasn't invited to the NFL Combine.

On draft night, he received calls from teams, including the Pittsburgh Steelers. The Steelers told him if they didn't draft him, they'd sign him as a free agent. They also told him he'd be the only defensive back they'd sign.

Jovon said his agent, however, pushed for a deal with the New York Jets, who had already drafted a cornerback in the sixth round. Jovon was released from the Jets three times in eight weeks, after which he landed in Pittsburgh.

The first player Jovon met when he arrived at the Steelers' facility was Troy Polamalu, who was in the players' lounge reading a book.

"He was a student of the game," Jovon said. "(He had) outstanding athletic ability, but he really studied it with laser focus on the teams that we would play. He would know things and be able to do things that were (inhumanly) possible because he studied so much."

Once again, Jovon was underestimated because of his size. The locker room ceiling was 11 ½ feet high, and players would try to touch the ceiling. Joey Porter, who knew of Jovon's jumping ability, would bet other players hundreds and even thousands of dollars that Jovon could touch the ceiling.

Jovon's hand would make contact with the ceiling and a player would be out some money. Some would even bet that Jovon couldn't repeat the feat, and they'd be out more money. Joey raked in the cash and gave some to Jovon.

The bets were fun and games, but the players were all business. Jovon noted their work ethic, attention to detail and level of greatness. He also knew not to take anything for granted.

"They tell you from day one as an NFL player, that every day they're looking to replace you," Jovon said. "You don't get to take days off."

With Erie so close by, family and friends supported Jovon and came to his games. He spent the first eight weeks of the season on the practice squad before being bumped up to the active roster. He recorded one solo tackle and assisted on another for the season.

Pittsburgh head coach Bill Cowher was impressed with Jovon.

"If Cowher had stayed, I would have probably played in the NFL for a long time," Jovon said.

But Cowher retired after the 2006-07 season. Jovon continued to play well, scoring a touchdown in a 2007 preseason game and regularly intercepting starting quarterback Ben Roethlisberger in practice.

However, the Steelers had just drafted corner William Gay, and Jovon said they were still waiting on 2004 draft pick Ricard Colclough to show promise. When it was time to release a cornerback, Jovon was the odd man out.

His agent told him teams weren't offering workouts to players who had just been released, so after the preseason he received no interest from other teams.

"It was discouraging, because I knew I was the type of player that could play at that level, and play at a high level," Jovon said. "The plays that I was able to make, it was like going through college all over again, and I just didn't get a fair opportunity."

Jovon was recruited by the Saskatchewan Roughriders of the Canadian Football League, and went up north in 2007.

Jovon said the Roughriders' general manager had recruited him to play, but they put him on the developmental squad for the first week and he only made $500. Knowing he could have gotten a nine-to-five job in Erie for that much money, he had a talk with the GM.

"If I don't play or at least get paid a normal paycheck, I'm definitely going back home," he told the GM.

Jovon started in the defensive backfield in the next week's game.

Though he made several tackles, he was criticized by the coaching staff for shying away from hits.

"I've never been the type of player to avoid contact, so that's not true at all," he said.

Though he dressed in eight games, he only played in two. He had made a joke about something the team's offensive coordinator had said during a practice, and was called into the office and chastised for mocking a coach.

He was bumped back to the developmental squad for the Roughriders' 23-19 win over the Winnipeg Blue Bombers for the Grey Cup championship. His paycheck was $500, as opposed to $18,000 for active roster players.

"I sold my Grey Cup ring, to say the least," Jovon said.

He returned home, where he played in 2008 with the Erie RiverRats of the now-defunct American Indoor Football League. He tallied 12 interceptions in eight games.

"It was fun, but I knew I was a better player than what I was playing against," Jovon said. Through all the moves, all the uncertainty, Jovon stayed focused.

"I just was determined to prove people wrong, and no matter how that came about I was willing to do it," he said. "I knew I was able to play, and I knew I could play (professional football) for a long time.

"But it was just a matter of showing people wrong. I didn't want to go back home and have one of those stories where that, shoulda-coulda-woulda-type thing, so I just stuck to it."

It was here that the discipline and self-reliance Jovon learned as a preteen man of the house paid off. Jovon, as he put it, was on the field with "ghosts" as he went through his progressions.

"I never really had anybody to push me to my limit or wake me up in the morning and say, 'You gotta work out,' so I was comfortable with that," he said.

The following season, Jovon signed with the Winnipeg Blue Bombers. He picked off three passes and led the team with 60 tackles.

He returned to Erie to play with the RiverRats, but was forced to quit because he was under contract with the Blue Bombers and they didn't want him to get injured.

In September 2008, tragedy hit home. Jovon's brother, Daquan, was 15 when he was an innocent bystander, caught in the middle of an argument between his friend and another teenager. Guns were drawn by the two having the argument, and Daquan was killed.

"I was in shock," Jovon said. "I didn't believe it. I didn't want to believe it."

When he talked to his mother, he was able to accept what had happened.

"That's when I knew it was real, and the emotion was just uncontrollable," he said. "That's the only brother I had."

Plenty of friends and family sent cards, letters and words of motivation to Jovon. They checked on his wellbeing and offered positive reinforcement.

Jovon, however, dealt with his brother's death the way he dealt with all the other pain in his life: by going all out on the football field.

"(The support) was good," Jovon said. "It was probably what I needed at the time, but football for me was still controlled violence. I got more fuel to the fire, more pain that I could unleash on people without even getting in trouble for it."

The 2009 season was Jovon's breakout year. Every time he stepped onto the field, he'd pray in the end zone, rub his bicep and point to the sky in tribute to his brother.

"From that point forward, I was locked in," he said. "I was in the zone. There was nothing that was gonna take me out of that zone."

He tallied 76 tackles and six interceptions to be named a 2009 CFL All-Star. Still, the Blue Bombers struggled. They went 7-11 in 2009 and 4-14 in 2010, while Jovon was named an East Division All-Star.

2011, though, proved to be a landmark year, both for Jovon and Winnipeg. Jovon recorded 55 tackles and eight interceptions — including two he returned for touchdowns — to be the first defensive back in CFL history to be named Most Outstanding Defensive Player.

"The way I was able to accomplish that was the guy that played next to me (Jonathan Hefney), he probably could have won it, too," Jovon said. "We kind of fed off each other's energy."

Jovon, Jonathan, Alex Suber and Clint Kent made up Winnipeg's stellar defensive backfield, and dubbed themselves "Swaggerville" for their style of play.

"We played with outstanding effort, and we had so many different playmakers that we wanted to impose our will on teams," Jovon said. "And we were gonna celebrate and have fun while doing it, so that's how (Swaggerville) came about."

The players would plank in the end zone, fly around the field like an airplane and say "Swag, swag, swag" to the TV cameras after making plays.

As much fun as they had, Clint said they excelled because they watched film. In particular, he credited Jovon as a student of the game.

"(He had) instinct and he was very smart, so when you have those two things you're gonna make a lot of plays," Clint said.

Swaggerville was instrumental in Winnipeg's jump from last place in the East Division in 2010 to capturing the division title for the first time in a decade in 2011.

Off the field, Jovon became a fan-favorite in Winnipeg for his personable nature.

"I wasn't one of those guys people (felt like) they weren't able to come up to and talk to," he said.

Back in Erie, Derick bragged about his superstar nephew.

"Not too many people make it out from where we came from," he said.

Jovon's CFL success drew attention from the NFL. In 2011, he worked out for the Cincinnati Bengals, Jacksonville Jaguars and Miami Dolphins. All three teams wanted him to sign a futures contract heading into training camp, but offered no signing bonus. Jovon opted to stay in Canada.

"My experience with the NFL politics prior to that showed me what it was all about, so I wasn't going to risk doing that for free," he said.

Jovon said his size factored into NFL teams not showing more interest in him.

"When you look at me, I'm not a prototypical-size corner," he said.

All the while, Jovon maintained a presence in Erie. He lived there for six months out of the year, training at Mercyhurst University and lifting weights with top Erie fitness trainer Steve Spearman.

By 2012, the word was out on Jovon. He said no one wanted to throw the ball anywhere near him.

"After winning (Most Outstanding Defensive Player) everybody kind of stayed away from me," he said. "I didn't get a chance to make the plays I was used to making. It was frustrating."

He made just one interception in 2012, but still tallied 55 tackles and was named an East Division All-Star. In 2013, he was moved to linebacker and made 62 tackles.

Though he didn't re-sign with Winnipeg heading into the 2014 season, he looks back on those years with pride.

"The amount of success (for) a lot of those years was just so special," he said.

Jovon joined the Ottawa RedBlacks in 2014. The team was a new franchise and went 2-16 that season while Jovon dealt with a torn bicep.

The next season, the group returned a year wiser and stronger and went 14-4 on their way to a runner-up finish in the Grey Cup.

"It was night and day," Jovon said of the difference between the two seasons.

That season, he had 56 tackles and five interceptions to be named an East Division All-Star for the final time of his career.

While in Ottawa, Jovon met a woman named Veronique Ayling who had survived Lyme Disease and ran V's Bakery. Inspired by her story, Jovon began raising awareness and funds to battle Lyme Disease.

"It was one of those moments where I started to realize that I didn't know everything," Jovon said. "It was a really humbling experience to have somebody teach you something that you didn't know anything about."

He estimated the fundraisers resulted in roughly $25,000 to fight Lyme Disease.

Jovon said that, following the 2015 season, Ottawa's general manager told him he didn't value cornerbacks enough to be able to continue paying him the same amount of money.

Faced with the prospect of a drastic pay cut, Jovon opted to sign with the Montreal Alouettes in 2016. He played halfback, which is the CFL's equivalent of the nickel spot, and recorded 59 tackles, six sacks and three interceptions. However, he was released after training camp in 2017.

That same day, Saskatchewan's general manager called and offered Jovon the same contract he had had in Montreal. He started in the Roughriders' defensive backfield throughout 2017 and through 10 weeks in 2018.

After that, they opted to go with someone younger, and Jovon was relegated to a reserve role.

"I knew at some point it was gonna come to an end," he said. "It was just a matter of time. Can't play forever."

He hung up his cleats after the 2018 season. In March 2020, Jovon signed a one-day contract to retire as a Winnipeg Blue Bomber.

"My memorable moments were all in Winnipeg, so that's why I chose Winnipeg," he said.

Jovon began his coaching career in 2019 as the defensive backs coach at Defiance College in Ohio. He quickly rose to be the defensive coordinator.

He said he draws inspiration from his former coaches — legendary Steelers defensive coordinator Dick LeBeau and longtime Iowa coach Kirk Ferentz — when coaching his players.

"To see them every day, and their personalities, their commitment to the game kind of shaped mine," Jovon said. "I was very committed to my players and their success on the field and off, and (considering) part of my journey to get where I am now, I can teach them from experience."

When Derick thinks of Jovon's success, two things stick out to him: drive and commitment.

"He wanted to do something (and) he did it," Derick said.

Jovon still visits Erie, where he runs a youth football camp. He's still underestimated because of his size, but he's able to shrug it off.

"Even to this day I'm always gonna have to face the reality that I'm 5-9, and you know people still doubt that I can do different things even though I've proven it over the years," he said. "It's just who I've become. I'm used to it. It doesn't even bother me now."

The kid from the Harbor Homes overcame a mountain of adversity to become a superstar. Jovon, now in his late thirties, carries valuable lessons from his climb as he goes about his day-to-day life.

"I found out that no matter how much adversity and struggle you might go through, that doesn't stop you from being successful, stop you from accomplishing your goals and dreams," he said. "It just puts a little roadblock, and you'll see how you respond to it."

Photo by Snodgrass Photo

The 2006 General McLane football team poses for a victory photo following its 28-23 win over Pottsville High School to become the PIAA Class AAA state champion. Several members of McLane's football team helped comprise the 2006-07 Lancers boys basketball team, which also captured a state title. The wins cemented General McLane as the first school in Pennsylvania history to win state championships in football and boys basketball in the same academic year.

Back to Back

By Steve Orbanek

Steve Orbanek is a McKean native. He graduated from General McLane High School in 2006, just one year before the school's historic dual state-title run. His book, General McLane Athletics: Stories From the First 50 Years, *was published in 2010 by Reedy Press. He received a bachelor's degree in journalism from Duquesne University in 2010 and a master's degree in communication studies from Edinboro University in 2012. He is currently the Associate Director of Communications at Temple University's Fox School of Business in Philadelphia, where he resides with his wife, Marissa, his daughter, Jemma, and their two hound dogs.*

Author's note: Interviews for this story came from the reporting done while writing General McLane Athletics: Stories From the First 50 Years.

It's March 21, 2006, at the Louis J. Tullio Arena. Members of the General McLane boys basketball team walk off the court as the final seconds of the game just ticked away.
Final score: Franklin 58, General McLane 52.
This was the third time the Lancers had met the Knights that season, and on two other occasions General McLane was victorious. First, the Lancers beat Franklin, 64-51 during the regular season. They then defeated the Knights, 54-48 in the District 10 Championship.
Yet here, under the bright lights of the PIAA Class AAA West Final, the Lancers fell short.
The scene was eerily familiar to one just a few months earlier. General McLane's football team fell 26-21 to Franklin on December 1, 2005, in the PIAA Class AAA West Final.
Both the boys basketball and football teams comprised the same core group of guys, and they both suffered the same fate.
So close. But still so far away.
"The western finals is literally the hardest game to win in high school sports," said Bob Stauffer, a 2007 General McLane graduate who

played guard and defensive back for those teams. "When you get to the state championship, it's easy because you're there. You know you're at least going to get a trophy. In the western finals, if you don't win, you don't get remembered."

The next year, the General McLane football and boys basketball teams made it back to the PIAA Class AAA West Final in both sports. Only this time, they won. They advanced to the PIAA Class AAA State Championship game in both sports, and brought home state titles both times.

The historical significance of what those teams accomplished cannot be understated. They made General McLane the first-ever school in Pennsylvania to win a state championship in both football and boys basketball in the same academic year. What makes this feat even more impressive is how close they were to accomplishing it twice.

The cliché is that players don't win championships, teams do. It's never been more apropos than it is in the case of these two General McLane teams.

"Just because we won two state championships doesn't mean we're the best," said Drew Astorino, who played guard and quarterback on the two teams. "But do I think we were the most accomplished? Yes. Does that mean we had the best players? No. But do I think we had the best chemistry? Yes."

In Lancer Country, the legend of Drew Astorino is very real. In the 2006 PIAA Class AAA State Championship game against Pottsville, he ran for a record-tying 172 yards while operating out of the Lancers' patented triple-option offense, all while leading McLane to a 28-23 victory.

Then, against Greencastle-Antrim in the 2007 Class AAA boys basketball state title game, Astorino hit a baseline two-point jumper with just 2.3 seconds left to lead the Lancers to a narrow, 57-55 victory.

Anybody who ever saw him play knew just how special Astorino was. His field vision was extraordinary, as he could see lanes develop before they ever did. That skill made him lethal against competitors, and it was not uncommon to see him take a punt or kick return back to the house.

Yet, despite his athletic prowess, scouts thought he was undersized. He was the only player on either championship team to go Division I, and his offer from Penn State did not come until after he earned PIAA Class AAA Player of the Year honors after leading the football team to a state championship.

Like his teammates, he was still an underdog. But along with them, he continued to prove all of the naysayers wrong, just as he did at Penn State. As a Nittany Lion, he was a three-year starter at safety and left the school ranked No. 10 all-time in tackles.

Following the double heartbreak of 2005-06, General McLane was optimistic about its chances in both sports in 2006-07. In addition to Astorino, key contributors for both teams including Stauffer, Dan and Ryan Skelton, Shawn Walker and Kelley Ponsoll would be returning. The cores of these teams were still very much intact.

Beyond that, each team fielded a veteran coach. In football, coach Jim Wells was known for perfecting the triple option, and no team operated it as methodically as this one did. In basketball, Andy Schulz had already been through some wars. The previous season was actually his second time taking a team to the West Final. The Lancers fell short the first time as well.

Based on the teams' seasons during the 2005-06 academic year, most would assume that the Lancers just steamrolled through their competition to win state titles. But it's a bit more complicated than that.

As Astorino mentioned, these teams had outstanding chemistry. They had been through so many ups and downs together. They were, essentially, a family.

But what's consistent with all families? They go through struggles.

In October of 2006, General McLane faced the Strong Vincent High School Colonels in a highly anticipated contest between two District 10 Class AAA powerhouses. The game actually happened to fall on Friday the 13th.

The superstitious among us couldn't be blamed for seeing that as a bad omen.

Essentially, everything that could go wrong for the Lancers did. What made it even more challenging was the fact that McLane had beaten Strong Vincent twice in the previous season.

It only got worse from there. In the next game, General McLane faced Cathedral Prep. The year before, they had defeated Prep, 35-28, but in this contest, they found themselves down 21-0 at halftime.

"I remember we were like, 'What are we going to do? This isn't fun anymore,'" said Dan Skelton, who played running back and safety on the team.

"Once we got those two losses, it made us step back and say, 'Hey, there's good teams out there. We're not better than everybody,'" added Ryan Skelton, who played at fullback and linebacker.

According to Stauffer, the impetus for the Lancers' turnaround came during halftime of that Cathedral Prep game. Faced with a 21-0 deficit,

McLane had two choices.

"We were down 21-0, but we all kept our heads up," Stauffer said. "We said, 'Hey, we can either go out there and let them beat our butts 42-0, or we can come out here and fight back.'"

The Lancers lost 21-7, but outscored the Ramblers 7-0 in the second half.

"I think that was a big turning point in our season," Stauffer said.

The loss to Prep was the Lancers' last of the season. From then on they went undefeated, avenging a loss against the Colonels in the District 10 Championship with a 19-7 win.

The key moment of the season, aside from the actual PIAA Class AAA Championship, was the West Final in which General McLane faced Thomas Jefferson High School. Perhaps no one outside of the McKean and Edinboro communities gave the Lancers a fighting chance in that game.

That was a mistake.

Astorino's typical greatness was on display throughout, as he carved up the Thomas Jefferson defense with 174 rushing yards and three touchdowns en route to a 28-7 victory. Overall, the Lancers out-rushed TJ, 334 to 96. If not for his encore that would come one week later, this would have been the finest performance of Astorino's high school career.

Against the Pottsville Crimson Tide on December 15, 2006, Astorino was once again spectacular. As previously noted, he ran for a record-tying 172 yards. The game was a back-and-forth battle, but the Lancers answered back on every occasion.

McLane led 14-6 at halftime, but Pottsville responded by tying the game at 14 in the second half. Then, on the next possession, Astorino once again provided an answer, scampering 71 yards to give the Lancers a 20-14 advantage. The Crimson Tide took the lead on the next drive as their running back, Tom McFarland, scored from 24 yards out to give his team a 21-20 lead.

Then, in what was perhaps the defining stretch of the game, Astorino orchestrated a nine-play, 87-yard drive that ate up nearly five minutes of the clock. The drive included Astorino runs of 45 and 20 yards, the latter of which found him in the end zone. A 2-point conversion put the Lancers up 28-21.

On the next drive, McLane's defense bent, but did not break. Pottsville fell inches short on a 4th-and-3 attempt at McLane's 15-yard line.

Then, Astorino stalled on repeated plays, even taking an intentional safety on 4th and 7, which allowed the team to burn an additional 11 seconds off the clock. With 16 seconds to go, McLane recovered its own squib kick, and the rest is history.

With the 28-23 victory, the Lancers became the first public school in Erie County to win a football state title since Strong Vincent had won it in 1991.

"I think a part of me will always be there," Wells said when recalling the moment. "I think it's something for all of the players, coaches, managers and for all of the townspeople involved. It's something you can never take away from this community."

With phase one complete, there was only one thing left for this spectacular group of high school athletes to do: win another state title. But things were already complicated. It was almost Christmas by the time football season ended, and basketball season was well underway. And for athletes, there's a big difference between "football shape" and "basketball shape."

The basketball team had gotten off to a rough start, losing four of its first six games while Stauffer, Ponsoll, Astorino, Walker and the Skelton brothers were still playing football. Even when they returned, things were far from perfect.

On February 9, the Lancers headed to Warren. They barely defeated the Dragons, 58-56 in a Region 5 matchup. The game was very important because if the Lancers had lost, they would have lost the region and seeding for the playoffs would have been different. Even with the win, the team's uninspired play had Schulz very concerned.

"The next day, I called Drew (Astorino), and I was like, 'What the hell's going on here? I don't get it, I don't get it,'" Schulz recalled. "I told him, 'I don't know, I don't get it, we're not gonna do this, we're not gonna get this done.' And Drew was mad, you know, at the way he played. He said, 'OK, I want to have a meeting with the players, just me, the captains and the players.' So I said, 'Go ahead.'"

Call it therapeutic. Call it cathartic. The fact is that the meeting lasted two hours, and it might have saved the Lancers' season.

Schulz always remembers his players being jovial during meetings. When he walked in at the tail end of this one, it was pure silence.

"We said everything," said Ponsoll, who played forward on the team. "Whatever was on someone's mind, they said it. Who cares, just say it and get it off your chest."

"Most of the stuff wasn't very nice," Stauffer added. "But the season is not all smooth sailing; people don't understand that. When you go through a season, there are going to be fights between players. We're all buddies, but sometimes you just have to let the other person know how you're feeling."

The sheer amount of time that players spent together could also be tiresome.

"You have to remember that year-round, every single one of us had been around each other for every single day for the last three years," said Walker, who played center and led the team in scoring. "We all do football. We all do basketball. We have the same practices. We see each other every day."

As was the case with the halftime discussion for the football team, following this players-only meeting, a new General McLane basketball team emerged.

"From that point on, we were on a different level," Schulz said.

The Lancers did not lose for the remainder of the season. In fact, they did not even really get all that close to losing until the second half of the PIAA Class AAA State Championship game against Greencastle-Antrim.

There, they faced a 35-29 deficit. The Lancers fought back, chipping away in the second half despite an incredible performance by Greencastle-Antrim's star, Demeatric Scott.

With 15.1 seconds left in the game, the score was tied at 55. There has been some debate as to whether the final play call was run in the wrong direction, but there's the one thing that remains clear. The call was to get the ball into Astorino's hands.

"I see Drew out of the corner of my eye," Stauffer said. "I just throw it to him, and the rest is history."

With high school basketball's brightest lights shining on him, Astorino hit a jumper to once again lift the Lancers to a state championship. Only one year earlier, General McLane had fallen just short of competing on the state's biggest stage. But this year, they would not be denied, becoming the first Pennsylvania high school to win state titles in football and boys basketball in the same academic year.

While Astorino was excelling at Penn State the following year, the Skelton brothers, Walker, Brian Roberts (a contributor on the championship football team) and Ponsoll played football at Division II Edinboro University. Stauffer went on to play basketball at Edinboro. Blidi Wreh-Wilson, a key contributor as a junior on the championship basketball team, was not a member of that year's football team. However, he went on to play Division I football at the University of Connecticut after he joined the McLane football team and made a strong impression in his senior year. He was later selected in the third round of the 2013 NFL Draft by the Tennessee Titans, and currently plays for the Atlanta Falcons.

But for all their athletic success, this was ultimately a rather ordinary group of high school athletes. Again, only one member from the football team played at the Division I level. Only one member of the basketball team played collegiate basketball at any level.

So, how'd they do it? Why was this team so poised to make history?

"I just always knew we had special kids," Schulz said. "It's not like you could look at them and say, 'Man, this team is better than everybody else. They're just superior.' That wasn't the case in football or basketball.

"But they were overachieving kids who just believed in what they were doing. They believed they could do it."

Photo by Snodgrass Photo

Photo provided by Courtney Oberlander

Allania Banta (left) makes a pass with Julie Pace looking on during a Fort LeBoeuf volleyball match in 2012. The Bison won the PIAA Class AA State Championship that season to become the first school in Erie County to capture a volleyball state title.

Never Let You Down

By Aaron McKrell

LeAnn Johnson was utterly befuddled.

All fall, the 2012 Fort LeBoeuf volleyball team had aced, spiked and dumped its way past the competition. The Bison never so much as went five games in a match on their way to a District 10 championship and state playoff berth.

But now, in a gym at Slippery Rock University, they looked lost in the Pennsylvania Interscholastic Athletic Association Class AA western final against Mars High School. LeAnn, LeBoeuf's head coach, wanted to know one thing: What happened?

"We couldn't walk and chew gum," LeAnn said, years later. "It was just the perfect storm of a hot mess."

With her team down 2-1 and on the brink of elimination, LeAnn took her players to a secluded area away from the view of the crowd.

"(I) couldn't believe it," LeAnn said. "All the hard work in the trash right now because they are tripping over their own two feet?"

But LeAnn, who was not averse to yelling to make a point, took her team aback with quiet intensity.

Eyes shining with tears, the typically Teflon coach implored them to follow through.

"Have some heart," she said.

In that moment, they realized just how much LeAnn cared for them. She left them to talk amongst themselves, and they found new life in their coach's fervor.

"We need to come together after every single point and scream as loud as we can," senior Maria Peluso, the fiery outside hitter, told her teammates. "We need to put the other team down. We need to let them know that we're not gonna just roll over."

That's exactly what they did. The Bison reinvigorated their loyal fans as they took Game 4 before winning 15-13 in Game 5 to clinch the match and a trip to the state championship.

After the game, their parents, friends and classmates wanted to know: What did LeAnn tell them that sparked the turnaround?

Even if the players had told them, they could have never truly grasped the emotional weight of that moment. LeAnn's words could only mean so much unless one had spent late nights at team sleepovers and early mornings running suicide drills for her, for each other and for a bond that was strengthened over years of trials, tragedy and ultimate triumph.

"We were there the entire time with (each other)," said Courtney Oberlander, who was a junior and defensive specialist. "We didn't let anybody fall down."

The Bison held each other up all the way to York, Pa., where they completed a perfect, 21-0 season and became the first volleyball team in Erie County history to win a state championship. Not too long before that, opposing teams couldn't even say their name correctly.

Fort LeBoof?

Outside of District 10, most teams didn't have any idea where Fort LeBoeuf High School was, and mistakenly called it "Fort LeBoof."

"They could never pronounce our name," LeAnn said. "It was great."

To be fair, the Fort LeBoeuf volleyball program hadn't had a long history of success. Before LeAnn, the team was consistently competitive within Erie County, but had never won a District 10 title, let alone earned a berth to the state playoffs.

"When I came into the program it was girls who were athletic and enjoyed the game, but we just needed to take it to the next level," LeAnn said.

LeAnn, who was practically raised in the gym by two coaching parents — Windber High School head coach Sheila Byer and her husband/assistant Don — was the ideal person to elevate LeBoeuf's game.

Taking cues from her parents both genetic and learned, LeAnn developed an extraordinarily intense style of play at Windber, which she fine-tuned in the high-stakes collegiate atmosphere of Gannon University.

While playing as a Golden Knight, LeAnn was also studying to become a teacher and completed student teaching in her senior year. Her student-teaching supervisor knew Fort LeBoeuf School District's superintendent, and told LeAnn that LeBoeuf had a need for both a teacher and a high school volleyball coach.

"The stars aligned, and it worked out great," LeAnn said.

She took the varsity helm in 2006 and brought the diehard culture of collegiate volleyball with her to Waterford. She quickly worked on constructing a program from the bottom up, running camps for fourth and fifth graders. She soon after became LeBoeuf's eighth grade volleyball coach.

Some of those grade-school-aged kids at LeAnn's camps would help comprise the 2012 state title team. One of them was Abby Rose, who in sixth grade went with her father to watch the varsity team in a playoff match. A young Abby was in awe of LeAnn.

"She took no B.S.," Abby said. "She commanded a lot of respect." However, most of the players didn't truly get to know LeAnn until middle school, when she was their seventh grade social studies teacher. Maria said LeAnn's class required more work and preparation than most of her other middle school classes.

"(She was) very strict," Maria said of LeAnn. "And then when I tried out for volleyball, I felt the exact same way."

Maria, along with defensive specialist/libero Allania Banta and defensive specialist Julie Pace, was part of the 2008 eighth grade team that went undefeated. The seventh grade squad, which included Courtney, Abby and middle hitter Jolene Young, also finished its season with a perfect record. The seventh graders' prowess was not lost on LeAnn, and was something she was quick to remind her eighth graders of if their play was lackluster.

"I'm gonna have some of the seventh graders come play if you guys don't play better," LeAnn would tell them.

Both groups had large numbers and good chemistry, and LeAnn saw potential in them. Just how great they would end up being, though, she had no idea.

A World of Hurt, A Culture of Love

By 2010, the eighth graders had become sophomores, the seventh graders had become freshmen and LeAnn's tenacity was becoming the stuff of legend.

She expected hard work, efficiency and focus from her players at all times. The ball was not to hit the floor, and if it did, they had better be laid out along with it.

"If you were in practice or a game, you had to be there or it would be a world of hurt," Abby said.

LeBoeuf's secret sauce, as Abby said, was discipline. LeAnn's expectations for her players were never any lower away from the gym than they were in it. Abby and Jolene found that out the hard way during a summer volleyball camp in Juniata County, when the pair thought it would be a good idea to order pizza to their hotel.

LeAnn was strongly averse to their stuffed-crust aspirations. She also made good and sure they wouldn't have anything to drink to go along with their pizza. The accompanying pop they had bought was promptly and unceremoniously dumped out before their eyes.

"She was one of the most intense coaches that we had ever had," Courtney said.

Rather than shy away from LeAnn's intensity, her players strived to match it. It wasn't long before they realized how well they gelled with her style, and LeBoeuf's coaching staff and roster fed off each other's drive and determination.

"That's a lot of the reasons why it worked," LeAnn said.

LeAnn's assistants — her husband and former Medaille College star Sean Johnson, former Mercyhurst College (now Mercyhurst University) standout Rob Cierniakoski, and former General McLane High School star Tara Kaczmarek — were ideal complements to LeAnn's style. LeAnn and Sean were a fantastic pair, even if their first meeting was more *Meet the Parents* than *(500) Days of Summer* (Sean accidentally spiked LeAnn in the face during a volleyball game). Sean, standing at 6-foot-5, and Rob, who is 6-3, held nothing back as they practiced against their players. They thickened Maria's skin with an endless stream of trash talk, while targeting Courtney in the back row.

Courtney's response?

Bring it on.

"I loved it," she said.

Even the tallest girls on the squad couldn't stand shoulder to shoulder with Sean or Rob, and every point was a challenge as the two former college players skyed for kills and blocks.

"They would always say, 'If you can play well against us, you can play well against any team,'" Abby recalled.

As tough as in-practice scrimmages could be, they were nothing compared to the rigorous conditioning LeAnn put her players through.

"If we get to Thursday and it's Game 5 and we lose because you're tired, that's my fault," LeAnn said.

The Bison ran up and down the steps of the school's football stadium, around the town of Waterford and up steep, daunting hills. Setting the pace was Julie, who was always one of the first runners to reach the top of the hill. Rather than catch her breath, she'd run back down and run up again, keeping in step with the others to encourage them.

Once, Julie lost her lunch at a street corner, straightened up, and kept running.

"We knew what we had to do, and it's like, no matter what obstacle we had, we just had to keep going," Julie said.

Their tireless conditioning gave them not only an edge in tight matches, but a reputation as some of the best-conditioned athletes at LeBoeuf.

Once, Julie was at Fort LeBoeuf Middle School and there were football players messing around in the weight room. One of the football coaches saw her and decided to make a point to his players.

"'Hey, Pace, come here,'" Julie recalled him saying.

She walked over to them.

"'Drop and give me five pushups,'" she recalled him telling her.

Without hesitation, Julie hit the floor and did pushups with ease. When she was done, she got up and left without a word.

The coach told her later that she could have heard a pin drop in that weight room after she was gone.

"We were the best-conditioned team," Allania said. "One hundred percent."

When the Bison weren't toning their muscles, they were strengthening their minds. They studied film extensively to the point where they would know where a given opponent's middle hitter would place 98 percent of their balls.

"We knew every step people were gonna take," Julie said.

As underclassmen, the players learned not only from each other and their coaches, but also from the older players who mentored them. Abby, who earned valuable playing time at setter as a freshman at tournaments, took her cues from senior setter Taylor Welch.

"She was very good, and I was very acutely aware of the big shoes that I was going to have to fill," Abby said.

Others, such as the never-say-die Jordan Rogers, Cassie Pietkiewicz and Jamie VanDamia, set the standard for poise and work ethic.

But it was Lindsay Bean, the loud, proud, basketball-shorts-wearing middle hitter who set the most memorable example for her younger teammates to follow.

Balancing boisterous humor with uncommon grit, Bean, who graduated in 2012, once broke her hand at a tournament and proceeded to finish the season with her hand taped up, witty jokes aplenty and no complaints.

"(She was) so intense, but so funny," Courtney said.

It wasn't long before the underclassmen took the lessons learned from their older counterparts to the court themselves. Jolene, Maria and Courtney earned starting spots as freshmen, while Abby, Allania and Julie started as sophomores.

"That's when you know that you've got some special athletes, is when they're playing as freshmen and sophomores on your varsity team," LeAnn said. "You know that you're doing something right."

As they grew together, they grew closer with each other. They'd make the trek to High Street to get cupcakes and cookies at Sweet Temptation in Waterford before matches. They did homework with each other in LeAnn's classroom. And they had pool parties and team sleepovers at Maria's house.

All this time spent together formed a sisterhood that transcended their sport.

"We all knew we had each other's back," Jolene said.

In turn, that bond transferred onto the court, where their chemistry strengthened their performance. They knew instinctively how each other moved, what their tendencies were and how they would react to any given scenario in a match.

"Being (friends) for so long, we had a lot of trust with each other," Courtney said.

And together, they developed a relationship with LeAnn that was deeper than player-coach. "Coach was like the missing puzzle piece," Julie said. "She kind of held us all together. She wasn't just our coach, she was our mom."

LeAnn was always there for them, steering — or at least, trying to steer — them away from troublesome boys, and keeping tabs on whether or not they were in class on time.

"She just knew everything, whether you thought she did or not," Julie said. "No matter what we did, she was always there for us."

And they for her. LeAnn appreciated how she could be tough on them without having to sprinkle sugar on her criticism.

"They could handle honesty when they needed it," she said.

LeAnn knew that, for her players to give her their best, they had to know she cared about them. But her compassionate gestures were more genuine than strategic. She had known them for several years by this point, so when she sent weekend texts reminding them to ice their ankles or to thank them for allowing her to do what she loves and coach, her words were straight from the heart.

"They were my children, and it was really fun," LeAnn said.

Before long, other teams and coaches began to notice the remarkable chemistry the Bison shared. They played on the 15-and-under Epic Volleyball Club team, and LeAnn sat and watched one of their matches. Afterwards, opposing coaches approached her with nothing but praise.

"'Man, that team is talented,'" she recalled them saying.

The improvement was easy to overlook if you were in the thick of things with them, sprinting, sweating and striving every day at practice. But the Fort LeBoeuf volleyball team was becoming something much greater than the sum of its parts. And in 2010, they had only just begun.

YES!

Each year, the players wore shirts with slogans on them. One year, it was "Get It, Girl," another it was "Always Go for the Jugular" (a sure-fire Seanism), and once it was simply, "Yes." The Bison would proudly and obnoxiously yell "Yes!" after a big kill or clutch ace.

Their enthusiasm was in step with their progress. The 2010 squad was the District 10 runner-up to Meadville, and became the first-ever LeBoeuf volleyball team to earn a trip to the state playoffs.

With several freshmen and sophomores clocking minutes and not one player on the team with state playoff experience, the Bison were caught by the moment.

"We were all just kind of like a deer in the headlights," Maria said.

They went 0-3 in pool play, but their first glimpse of the big stage would be useful down the line.

"That was great experience for them, and gave them a taste of what was coming," LeAnn said.

Though the 2011 season would prove to be a big step forward for the Bison, it didn't come without heartache. They were on their way to a preseason match when they learned that one of their teammates, Savana Stephens, had died following a car accident at age 16.

The players were in shock that someone so young whom they knew so well had died.

"That was definitely a challenge for all of us," Allania said.

The team pulled together, though, with the help of Savana's other friends, family and the tight-knit community of Waterford.

Once again, they were the unknowns. The Bison relished their underdog status.

"I liked being the team that nobody had a clue (about)," LeAnn said.

The squad claimed its school's first-ever District 10 volleyball championship with a win over General McLane, and earned another trip to the state tournament.

But the Bison, who excelled in part because of their extensive preparation for each opponent, did not favor the round-robin format of the playoffs. The schedule found all teams playing match after match, with little time between competition. Even the Bison, who were in excellent shape, were affected by the claustrophobic, exhausting atmosphere.

LeAnn questioned how any team could be at its best in such a frenzied format.

"It was just foolish," she said.

The Bison went 1-2 in pool play before being edged out by Freeport, 25-23, in a late-night tiebreaker game that ended their season.

No matter. They finished eighth in the state in Class AA and were returning most of their core of starters. After the loss to Freeport, LeAnn's focus on the next season could not have been any tighter: *Can we start tomorrow?*

Goodie Bag

The players' expectations for the 2012 season ranged from unassuming optimism to blazing confidence. But all of them knew what they had in terms of talent, skill, drive and chemistry.

And they weren't going to let an opportunity go to waste.

Abby took private setting lessons from then Fairview head coach Ashley Cottengim, who had been a middle school and JV coach for LeBoeuf (she is currently a Bison assistant again). The Bison were a fixture at summer camps to hone their skills against prospective opponents.

Before the season started, another piece of the puzzle fell into place. The PIAA announced the state tournament format was changed from pool play to single-elimination and that matches would be played on separate days. This was nothing but good news for the strategy-obsessed Bison.

"That was a big help," LeAnn said of the change in format.

No one was more encouraged by the structural change than Maria, who was certain they were going to go all the way. She stood in the locker room on the first day of preseason and struck fear into the hearts of a few frightened freshmen.

"I don't care," she told them. "I know you guys are young and you're freshmen, but we're winning state this year. So you better play well."

But neither their confidence nor a top-10 state ranking could take their focus off the moment.

LeAnn simply would not allow it.

"We gotta get through Tuesday and then we'll worry about Thursday," she said of her mindset at the time.

She wanted her players to enjoy each moment, not just in matches but in practice. The team had advanced to the point where there was more gameplay in practice, and LeAnn even incorporated team-building exercises like a scavenger hunt and Zumba.

And yet, they were as focused as ever. Practices held a game-like intensity, and anyone from outside the gym could tell the Fort LeBoeuf volleyball team was practicing from their constant stream of chatter and cheering. Rappers such as Kanye West soundtracked their drills, with Kip Moore's "Somethin' Bout a Truck" mixed in for their country-loving, senior opposite hitter, Amanda Krolzcyk.

Practices featured fierce-but-friendly competition, and come match time, their blend of personalities bolstered a sense of unity.

Allania was the team's vocal leader on the court, yelling not at them, but to them to direct, motivate and encourage their play.

"She kind of held our team together," Jolene said.

Maria and Jolene were just as aggressive. Whether there were five people in the stands or 5,000, Maria played with a kick-butt ferocity and a singular focus on winning.

"The moment could not get bigger than her," LeAnn said.

Just as the Bison complemented height in the front row (Maria stands at 5-8 and Jolene is 5-9) with speed in the back, they had calmer players to balance out their fearsome hitters.

Julie doubled as the team's on-court mom and the Maria Whisperer, the only one who could talk Maria off a ledge in intense moments and keep her from running through a wall with her fist cocked like Fort LeBoeuf's version of the Kool-Aid Man.

Abby also was communicative and impassioned, and relied on the even-keeled Courtney to bring her back to earth when she needed it. That didn't mean the back row was docile. Courtney had a knack for clutch plays and improbable digs that left her teammates asking, "How did she get that?"

"Everybody says you need a leader on your team," LeAnn said. "No, you don't need one. You need four or five different people in different ways."

LeBoeuf also had role players who sprinkled in their own contributions to complete the whole package. One such player was junior Caitlin Ebert, another calming presence who displayed a steely work ethic. Nearly cut from the middle school team as a tall, lanky seventh grader, Caitlin willed her way to a spot on the roster and ended up with a handful of kills in LeBoeuf's state title match.

"I've never seen anybody work as hard as she did," LeAnn said.

Amanda was quietly consistent, not prone to wowing the crowd with a forceful kill but offering steadfast reliability.

Junior Alex Carroll was a steady defensive presence for the Bison, while quiet sophomore Larissa Cass soaked up game from Maria and stepped to the net to provide service with a smile.

Julie likened their roster to a "goodie bag," and said LeAnn knew when to reach into the metaphorical bag to grab the right "goodie" at the right time. A kill here, an ace there, and loud cheers reverberating around the gym after each point won.

"It was just a good, good mix," Jolene said.

Once out of necessity, Julie, standing all of 5-2, played middle hitter. The result? They won the match.

"I need to go... This is my team."

After toiling in anonymity for years, the Bison began to make waves across the state in 2012. They were quite the sight; decked out in matching headbands and running onto the court to Kanye's "All of the Lights" with a come-get-it swagger, assured by the knowledge that, should one of them slip, the others would be right there to catch them. Their uncontainable energy was matched by their massive, raucous student fan section, dubbed the "Blue Crew." The Blue Crew showed up to games in large numbers, prompting complaints from other schools but also motivating General McLane and Corry High School to attempt to match their crowd.

"It just made it way more fun," Abby said of the Blue Crew.

The Bison won every match in either three or four games to enter the District 10 tournament undefeated. They rolled through the district before beating Meadville to capture their second consecutive D-10 title, but the victory over the Bulldogs was a mere appetizer for the state playoffs.

The Bison were correct in their hunch that the change in playoff format would benefit them.

They pored over game film and analyzed their opponents down to their shoelaces.

Their focus never went past what was right in front of them. Unlike other teams, the coaching staff didn't book hotel reservations for the state championship match.

LeBoeuf's focus came to fruition. The Bison swept Ambridge High School in the first round before upsetting No. 1-ranked Hopewell High School in three games in a state quarterfinal match.

The players were over the moon. They had a postgame celebration at Quaker Steak and Lube, where they chowed down on chicken wings and onion rings while LeAnn opted for a spinach salad that ironically made her sick.

The next morning, Courtney woke up still on the victory high from the night before. She milled around in a volleyball T-shirt on what seemed to be a typical Sunday morning.

Then the phone rang, and Courtney's mother answered it. It was a friend of theirs, offering condolences over Courtney's grandfather. Confusion turned to stunned grief as they learned that her grandfather had been in a bad car accident and did not survive. All they could do was stand around the house, unsure of what to do next amidst a revolving door of visitors. Courtney did have one idea of what her next step should be. That night, the Bison were scheduled for a film session on Mars High School, their opponent in a state semifinal. LeAnn told her she didn't have to come, but Courtney was resolute.

"I need to go," she told her mom. "This is my team."

As they had been for years, Courtney's teammates were there for their quiet, loyal, determined friend.

"(She was) just the sweetest little girl, and you felt so terrible," Maria said.

LeAnn had the unenviable task of balancing compassion for Courtney and her family with consideration for everything the team had worked for.

Courtney made it easy for her. Despite LeAnn telling her she didn't have to play, the thought of sitting out the semifinal never crossed Courtney's mind.

"Yes, this is tragic, this is what happened, but this is still what we're doing next," Courtney said of her mindset at the time. "And I knew that (my grandfather) wouldn't want me to stop and not play."

Courtney's teammates gave her hugs and offered to help in any way she needed. On Monday, the day before the semifinal, Courtney sat in the locker room and cried. Caitlin was there next to her with kind words and a comforting hug.

"It was the best support I could have had," Courtney said.

Yet, there was still a match to be played. Courtney's family had always been big on sports, and scheduled the funeral arrangements around the match.

The match was a positive outlet for not only Courtney but her entire family. No matter what she was feeling outside of the gym, she could block it out when she stepped onto the court.

"Volleyball was just my escape from life," she said.

The comeback victory over Mars was just what her family needed. After the game was over, as fans stormed the court in celebration,

Courtney's mother approached LeAnn and thanked her for continuing the playoff run.

The little borough of Waterford was lit up like a Christmas tree with excitement. Fitting, since they were well into November and the holidays were just around the corner.

The state championship match was set for Saturday, November 17 at Central York High School in York.

They departed for York on Friday and received a hero's sendoff from the school and town. Their family, friends, classmates and neighbors lined the hallways of Fort LeBoeuf High School, holding up huge poster boards with the players' names and faces on them. Excited children sat atop their parents' shoulders to get a glimpse of the players, as if it were wartime and they were bidding soldiers farewell before battle. The stakes could not have been higher.

"'Well, this is your opportunity,'" Maria recalled a teacher telling her. "'You better not come back without a gold medal.'"

OK, Maria thought. *No pressure*.

The Realization

Whatever pressure the Bison may have felt, it wasn't present on the bus they took to York. The girls spent the ride down blasting music and projecting an excited confidence for the weekend ahead.

Rob couldn't make the trip with them, as his brother was getting married that weekend. But Sean was there, practicing with them in a Nicki Minaj T-shirt.

There was, somehow, no practice time allotted for out-of-town teams. So the Bison booked a YMCA in nearby Harrisburg. It turned out to be the gym of doom. It was, as LeAnn put it, a "horrifying" setup with brick walls lining the floor just a few feet from the court.

Allania sprained her ankle during practice, but was good to go the next day.

As dungeonesque as the gym had been, that's how lavish the beautiful hotel and resort they had booked was. They ate a delicious breakfast the morning of the game before working out their nerves in a pregame practice at York College.

LeBoeuf's opponent was Delone Catholic High School of McSherrytown, which was about a 20-minute drive from York.

The Squires boasted a lineup that included future University of Pittsburgh at Johnstown standouts Cambria Wierman, an outside hitter, and Allison Mondorff, a setter.

It was Delone Catholic's first trip to the state final as well, and the Bison didn't know much about their opponent. They were underwhelmed by what they saw from the Squires on film, and planned to have Abby dump the ball over the net to exploit an opening in the Squires' scheme.

As the Squires were so close to Central York High School, they were able to sleep in their own beds the night before the match. However, proximity didn't translate into strength in numbers, and Delone Catholic's crowd was minuscule compared to the bus loads of family, friends, neighbors, classmates, teachers and Blue Crew who showed up to hype up the Bison. Maria's brother dressed as her, wearing a red wig and an old jersey of hers to her utter mortification.

Meanwhile, the superstitious Maria was the lone Bison donning one of the headbands that her teammates had long since stopped wearing. Courtney's grandmother, still processing her husband's passing, was not at the match but tuned in to watch on video.

Once the match began, the nerves the Bison had shaken off at York College returned. They also came to find out that what they saw on film of Delone Catholic was a poor representation of the team's abilities.

"The film did not do them justice," LeAnn said.

Instead of imposing their will on the opposition like they had done so many times throughout the season, the Bison found themselves scrapping to keep the ball alive in long rallies. LeAnn was just as nervous as her players, and wondered for a moment if she had prepared them well enough. She realized they would have to outlast the Squires and make fewer errors, because there weren't going to be any easy points in this match.

Maria tried every which way to get a kill, but the Squires blocked or dug out everything she sent their way.

"It took me a while to get my wheels rolling, she said. "They just had an amazing defense."

Meanwhile, LeAnn offered encouragement to her servers.

"You've served a million balls in your life," she told them more than once. "Just get back there and do what you know how to do."

She also encouraged them to do what they did best: be chatterboxes to talk out their nerves. They stayed in the fight. Julie covered a block. Alex got the next one. LeAnn knew they were all in.

All right, she thought. *We're ready to go.*

The points didn't come easy, but they came, and the Bison began to relax.

"We scored a couple points and we said, 'This team is human just like us,'" Abby recalled.

The points kept coming, and LeBoeuf won, 25-20, to head into Game 2 with a 1-0 match lead. For some reason, the traction LeBoeuf had gained in Game 1 was lost. The Squires picked up steam, and Allania got stuck in her own head as they sent ball after ball her way.

Delone Catholic won Game 2, 25-15, to even the match. But the Bison were unfazed.

"What you do after you lose a set, how you come back from that shows who you really are as a team," Maria said.

Allania switched shirts with Courtney in between games so Courtney could take her spot as the libero in Game 3.

It was a mark of both Allania's selflessness and the extraordinary bond they all shared that she was not only willing but also confident in going along with the change. It wasn't the first time they'd switched shirts, and each time Allania knew it was for the good of the team.

"In the end, I was OK with it because I knew that (Courtney) was gonna have my back and that she was gonna do what I couldn't that day," Allania said.

When Allania reentered the match, she had regained her composure. Her teammates rolled right along with her, surging on a long service run to claim a 25-20 win in Game 3. Up 2-1, the Bison found themselves 25 points away from a state championship. But just as Delone Catholic was desperate to stave off elimination, LeBoeuf was fervently trying to avoid a fifth game.

"Nobody wants to go to a fifth game, because (in) fifth games anything can happen," LeAnn said.

The two squads challenged each other throughout Game 4. LeAnn had heard horror stories of coaches going into big matches with the wrong lineups written down on their cards, and had been determined to avoid any and all mental mistakes. But with the score tied at 22, she asked the down referee if she had another timeout available. The ref told her she did, so she called timeout.

Unbeknownst to both of them, LeAnn had already used her two allotted timeouts for Game 4. Even though the referee had been mistaken, under PIAA rules it was the Bison who were penalized. The Squires were awarded a point which gave them a 23-22 lead. LeAnn was devastated.

"(I) wanted to go, 'Oh, my goodness,' and stick my head in a fire," she said.

LeAnn shook off the mistake as best as she could, and gave her team clipped instructions.

"I'm sorry, go — do it," she told them.

With Maria behind the service line, the Bison won the next two points for the 24-23 lead. On the next volley, Amanda was set up for the kill. She did what she always did; she put the ball where people weren't. It wasn't a pounding spike, but the ball lofted to the back corner of the court. The Bison's heads turned in unison, watching the ball for what seemed like a lifetime.

The ball dropped to the floor. 25-23. They were champions.

It was as if a powder keg exploded in the gym. The Bison jumped into the air in celebration. Their family, friends and fans flooded the court to meet their heroes, who were crying tears of, as Julie put it, "pure joy."

"It was literally the best feeling of your whole entire life," Julie said. Courtney shared a celebratory moment with her grandmother over the phone. She didn't know whether to be happy they won or sad that it was over. Abby was in a haze of surreality. All of the players and coaches were trying to make their way through the swarm of fans to shake the Squires' hands. It was delightful pandemonium, and it wasn't over yet.

The six-hour bus ride home only bolstered their excitement as they were escorted back into Waterford by ambulances and fire engines. They were greeted by town-organized fireworks and an enormous crowd in Fort LeBoeuf's gymnasium. It was nearly midnight, but the victory party went on with Queen's "We Are the Champions" booming through the loudspeakers.

The Bison hadn't even realized until someone told them that they were the first volleyball team in Erie County history to win a state championship.

"We just knew we wanted to win, period," LeAnn said.

It was a win for all of Erie, and the players received a flurry of congratulatory messages from opponents across the county.

Something else had dawned on the Bison when they were still in the gym at Central York High School.

As they lined up to receive their medals, a realization dropped into Allania's head. She turned to LeAnn.

"Coach," she said. "That's a perfect season."

...Like it was yesterday

Fort LeBoeuf made it to the state title match in each of the next three years, but the 2012 team remains the only Bison team to win it all. Several of the alumni from the 2012 squad went on to play college volleyball. To their surprise, the difficulty of their college practices and conditioning paled in comparison to the rigors of Fort LeBoeuf's program.

"When we got to college, we only had to run like two suicides," Courtney recalled. "We're like, 'That's it? OK.'"

As it inevitably happens in life, these high school best friends veered down separate paths. They've entered fields such as nursing, education, pharmacology, sales and accounting. Some still live in the area, while others have moved for their careers.

But they are all bound together by the lessons they learned from LeAnn in the gym at Fort LeBoeuf High School.

"She gave me every single tool that I needed to succeed in life," Maria said.

They have taken these tools and passed them down to others. Abby, Julie and Maria all coached in LeBoeuf's program for a time, and Courtney is an assistant to LeAnn on the varsity level.

Her goal is to get a job that allows her to work volleyball around her schedule.

"Volleyball has been my life," Courtney said. "I just cannot give it up."

Allania is engaged to be married and has a toddler. While she already balances her family duties with her role as an accountant at Scott Enterprises in Erie, she still hopes to become a volleyball coach.

She looks at the example set by LeAnn, a family woman and teacher who still found time to lead a team to a state championship. And when her fiancé is out of town for work and she must take care of her child by herself, Allania sometimes wonders how people can do so much.

But then she thinks of LeAnn and Sean, and how their shared passion of volleyball brought them closer together.

"They have a very healthy relationship and two very beautiful, healthy kids, so it's definitely possible," Allania said.

It's a lesson LeAnn intended to impart, that one can be a strong, independent woman with a spouse and children, and can still pursue their passions.

"Most days you're gonna feel like you're going nuts, but it's absolutely, 100 percent possible,"

LeAnn said. "And you don't have to put somebody else's needs in front of you."

But LeAnn also learned something from the players of that 2012 team. Even — or rather, especially — on a bad day, you have to set yourself aside and be present in the moment.

"You're not gonna love your job every day," LeAnn said. "You're not gonna love your spouse every day. There's times when they drive you a little crazy. But you made the commitment, and you need to find ways to get through those days where it's not all rosy and wonderful."

Having children taught LeAnn that there's more to life than volleyball. However, that doesn't mean she's any less competitive. The Bison were bumped up to Class AAA after barely making the class-size cutoff. They remain formidable at the district level, and were District 10 runners-up to Conneaut High School in 2020.

LeAnn is with LeBoeuf for the long haul, and hopes to add more former players to her coaching staff.

"What better manpower than the girls that you coached for seven years?" LeAnn said. "They're gonna do exactly what I'm looking for."

The players, now in their mid-twenties, don't see each other as often anymore. But they remain friends, and when they reunite, they greet each other as if they had just been together the day before.

"It doesn't matter that we don't see each other for years to come," Jolene said. "We'll always pick up where we left off."

Abby will be getting married in 2021. Lindsay Bean will be her maid of honor, wearing a dress instead of basketball shorts. Courtney and her sister, Jordan, will be bridesmaids.

And, of course, LeAnn will be there.

"She was my favorite coach I ever had," Abby said.

Jolene and Allania also will be marrying their respective fiancés in 2021. No doubt the weddings will also function as reunions for the players, who love to reflect and reminisce on their accomplishments. Especially their state championship.

"To be a part of that team and bring home a gold medal for our school, (it was) being a part of something bigger than we are," Julie said.

And they haven't forgotten the root of it all.

"(You need) somebody that's going to push you to a level that you didn't think you could achieve yourself," Jolene said. "(LeAnn) did that for all of us, and that's why we were so successful."

The girls are women now, and they know these things to be true: Hard work pays off. Time management is essential. You might fall on your butt going for a ball. That's OK. Pick yourself up and get the next one. It's OK to laugh, even at yourself. It's OK to cry. Thou shall not order pizza at a volleyball tournament.

Show gratitude. Be selfless. Be a team player. Know that everyone is different, and relate accordingly.

Being yelled at is not the end of the world. High expectations are a good thing. Stay consistent. Stay disciplined. If you throw up mid-run at a street corner, you have to straighten up and keep going.

And if you do these things, you won't have to do them by yourself.

As these ladies know, your sisters will be beside you every step of the way.

Photo provided by Dan Brabender

Dan Brabender (above) announces a Cathedral Preparatory School football game. Brabender, a Cathedral Prep alumnus and lifelong Ramblers football fan, has written four books about Prep and Erie sports.

A Life in Orange & Black

By Dan Brabender

Dan Brabender was born and raised in Erie. He is a lifelong Cathedral Prep sports fan and graduated from Prep in 1970 as a two-time letter winner for the Ramblers' wrestling team. Brabender is the author of four books about Prep and Erie sports. He spent more than 30 years as a defense attorney before becoming a judge on the Erie County Court of Common Pleas. Brabender remains a regular attendant at Cathedral Prep football games. He lives in Erie, and has many friends and two daughters, Alexis and Rachel.

High school football is the purest form of America's greatest sport. I learned this truth even before I reached the age of reason. When I was very young, my father, Dan Sr., would take me to Cathedral Preparatory School football games at the "Academy Stadium," as it was locally known, off West 26th Street between State and French streets.

The first game I actually remember was a 46-0 pasting in 1959, when Harborcreek High School got dump-trucked by the fully operational battle station that was the Cathedral Prep football team.

I'd be a Prep fan forevermore.

One of the few things that is inevitable in life is change. Change, that relentless force that picks you up and tosses you forward like a tidal wave. Once we get settled into a new school, job, town or relationship, change is always there to remind us that nothing lasts forever.

In my life, however, there has been one constant. One heart-pounding, soul-filling certainty that comes in the shades of orange and black. No matter how my path twisted and turned, I could always count on a few action-packed hours on a fall Friday night with my Ramblers.

To be sure, there are far more important things in life than high school football. But the joy I get from watching my favorite team has enriched my life in many ways. More than what goes on between the hash marks, the memories I've shared with friends made along the way hearken to the old adage: It's more than a game.

The Brabenders of Millcreek Township were a typical 1950s family. My dad was an auto salesman, and my mother, Jane, stayed at home to take care of myself and my two siblings, Mary Ann and Tim. I grew up like any other American boy at that time, playing football, basketball and baseball in my free time. I was an altar boy, a boy scout and a paper boy. I held my first job at 14 years old at the Red Barn on Peach Street, making 85 cents per hour.

You could say we were a traditional family, and that tradition included high school sports. My dad graduated from Prep in 1937, and played football for legendary Ramblers coach Father Walter Conway. My dad wasn't a star, but as an offensive guard was Prep's first substitute in games. Dan Sr.'s love for Prep football extended well into adulthood, during which he shared his love for the Ramblers with his namesake.

It was the perfect time for me to become a Prep fan. The Ramblers had won their first City Series crown in 1949 under coach Walt Strosser, kicking off a "golden era" that included 20 city titles in 29 years. Prep left an indelible impression on my young mind. When you're a kid, you don't want to root for losers. And there was no doubt in my mind that I was going to attend Prep. I was a Rambler all the way, from beginning to end.

The atmosphere of the high school sports culture in those years was like something out of a dream. I pored through the lineups and game summaries in the sports pages of the *Erie Daily Times*. My friends and I studied the box scores and the standings of the City Series and Erie County League as if they were sacred scrolls. We were mesmerized by the images of stately-looking team uniforms, exciting touchdowns, larger-than-life heroes and thrilling battles.

These games were without a doubt the social events of the week. I can clearly recall walking amongst the thickness of the crowds approaching Erie Veterans Memorial Stadium, a venerable, old, brick-walled building that sat in front of Academy High School. I caught the aroma of hot dogs and popcorn as I took in the beating drums of the bands parading around the track. I watched the games with rapt attention as the constant noise and organized cheering of raucous fans both young and old swirled around me.

Once the roaring voice blasted through the loudspeaker to announce the lineups, the gridders made their grand entry down the stone steps before busting toward the sidelines. At times, the stadium was so packed that police officers had to clear fans from the steps just so the players could reach the field to warm up.

I enthusiastically supported the Ramblers, who had a reputation for taking no prisoners on the field. The reverberations of the mental and physical beatings they laid on opponents were felt for weeks to come. Regular kids from our neighborhood such as Jimmy Jobes, Donny Wurst, Pat Lupo and others transformed, in my eyes, to athletes of mythical proportions. My friends and I were captured, hook, linemen and sinker.

Perhaps it was the local angle, or maybe the idea that on any given weekend, any team in the city was capable of beating another, that made high school football in Erie such an enthralling experience for so many. Whatever the case, between 5,000 and 16,000 fans regularly showed up to support their heroes.

I remember those games well, including the Ramblers' trio of wins over Tech Memorial and the Biletnikoff brothers — future Pro Football Hall of Famer Fred and future New York Yankee Bobby — from 1960-62. Fred was an outstanding football player, but in my mind Bobby was the greatest all-around athlete Erie has ever produced.

I also recall the inception of the now storied rivalry between Prep and McDowell High School. After Prep had won the first 11 contests between the two schools, the Trojans, led by legendary coach Joe Moore and stars such as Jeff Davis, Doug Fabian and Roger Gunesch, laid waste to and napalmed the Ramblers for seven straight years starting in 1967. From that point on, the Prep-McDowell rivalry would be the fiercest in town, and remains so to this day.

By the fall of 1967, just after the Summer of Love, I was a sophomore at Cathedral Prep. While I had played football in my grade school years, I opted to focus solely on wrestling as a high schooler. We always regret the things we didn't do. But I still supported Prep and was there when the Ramblers upset the mighty East High Warriors that fall.

Jack Polancy, sports editor of the *Erie Morning News*, labeled East the heavy favorite, which boosted the spirit of the Rambler faithful tenfold. We took it personally, taking from Polancy's colorful write-ups the assumption that he actually *wanted* Prep to lose. After a Friday pep rally before the big game, about 250 of us stormed the newspaper's office building, shouting, "Polancy's always wrong!" Jubilation came more often than not at the end of the season, when the Ramblers would claim many city championships. Thousands of Prep fans, including a future judge on the Erie County Court of Common Pleas, marched right behind the school band down State Street to the docks of the bay, raising hell all along the way.

The rivalries between city schools in those days were intense. Before one Prep-Academy game, the letter 'A' was burned into Prep's front lawn. Monsignor Robert McDonald, then headmaster at Prep, was beside himself.

"They don't respect you!" he yelled to the student body. "They don't respect your parents!"

He revved up this group of rowdy altar boys so much that, by the time we were dismissed, we were like the guys from *Animal House* after Bluto's big speech. As it turned out, Strong Vincent High School students were the culprits of the lawn-burning.

I was the team captain of the wrestling team in my senior year. I learned so much from wrestling, including the values of hard work and perseverance, which carried me through every phase of my life. I graduated from Prep in 1970 and was off to the University of Dayton, in Ohio, to study pre-law and wrestle for the Flyers. While there, I picked up rugby, and ended up as the captain of Dayton's rugby team. I guess you could say that was the closest I came to playing high-level organized football.

While I immersed myself in campus life, I remained in the loop about Prep football with the help of my best friend, Bob Smith. I earned my undergraduate degree in 1974 and stayed at Dayton for four more years to get my law degree.

During this time, in 1976, the City Series was abolished in favor of the Metro League, which included the five city schools and suburban McDowell. The Ramblers had some solid players in those years, such as Fran Mifsud, Tim Dougan and Tom "Smokey" Smogorzewski, but they could only muster a 15-32-1 record from 1975-79. It was a tough pill to swallow for fans who had become so accustomed to success. Even coaching changes didn't help matters. It was like doing a crossword puzzle in a Sunday edition of *The New York Times*. Gimme a six-letter word for unhappiness at Cathedral Prep. Try "d-e-f-e-a-t." Did it fit?

Meanwhile, I graduated from law school in 1978. I spent a summer in Pittsburgh studying for the bar exam, and in the fall of '78 I joined my uncle Richard Brabender's law firm, Carney, Good, Brabender and Walsh, located on West Sixth Street in Erie.

While I continued to root for the Ramblers, my primary focus was on getting my law practice established. I also moonlit as a bartender at

Wagner's Side Door, a popular downtown hangout.

Just as I transitioned into a law career, the Ramblers made their way into a new era.

Headmaster/Father John Dollinger was determined to make the football program a winner, and a resurgence came with the hiring of former East High star and St. John Kanty Prep mentor Michael "Mina" George as the new head coach. This appointment was greeted with much enthusiasm by Prep football fans, who felt there was plenty of talent on hand and that George was just the man needed to return the Orange & Black to its glory.

After back-to-back losses to start the 1980 season, Prep dumped McDowell, 20-7, en route to an eight-game win streak and the Ramblers' first Metro crown. Local fans began talking Rambler football again, and it was in championship terms.

As Prep's football team took off, so did my law career. I enjoyed practicing law and I cared about the people I represented. I am grateful to say I never had any financial worries, and even bought a BMW as I went through some yuppie years.

George, who was mentored by Joe Moore and my uncle, former East High coach Billy Brabender, was a real character. He rarely humiliated his players publicly, but privately he had no qualms about reaming them out. During one game in 1994, Prep's Jake Merski muffed a few punts. George screamed at him on the sidelines that he wasn't welcome on the team bus and he needed to find his own way home. Later, with three seconds left in the game and Prep trailing 14-13, Merski kicked the game-winning field goal for the 16-14 upset. Just like that, he was back in George's good graces, all pretensions of a ride from a family member or hitchhiking forgotten.

In 1988, local football championships lost their prominence with the advent of the Pennsylvania Interscholastic Athletic Association football state playoffs. The focus in the Erie area, particularly as city schools closed in subsequent years, became squarely on the quest to become a state champion.

Prep's 1990 squad, led by running back Tim Colicchio, came close. Prep was ranked amongst the top 10 high school football teams in the nation by *USA Today*. I remember being in awe as I learned this from a newspaper article. It made me just want to sit there and stare at the paper for a while.

The Ramblers, who played in Class AAAA (the largest division) went 10-0 in the regular season to garner an invitation to the PIAA's four-team bracket. However, they fell to North Allegheny in what was considered the western final.

The next year, Erie was alive with excitement over local football. Not only was Prep primed to make another deep run, but Class AAA Strong Vincent, coached by former Cathedral Prep football standout Joe Bufalino, also had a shot to win state. The two teams met during the regular season in a heart-thumping, 7-0 verdict in favor of the Ramblers.

Prep pulled off an improbable, come-from-behind victory over Connellsville High School to reach the state title game. After more than 30 years of watching and following Prep football, we were finally here. Prep was slated to face the dynasty that was Central Bucks West for the ultimate prize.

But the ride down to the game was ominous. It was the last day of buck-hunting season, and as I drove through scenic Pennsylvania, I saw orange-clad hunters in the woods, hoping to slay the bucks. Talk about symbolism.

I sat and watched the game with my friends, renowned sports radio host Jim LeCorchick and fellow Prep grad Phil Trapolsi. We watched as the wind howled mercilessly and the Ramblers committed three second-half turnovers.

Prep lost, 26-14, in what was a great effort against a great team. Strong Vincent, meanwhile, became Erie's first football state champion, with a 15-1 record. Though this was one of those times I was disappointed as a Prep fan, my dismay never prevented me from enjoying the ambiance of high school football. And, no matter my interests in Dayton athletics or professional sports, the Ramblers remained the nearest and dearest to my heart.

On October 31, 1993, my parents were driving back from Dayton after visiting my brother and seeing their first grandchild. Someone cut in front of them, causing an accident. My mother died after seven hours in surgery, while my dad was in critical condition. He never truly recovered, and died on June 17, 1994 — interestingly, the same day as O.J. Simpson's infamous white Ford Bronco chase.

Right around the time my mom died, I started to write a book about Cathedral Prep football. It kept my mind off the terrible tragedy of losing her. I took a break from writing as my dad's health continued to decline, but a few months after he died, I went to the Mercyhurst

College (now Mercyhurst University) library to look up the 1935 Prep football team that my dad had been a part of. This snowballed into the popular *RAMBLERS: The History of Cathedral Prep Football, 1924-1999.*

Writing the book had been in the back of my mind for several years. I felt like it was up to me. I had a genuine interest in the history of Prep football, and I thought that if I didn't write it, this history was going to be lost forever. To my delight, the region and beyond seemed as interested in the history of Rambler football as I was. And, to my relief, no one told me I was nuts for writing an extremely detailed, nearly 1,000 page book. In fact, the inclusion of so many familiar names turned out to be its charm in the eyes of many.

While I was writing the book, Prep football had again fallen on hard times. George's last few seasons were nowhere near the Ramblers' dominance of the early '90s. Still, he retired in 1995 as the winningest coach in program history with a record of 131-44-2. George had a lot to be proud of. He was named the state's Big School Coach of the Year in 1991, and coached three players — Mark Tate, Charlie Baumann and All-Pro Mark Stepnoski — who went on to play in the NFL.

Even as the McDowell Trojans emerged as the kings of local football and Prep slipped into the shadows, I wasn't concerned. We had been here before. Everything is cyclical, and you can't go 12-0 every year. Sure enough, a Cathedral Prep renaissance was on its way. The Ramblers hired their successful freshman team coach, 28-year-old Mike Mischler, to take the helm on varsity. At his side? The one and only Joe Moore, who had coached McDowell to great success and had been an offensive line coach at Notre Dame University.

The 66-year-old Moore, who had once punched a referee in the face out of anger over a no-call, was a compelling yin to Mischler's yang. The young Turk and the grizzled veteran made for a promising duo, and hopes were high for a resurgence.

The results were immediate. Prep went 9-5 in 1998 and reached the western final. Wins over powerhouses such as McDowell and State College boosted the Ramblers' confidence that they could hang with anyone in the state. The 1999 season gave reason for more optimism. Returning were senior Demond "Bob" Sanders, who for my money was the most exciting player to grace the turf at Vets since East High's Eddie Woodward some 30 years before; Charles Rush, one of the most highly recruited junior lineman in the nation; junior Ed Hinkel, who I argue is Erie's greatest high school football player ever; and a heady senior quarterback in Eric Carlson.

The Orange & Black did not disappoint. Prep was ranked ninth in the nation by *USA Today*, and reached the state final to face — who else? — Central Bucks West. It would be the "Game of the Millennium," as it was the first time ever that two top-10 nationally-ranked teams — the Bucks were ranked fourth — would meet in a state title game.

In that 1999 Quad A title clash, Prep had outplayed and was leading superpower Central Bucks West, 13-7 after the first 45 minutes and 8 seconds of play. The Ramblers were about to crack a 44-game win streak and dethrone a dynasty.

Then came a fellow by the name of Andrew Elsing, the Bucks' star defensive end, who bolted through the line and blocked Ed Hinkel's punt. The leather-encased bundle of wind bounced to Elsing's left, where he stumbled before unconsciously gathering it and diving into the end zone for a touchdown. The extra point sailed through and CBW shockingly rallied ahead, 14-13.

The Bucks held on to win their 45th straight contest and third consecutive PIAA crown. It was a classic, legendary battle, considered to be the most exciting state title game ever played in the Keystone State.

It was a game in which the Ramblers left their hearts on the field, outplayed CBW for most of the game and, by many metrics, should have won. It was a painful, devastating loss that left Prep fans everywhere wondering why life wasn't fair.

Patience, as they say, is a virtue. Sanders — who went on to play for the Indianapolis Colts and become the 2007 NFL Defensive Player of the Year — was gone, as was Carlson. But the 2000 Ramblers still had a great, experienced core returning. Rush. Hinkel. Jason Easter. Joe Dipre. Josh Lustig, Eric Field and Jawan Walker. These all-staters and future college football players were back, along with other strong seniors such as Tim Dance and Ed Brown.

The Ramblers steamrolled their competition all the way to the regional final. Prep was to host at Vets, which had been covered in 44 inches of snow. Dozens of local fans worked tirelessly to remove snow from Vets' turf to avoid the prospect of a venue change.

Meanwhile, Altoona was dispatched to Erie to knock the ears off the Ramblers, who were ranked No. 1 in the state and sixth in the nation.

The Mountain Lions came in optimistic and hungry. They strategically devoured the game clock to prevent Prep's offense from running wild, and held a 7-6 lead late in the game. After a touchdown pass from Hinkel to Dance was called back on a questionable offensive interference penalty, the Lions picked off a pass and returned it to Prep's 10-yard line. Rambler fans, myself among them, were sick. Many began to leave.

I remained in my seat. I had never quit on my Ramblers before, and I wasn't about to start now.

With the Lions at Prep's 4-yard line after two plays, Mischler made a brilliant call:

"Let Altoona score on the next play."

Prep backed off, and Altoona crossed the goal line. The PAT was missed, but the Lions still led, 13-6, with a little less than two minutes remaining. Someone had to step up.

Tim Dance was just that someone. He scooped up the ensuing kickoff at Prep's 15, and the speedy Dance tore up the middle on the strength of strong blocks by Brad Wernicki and Brian White. He broke one tackle, then another, before breaking away for an electrifying 85-yard touchdown return. Rory Maloney nailed the pressure-packed PAT to deadlock the game at 13. Overtime, baby. The tension at Vets that day was as thick as Mississippi molasses in May.

The Lions took a 20-13 lead. Prep took over and was facing a 4th-and-3 situation when Hinkel hit a diving Lustig with a lightning bolt for the clutch TD. Maloney came through again to tie it up at 20.

Prep got the edge after Hinkel scored on a 10-yard draw in the second OT. The Ramblers' defense held strong to give Prep the win and cause the wildest postgame celebration I had seen at Vets in a very, very long time.

Prep blew by Mount Lebanon in the western final to make it to state. And, once again, they faced Central Bucks West.

For the Ramblers and their fanbase — myself included — it was payback time. We gladly made the pilgrimage to Hershey in the hopes that our beloved, orange-clad heroes would finally claim the throne of Pennsylvania high school football.

I had some good company on that trip. My six-week-old daughter, Alexis, braved the cold with my then wife, Marci, and me. There we sat, in 28-degree weather, my daughter supporting Prep before she could walk, talk or crawl. In the distance, we could see Christmas lights adorning a giant, dormant roller coaster at Hersheypark.

The Bucks, riding high on a 59-game winning streak, out-muscled Prep to a 13-7 halftime lead. At halftime, I was concerned the

Ramblers would again fall short. But in the second half, the lead was traded a few times before Dance pulled off a state-title-game-record 90-yard kickoff return for a touchdown to tie the game at 21. Each squad would score twice more to send the game into OT tied at 35. Prep forced a field goal try, and 6-foot-7 defensive lineman Dale Williams stretched out his arm and blocked the Bucks' kick. Now, it was the Ramblers' turn.

As hard as it was to envision, the tension and drama buried that of the 1999 slugfest. Field general Hinkel shouted to his teammates, "We gotta get it in! Paybacks for last year!" It was third-and-goal on the 4 as Mischler began readying his field goal unit.

With the entire Prep sideline on their knees locking hands, Walker slashed through the left side against a blitz. He landed with a happy thud in the north end zone, ironically just a few feet from where Andrew Elsing stumbled into the house to win it for the Bucks just one year before. Walker stayed down with not only the football, but history in his hands. There was hesitation for a second, then a quick look around the field revealed no flags.

Walker had scored. It was 41-35. Prep had won!

A throng of Prep coaches, players, fans and friends alike poured onto the field in a sea of orange.

Finally, after years of frustration, my team had pulled it off. They were state champions. And I felt that anybody who was, like me, a real Prep fan and supporter, had a piece of that championship.

The year 2000 was pivotal for me in multiple ways. In addition to the birth of my eldest daughter and Prep's state championship win, my first book was released to fanfare from the Erie community. The state title run inspired me to write another book, *That Championship Season: The Story of the 2000 Prep Ramblers*.

My second daughter, Rachel, was born 17 months after her big sister. Life was good.

The Ramblers, though, faced another downturn. After a few lukewarm seasons, Mischler resigned. Former Prep football player Don Holl took over the program in 2005. The Ramblers entered another change when they dropped from Class AAAA to AAA, which was more fitting of their enrollment numbers.

Five years after he left, Mischler returned. That same year, I was elected to the Erie County Court of Common Pleas. I had truly enjoyed my time as a lawyer, but it was time for the next step.

While I acclimated to the bench, Mischler began to build a dynasty. His commitment to strong values and his relatability inspired his student-athletes to play for him, and play well. Indeed, it only took a few years before Prep was back in Hershey. Led by preseason All-American quarterback Damion Terry, the Ramblers defeated Archbishop Wood in 2012 to claim their second state championship. The next several years were an onslaught of accolades, championships and euphoria for Cathedral Prep football. Mischler went on to win the PIAA Coach of the Year award three times, once in the AAA division and twice in the AAAA division after the state's programs were reclassified.

Prep lost in the 2015 state title game to the Imhotep Charter Panthers, a powerhouse program out of Philadelphia. But payback came when the Ramblers — led by Mischler's son, QB Joe Mischler — defeated Imhotep for state crowns in 2016 and 2017. Prep pulled off a three-peat with yet another victory over the Panthers in 2018.

That first win over Imhotep, in 2016, remains one of the highlights of my 60-plus years as a Prep fan.

Since Mischler returned in 2009, Prep has won 11 straight regional titles, went eight straight years with no less than 11 victories each year, posted five undefeated regular seasons, appeared in five state finals and captured four state titles. Even though Erie's population has declined — and with it, Prep's enrollment — with Mischler at the helm of the football program and Prep's basketball team coming off a state championship win, the Ramblers are on solid footing.

There are still grumblings around the county that Prep's success is largely due to its recruitment of promising athletes. I can only meet these claims with a sigh and an eye-roll, because I've been around the game long enough to know that both private and public schools recruit. Personally, I am proud that Cathedral Prep has remained private and rooted in Catholicism.

The McDowell-Prep rivalry is always fun. The students get riled up and longtime Erieites still hold grudges. But those two schools need each other. They feed off one another and make each other better.

As I've enjoyed this blissful era of Prep football, life has gone on. I have no complaints, really. I have been blessed with great friends. Both of my daughters are progressing well and are in college, and I am still a judge at the county level. Because of my familiarity with Erie and the people who live here, I am able to relate to the people who come before me in the courtroom. A lot of that comes from the research I've done while writing my books. I published *Cathedral Prep Basketball Chronicles: 1924-2017* in 2017, and in 2019 I released

Sports Heroes of the Erie School District: 125 Profiles.

Though I don't have anymore writing projects on the horizon for now, I will never stop loving Erie sports. Particularly, I will never stop being a diehard Prep fan. Even if I move to Florida someday upon retirement, I will always come back for football season.

How could I not? Not only has Cathedral Prep given me more than six decades of exhilarating fandom, the school itself helped mold me into who I am today. When I think about that, Monsignor McDonald comes to mind. I think about how he always wanted Prep to be the best.

As I look back on all the amazing experiences I've had with Cathedral Prep, and I reflect upon the excellence of the Ramblers' storied program, I think it's safe to say that my old headmaster got his wish.

Photo provided by the Cathedral Preparatory School and Villa Maria Academy athletics department.

Adrienne (Kloecker) Kalivoda (above) makes a pass during a Villa Maria Academy girls basketball game. She was an integral part of the Victors' PIAA Class AA state-championship threepeat from 2009-11.

A Tradition Like No Other

By Adrienne (Kloecker) Kalivoda

Adrienne (Kloecker) Kalivoda, born and raised in Erie, was a guard on three state-champion Villa Maria Academy girls basketball teams from 2008-2011. She graduated in 2012 and went on to play at Mercyhurst University on a full scholarship. She was a 1,000-point scorer in her career with the Lakers. She is currently an assistant coach for the Victors and the head coach of Erie Irish AAU. She also is the funeral director at Kloecker Funeral Home and Crematory, Inc. and the supervisor of Kloecker-Bailey Funeral Home and Crematory, Inc., which are owned and operated by her father, Mark Kloecker.

You could say that, from birth, I had no choice but to be a Villa Victor. My family has always been very supportive of Cathedral Preparatory School and Villa Maria Academy, including their athletic programs.
At a young age, I started to see my potential in the game of basketball. I found that many of the top players in the city played on a travel basketball team, so after my fifth grade season I joined the Erie Saints 10U team.
The core of the eventual 2010-11 Pennsylvania Interscholastic Athletic Association Class A State Championship team was formed on that squad. Zhane Brooks, Karlee McBride, Lisa Mifsud and I played together then, long before we ever suited up for Villa. We continued to play together through our eighth grade season, during which we all transitioned to play for Scott Dibble and Erie Irish AAU.
That year, the team added Cierra Pollock, Rebecca Sweny and Abbey Steudler. As we grew older, it was apparent we would become something amazing.
I was definitely not the best basketball player going into high school, and many coaches in Erie will attest to that. The only advantages I had were my work ethic, leadership ability and confidence.
As a freshman, I did not make the Victors' varsity team. Instead, I took the court as the starting point guard for the junior varsity squad. I have to admit, I was disappointed. Many of my friends and longtime grade school teammates were chosen over me. I was disappointed and

feeling sorry for myself, but my parents — especially my father, Mark Kloecker — did not let me feel that way for long.

"What are you doing to get better?" he would ask me. "What are you doing to *prove* to the coaches that you *deserve* a spot on varsity?"

As the head coach of a middle school travel basketball team and an assistant coach at Villa, I find that many kids think the amount of playing time they get is solely based on the coach's opinion. It is hard to think otherwise as a young girl playing basketball, but half of that decision is on the player herself. I can't tell you how many girls who question playing time put all the blame on their coach. My father's lesson echoes as I ask them, "What are you doing to *prove* to me that you *deserve* to be on the court?"

It is a mental decision each player has to make: Either they will give up, or they will work harder. Villa taught me this lesson from day one. By the time the playoffs had arrived in my freshman year, I had earned a jersey for the varsity team. I was not guaranteed any playing time whatsoever, but I will always appreciate being a part of that team. The 2009 Victors were not the best in the state; we had a young starting five and we had graduated key, big-time players in 2008. What we did have was chemistry like no other. From the starting five to the managers, everyone had one goal: to be the 2009 state champions.

The traditions of Villa Maria girls basketball are so unique to the school. The spaghetti dinners the night before playoff games, the prayer in the locker room before games, the famous "We Ready" chant in the hallway before running out to the court, the hype from the bench — everything we do as Villa Victors today was handed down year after year.

My role on that team was to be a practice player, memorize the other teams' plays, guard future Notre Dame/WNBA star Kayla McBride to the best of my ability and be the biggest cheerleader on the bench come game time.

During those first couple of years at Villa, I learned the importance of each and every role on the team. Even though I barely played in varsity games, I knew I had an important role to bring energy to the game from the bench. Anyone who plays sports knows that if your bench is hyped, the energy of the game swings in your favor.

The morning of the state championship game, the front page of the *Erie Times-News*' sports section showed a young Adrienne Kloecker running onto the floor to give Kayla McBride a high-five. That was my role, and I loved every bit of it. As we came closer to the state final, we could tell there was so much riding on this season. Villa had reached the state title game before, but had always come up short. We were not going to let that happen this year.

We faced York Catholic in a nail-biter, but we came out on top, 56-51. It was enough of a margin for us bench players to get four whole seconds in the game!

Winning a state championship in any sport is a huge accomplishment. But in Erie, winning it all doesn't just make our school proud. It makes the entire city proud. The amount of support from the community was overwhelming. As a young girl, you don't grasp that accomplishment for what it was, but you know all the hard work it took to get there.

Not much had changed as I began my sophomore year. We lost a few seniors, but the same core group was back. The biggest difference between the 2009 and 2010 teams was the amount of pressure on us. The *Times-News* published a season preview of our team in its *Varsity* section, and the headline read: "Villa Basketball: The Sequel." All athletes take pressure differently. Some of our girls could really feel it, some said "Bring it on," and others blocked it out. I always was the player who loved the pressure, but in this case, I was just cheering from the bench. As my confidence grew and my basketball skills increased, I became a leader for the JV team while playing the dual role of hype player on the varsity bench.

Any person who has watched me play basketball will tell you about my energy. From a young age, my dad and my coaches would tell me how big of an impact my energy level made on the entire team. As a leader, if your energy is down, your entire team's energy takes a hit. That is a hard lesson to learn as an underclassman, and oftentimes I failed my teammates. It takes mental discipline to be energetic when you know you aren't playing well.

As the season went on, we knew we were going to make a run for a second straight state championship. We had most of the same team we had had in '09, and the chemistry between us was much stronger this time around. Kayla had been on varsity since her freshman year, and as a junior she didn't play much with the girls in her class. In 2010, the senior class was stronger than ever after playing so much together. In short, no one could stop us.

I remember the older girls always joking around with me, but I could take it with a laugh and give it right back. Particularly, Ashley Prischak and Kaylyn Maruca constantly gave me a hard time, but I loved those girls. They never handed things to me, they never let up their defense on me and I got better because of that. Of course, if I went as hard as I could they would give me a look like, "Calm down, AK, don't hurt us, it's playoff time."

That really was a fun year as a Villa Victor. We rematched with York Catholic in the state title game, and as the *Times-News* had predicted, we repeated as the state champs. Many of the girls cried after the game. Not only was repeating as a state champion almost unheard of, that 52-44 victory also was the last game with our seniors. The powerhouse starting five went out on the highest note possible for high school athletes.

Out of all my years as a Villa Victor, my junior year was by far the most exciting of my career. No one saw us coming. We had graduated our entire starting five, so people overlooked us. There really wasn't any pressure on us. No one thought we could possibly win another state championship without that starting five, and especially not without Kayla.

No one, of course, except us.

The only three players on our team that had previously seen any significant playing time on varsity were Lisa Mifsud, Abbey Steudler and Karlee McBride. All three eventually received full rides to play college ball. We also gained a transfer from Collegiate Academy in Zhane Brooks. Those four girls and I made up the starting five. As the year went on, the community began to realize that a graduating class does not stop the powerhouse that was and is Villa girls basketball.

As we were preparing for the playoffs, though, our team took a huge hit. Our coach, Scott Dibble, was asked to resign. We were devastated. We loved coach Dibble. Most of us cried for days. We couldn't dwell on it for long, though, because our next game was the start of the postseason. We suited up with Doug Chuzie taking the reins as head coach. From the start of the playoffs, we had a drive like never before. We wanted to win that championship so badly. Even losing our head coach was not going to stop this train.

I will never forget the semifinal against Seton LaSalle Catholic High School. Simply put, we were the perfect match. They had many of the same strengths we had.

The Rebels were the highest-scoring team in the Western Pennsylvania Interscholastic Athletic League that year, and they were crushing teams left and right. Their seven postseason wins came by an average of 27.5 points. We knew it would take perfect defense to win the game, and that's exactly what we came with. We forced nearly as many turnovers (32) as they scored points (34).

I remember making free throw after free throw toward the end of the game. I was never the highest scorer as a Villa Victor, and it was Lisa Mifsud who scored 21 points in that game, but those free throws meant everything to me. That win was such a huge moment for our team, and every one of us was crying in the locker room. Once I stepped out of the locker room, two of my uncles lifted me up on their shoulders. I felt like I was on top of the world.

The following Friday was the state championship game. By this point, everyone in our class thought going to the state final was the norm. For three straight years, everyone got to skip school on game day, ride the bus to Penn State University and cheer on their Villa Victors. But this time was different for our junior class. *We* were the starting five, and it was all on us to win this game.

We played Dunmore High School, which had pulled off multiple upsets to be the Cinderella story of the state playoffs. We didn't know much about this team.

We were very nervous as the game began. I made some stupid mistakes in the first couple of minutes as Dunmore started the game on a 6-2 run. During a timeout, we told coach Chuzie we could definitely get up on them and apply some pressure. We came out of the timeout and went on a 21-0 run, keeping them scoreless for nearly 12 minutes.

After that, they didn't have a chance. We won, 62-39, to capture our third consecutive state championship.

"This is unheard of!" I said over and over again.

That 2010-11 team was definitely one to remember. Through the highs and lows, through the doubts and negative forces around us, we still came out on top.

The 2011-12 team turned out to be even better than the previous one. Several of us were now seniors. We had experience, confidence — maybe a little too much — and each member of the starting five was offered a full ride to play college basketball. Our expectations were through the roof. It was going to be the perfect ending to a perfect high school career.

Even though we had improved from the year before, we didn't know how much harder it would be to earn another state title. Every team in PA was out to bring down the Villa Maria girls basketball powerhouse.

We still played great basketball together, and our defense brought us all the way to a PIAA semifinal.

Our final stop was a rematch with the Rebels, and they hit the court with a vengeance. A few years later, Seton LaSalle starting forward Natalie Piaggesi joined my college team at Mercyhurst University. We have talked about our rivalry plenty of times, and she told me the Rebels had one goal in 2012: Beat Villa.

That's what they did. The semifinal was the end of the Villa state championship run, and it was devastating. Not that we admitted it, but many of us had expected to go to the state final again.

Seton LaSalle took advantage of that confidence.

Although our senior year ended just one game short of our goal, our four years were one for the books: A four-year record of 107-12, four district championships, four regional titles and three PIAA Class AA state championships.

In 2018, coach Chuzie asked me to be a part of the Villa girls basketball team, this time as an assistant coach. Now that I am on the other side of the squad, I have an even greater appreciation for the hard work and dedication our coaches put into this program when I was a player. Coaches Dibble and Chuzie put so many hours into watching film, traveling to scout other teams, putting together practice schedules and coming up with game plans, all for us to have a chance to become state champions.

One thing I took away from both coaches is that, as a coach, you have to give credit to the girls at all times. I also learned that, if you happen to lose a game, you take the blame for that loss. I always admired that from both coach Dibble and coach Chuzie.

As an assistant coach at Villa and a head coach for Erie Irish AAU, I am able to take every lesson I learned from playing at Villa and share them with the girls I coach. I teach them that every role is important on the team. I also ask them, "If you don't like your role on the team, what are you doing to change it?" I emphasize that energy on the bench and attitude on the court can change an entire game. Last but not least, I instill in them the value of humility through both wins and losses.

Our Lady of Victory, pray for us!

Photos by Aaron McKrell and illustrations by Ernie Askins
(Access to illustrations provided by Lou Bizzarro's Ringside Restaurant)

These are photos of illustrations of Erie's Lou Bizzarro (left) and Roberto Duran. Bizzarro lasted nearly 14 rounds against defending lightweight champion Duran in a World Boxing Association World Light Title bout at the Erie County Field House in 1976.

L'evento Principale

By Aaron McKrell

In the fall of 1976, a film was released that forever changed American cinema.
Rocky, Sylvester Stallone's passion project, opened in New York City on Nov. 21 and hit theaters nationwide a few weeks later. This tale of a down-on-his-luck boxer rising above his circumstances resonated with audiences of all ages. The film became and remains a cultural phenomenon, grossing more than $117 million and spawning seven sequels. A statue of the fictional Rocky Balboa stands proudly atop the steps of the Philadelphia Museum of Art.
The film's premise is that Rocky gets a shot at the title fight because of a promotional stunt by defending heavyweight champion Apollo Creed. The most poetic aspect of the story is that Rocky didn't actually win. Rather, he proved his grit and character by "going the distance" and lasting all 15 rounds with Creed. This bittersweet theme connected to viewers who related to fighting the good fight even when the odds are against you.
Surely, the movie was adored in Erie as it was all around the nation. However, if even one Erieite had been nonplussed by the triumph of the underdog, no one could have blamed them. Though Erie's Lou Bizzarro was not the inspiration for *Rocky*, he had already embodied the film's pathos about six months before its release.
On May 23, 1976, Bizzarro fought Roberto "Hands of Stone" Duran for the World Boxing Association's World Light Title. Bizzarro did not win, but fought valiantly for nearly 14 rounds with one of the greatest boxers of all time. His courage, fortitude and perseverance embodied the spirit of strength and pride for which Erie is known.

Lou Bizzarro was not the first of his family to step into the ring. He may not even have been the most successful of his brothers who sparred. Born in Marcianise, Italy, just after World War II, Bizzarro emigrated to America with his family in 1948. Though they initially settled in Meadville, Pa., a town about 40 miles south of Erie, his family eventually moved to the city by the lake.

It was in Erie that Lou's older brother, Johnny Bizzarro, got his start in boxing. Lou said Johnny trained at St. Mark's Seminary Gym and was noticed by fight promoter Don Elbaum for his fearlessness.

Johnny set the tone for his family's long and storied history in the Sweet Science with a career that spanned a decade. In 1963, he fought Flash Elorde in Manila, Philippines, for both the WBA's and World Boxing Council's World Super Feather Title. Johnny lost the fight by decision, but went on to win the North American Lightweight Title in a 15-round decision over Paddy Read later that year. He'd get one more shot at a title in 1966, a year after he beat fellow hometown boxer Gene Toran in a ferocious match that Elbaum later told the *Erie Times-News* was "one of the greatest fights ever between two Erie fighters."

Johnny won by unanimous decision, and went on to fight Carlos Ortiz for the WBA's and WBC's lightweight titles in 1966. He lost by a technical knockout, as the match was stopped after he went down in the 12th round. Johnny finished his career in 1968 with an impressive record of 55-11-2. In 2016, he was inducted into the Pennsylvania Boxing Hall of Fame.

His brothers — Ralph, Angelo and Paul — also boxed. Lou said of Paul, "He hit you, one punch, he'd knock you dead."

But, out of all of Johnny's brothers, it was Lou who left the most lasting impact. Lou hung around St. Mark's Seminary Gym while Johnny trained with Father Tom Geddes, who taught at Cathedral Preparatory School.

Lou went from watching his brother to hitting the bag himself. Elbaum took notice of him, as he had all of his boxing brothers.

"All the Bizzarros showed me something," he said.

Elbaum, who was raised in Erie, began promoting boxing matches after a stint in the ring. Throughout his career, he promoted fights for the likes of Muhammad Ali and "Sugar" Ray Robinson.

Elbaum became a friend to the Bizzarro family. He said that every Sunday, he'd go to their house at West 20th Street and Greengarden Boulevard, where he'd be served a large plate of pasta.

Naturally, Elbaum developed an interest in Lou, who showed promise early.

"He could box," Elbaum said of Lou. "He wasn't a big puncher, but he had heart galore."

Lou began training with Stan "Stan Rocky" Rzodkiewicz, a devout Catholic and longtime Erie boxing trainer. Lou credited Stan Rocky with teaching him how to train, which would be essential in his bout with Duran. Lou opted not to lift weights because he felt it would compromise his speed. Instead, he ran four-to-five miles per day, followed by a gym workout that included hitting the speed bag and jumping rope.

His training allowed for a style that made him hard to hit. Lou, a lightweight, danced from side to side as frustrated opponents struggled to land punches. When Lou turned 18, Elbaum turned him pro without a single amateur fight to his name.

It didn't matter. With Stan Rocky and Sonny Liston trainer Joe Pollino in his corner, Lou won his first fight against Pittsburgh's Herman Dunbar by decision. Lou called Dunbar a "tough kid," but said it was an "easy" win. After that, though, Lou entered into a two-year hiatus. Elbaum had left Erie, and Lou said he didn't want anyone else to promote his fights.

In 1967, Lou asked another Lou, well-known local entrepreneur Lou Porreco, to manage him. Porreco had one condition: If Lou was going to do this, he had to be all in.

"'You work out, you do your homework right, I'll get you to fight for a championship of the world,'" Lou recalled Porreco telling him.

Lou responded with tenacity. He trained hard and won his first 22 fights.

"I didn't take nobody for granted," he said. "If I fought you today and won, (and) I fight you again, I'm gonna be in better shape."

In 1975, Lou fought and defeated both Hector Matta and Benny Huertas, both of whom Duran had already beaten.

The victory over Matta catapulted Lou into the top 10 of the lightweight division. With the ranking came esteem, and in 1976 Porreco made good on his word to get Lou a shot at the title.

According to Elbaum, Porreco helped put up the money for the bout with Duran. Elbaum was friendly with legendary trainer Ray Arcel, who returned to boxing after two decades away to train Duran. Arcel had trained 16 championship fighters before he was assaulted with a lead pipe outside of a Boston hotel in 1953. Though the culprit was never caught, it was later reported by the New York Post that the assault was a warning from members of the Italian American Mafia. Reportedly, Arcel had been helping to organize bouts for a television show that the mob saw as competition to a boxing program they endorsed.

Duran had won the WBA's lightweight title from Ken Buchanan in 1972 and had successfully defended it several times. Under the rules of the WBA, Duran was mandated to again defend his belt.

Elbaum said he approached Arcel about the possibility of a fight.

"Ray, I want to make my kid (fight with) Duran," Elbaum said.

"'Don, you gonna be able to afford him?'" Elbaum recalled Arcel asking him.

Elbaum's reply was doubtless: "I think this thing's gonna be great."

Lou recalled Porreco calling him to his office on Peach Street, where he asked his fighter if he would be willing to fight Duran. Lou didn't hesitate; he was all in.

Elbaum said Arcel agreed to the bout on the basis of their good relationship. He also said Duran was willing to fight Lou on the word of Arcel.

"Ray Arcel was like a father to Duran," he said.

Lou's slice of the pie was minuscule: a mere $10,000 to Duran's $125 grand. Notorious promoter Don King, who also was involved in the fight, was given $10,000.

"'I don't care,'" Lou recalled saying about the money. "'Because I'm gonna beat him, and I'm gonna make more money anyways.'"

Lou's confidence and optimism were not widely shared. Duran was known to be fierce, both in and out of the ring.

"Hands of Stone" grew up in "The House of Stone," the La Casa De Piedra district in the slums of Panama City, Panama. He earned his nickname because he punched fast and he punched hard. He also benefited from elite training, not only from Arcel, but also from Freddie Brown, an expert cutman who had been in Rocky Marciano's corner.

"At the time, he was just unstoppable," said Kipp Elbaum, Don Elbaum's son and a "gopher" who helped set up tables and run the weigh-in before the fight.

Don Elbaum offered even higher praise.

"Duran, in his time, was like Muhammad Ali," he said.

But while Ali was charismatic and personable, Duran — at least in front of the cameras — could be hostile and aggressive. Philadelphia boxing legend Joe Frazier later compared Duran not to another boxer, but to Charles Manson, the notorious cult leader who led his followers to commit nine murders in 1969.

By the time he was set to fight Lou, Duran held a record of 55-1-0, with 46 wins by knockout. Lou, though, had compiled an impressive record of his own: 22-0-0, including seven knockouts.

Lou's own cornermen were no slouches. In addition to Stan Rocky and Father Geddes, he had Luther Burgess, of Detroit's renowned Kronk's Gym, and veteran cutman Arthur "Artie Curley" Salzman on his side.

"I had a good team," Lou said.

Initially, the fight was set to take place in Monaco. However, CBS bought the television rights to the fight, and moved it, of all places, to Erie, Pennsylvania.

By today's standards, Erie being home to a world championship boxing match would seem far-fetched and wildly unorthodox. But back then, ranked boxers more commonly entered the ring in smaller venues, or even in their challengers' backyards. In 1975, Muhammad Ali defended his heavyweight title against Chuck Wepner in the village of Richfield, Ohio. Wepner nearly went the distance with Ali, and some — including Wepner himself — assert that he is the basis for the character of Rocky Balboa. A few years later, in 1978, "Sugar" Ray Leonard ventured to Boston to fight Dicky Eklund, of nearby Lowell, Massachusetts.

Lou, for one, was thrilled at the prospect of contending for a world championship belt in his hometown.

"(I wanted to) do something that's never been done before in Erie," he said. "The championship-of-the-world fight."

There was only one problem. When CBS got the rights, the network moved the fight to a Sunday. Pennsylvania's "blue laws" outlawed boxing matches on a Sunday. Don Elbaum said the Erie mayor at the time, Lou Tullio, contacted Pennsylvania Governor Milton Shapp, who in turn ensured the fight would go on as planned. He also said the fight was still sanctioned by the WBA.

Kipp, who was 19 years old at the time, recalled that the community's initial skepticism about the fight turned into excitement as the bout got closer and closer. Especially when Don King showed up.

By that time, King was already, as Kipp put it, "a friggin' legend." He got his start as a promoter with the help of Don Elbaum, and together in 1972 they organized an exhibition match for Muhammad Ali in Cleveland, Ohio. As for jump-starting King's career, Don Elbaum later was quoted in *Sports Illustrated* as quipping, "I've been apologizing to the world ever since."

King, who had promoted "The Rumble In The Jungle" between heavyweight champion George Foreman and challenger Ali, had an unmistakable charisma to him. Kipp described him as "very, very, polite" and "bigger than life." Talking to King, one may never have suspected he had served time in prison after stomping to death an employee who owed him $600.

"The crimes he had committed were known, but he had such a charm about him and such a way to look you in the eye and just say nice things, and just knew how to get to you," Kipp said.

National media outlets flocked to the event. This included Dick Young, legendary sportswriter for the *New York Daily News*. As the fight got play in the press, so did the city.

"That was a huge move for Erie," Kipp said.

With all the buzz, there was still the matter of the actual fight. Lou was an 8-1 underdog, with some predicting that he wouldn't make it past the first three rounds.

Known for his speed, Lou had one plan: never stop moving. He knew if he stood toe to toe with Duran, he'd feel the full force of his punches. Stan Rocky advised Lou to move side to side with the mind that, hopefully, Duran would tire out after 10 rounds.

Don Elbaum was confident the plan could work.

"Styles can beat you," he said.

Kipp agreed.

"Louie, I don't think he had a great chance, but he had a chance," he said. "He could slip and move, he was fast as hell — get in there, you know, stick and run. There (were) some hopes that he would frustrate Duran, and when fighters get frustrated they make mistakes."

As for Duran? Former highly ranked heavyweight and the fight's color commentator, Jerry Quarry, said during the match he had previously asked Duran what his plan was.

"'I'm gonna try like heck to catch him,'" Quarry recalled Duran saying.

To aid in Lou's strategy, Don Elbaum had a ring made that was larger than the standard 16-to-20 feet, and had a hard canvas so Lou could roam freely and quickly.

Though Lou was quoted as refuting the ring's larger size in Christian Guidice's *Hands of Stone: The Life and Legend of Roberto Duran*, Don Elbaum confirmed that it was 24 feet.

According to *Hands of Stone*, when Arcel saw the size of the ring, he told Don Elbaum, "I thought you had class."

The referee for the fight was Waldemar Schmidt, whom Lou and his team had thought was from Germany. To Lou's chagrin, he learned that Schmidt was from Puerto Rico. Due to Schmidt's heritage, Lou was concerned the ref would favor the Panama native Duran. Don Elbaum, however, said Schmidt "did a good job."

As the fight drew nearer, the lightweight champion of the world came to Erie. The young Kipp was tasked with showing Duran around. Despite the language barrier — Duran spoke very little English — they enjoyed each other's company. Smiling and laughing, Duran resembled more the man who entered boxing to buy his mother a house than the 133-pound terror with fists like concrete.

"Everybody's going, 'Oh God, I can't believe you gotta do that, because this guy's an asshole,'" Kipp said. "No, this guy's a great guy."

Duran loved riding around Erie's peninsula, and took a shine to Kipp. "I wasn't eating enough and he's looking at me like, 'I'm gonna get you more food,'" Kipp said. "He wanted to take care of me, also."

True to form, and as displayed in the 2016 Duran biopic *Hands of Stone*, the champ loved his ice cream. He and Kipp made sure to stop at the Whippy Dip on West 26th Street.

Duran, though, was anything but soft-serve during a pre-fight press conference. According to the book *Hands of Stone*, while Lou was friendly to his opponent, Duran stood up and said in Spanish what amounted to just a few words of English.

His translator said Duran declared he'd send Lou home in an ambulance.

Physically speaking, the fighters were nearly identically matched. Both men were 5-foot-7. Duran had the edge in reach, with 65 inches to Lou's 64, while Lou (134 pounds) had nearly a pound on Duran (133 ¼ pounds). Duran, at 24, was three years younger than the 27-year-old Lou.

By the time of the weigh-in, the city was alive with excitement. But there was one person who didn't want the fight to happen: Lou's mother.

A few weeks before the fight, Jennie Bizzarro pleaded with her son to call it off.

"'Louie, don't fight,'" Lou recalled her telling him.

"Mom, I got to," he told her.

"Don't fight," she persisted. "I'll call Lou Porreco and tell him I don't want you to fight."

Despite her assertions, the fight would go on as planned. And by the afternoon of May 23, 1976, it was time for the main event.

Nearly 3,000 fans packed into the Erie County Field House off Route 8. The Field House was chosen as the venue because it was the only place in Erie County big enough to host the event.

Kipp, who sat ringside at the fight, said Lou's team was far from fond of the Field House.

"It was concrete and tin, so there was no warmth to the place," he said.

If the venue was chilly, the excitement over the bout was smoldering. By fight day, nobody in Erie was bad-mouthing the match anymore. They just wanted to see the local boy knock the crown off the champion's head.

"The crowd was loud — that place was a real ringy place anyway, because of the way it was built — so when anything would happen, that crowd, it would just echo in that room," Kipp said.

The reverberations of enthusiasm from Lou's family — including cousins who had flown in from Italy — as well as his friends and supporters, both motivated him and put pressure on him.

"It was great," Lou said. "It was tough, though, knowing all these people were there. I wanted to look good, I wanted to do something."

Former Philadelphia Eagles defensive back Tom Brookshier was on to call the fight. Joining him was Quarry, a prominent heavyweight known as "The Bellflower Bomber." Quarry is perhaps best known for being the only Top 10-ranked boxer who was willing to fight Muhammad Ali following Ali's suspension from boxing after refusing entry into the U.S. Army.

As soon as the bell rang, Lou's feet were moving. He bounced around like a jackrabbit, dancing in and out of Duran's reach.

"(Duran) didn't like when a person moved," Lou said. "If you stand in front of him, that's what he loved. But that's where he'll knock you out."

He hit Duran with a few jabs early, but Duran responded with an uppercut.

"He's done the right thing, now," Quarry said during the fight of Lou's strategy. "But he's gonna have to use his jab a little more effectively if he's going to win this fight."

Round 2 began the same way, with Lou still moving like he was walking on hot coals. He landed a right hand, which caused Duran to smile. The title defender hit back, dodging a punch and uppercutting Lou.

Just as Lou stuck to his speed, Duran was relentless with his fists.

"He wouldn't back up or nothing," Lou said. "He kept throwing punches."

Another, more consequential punch came at the end of the round. The bell rang early, at about two-and-a-half minutes in. Duran's arm was already in motion when it rang, and he hit Lou with a hard uppercut to the ribs.

Lou was hurt. He had, for the first time, felt the full effect of "Hands of Stone."

"You look at him, say, '135 pounds, how hard can he hit?'" Lou said, before adding with a laugh, "Get hit by him, you'll see."

The effect of the blow slowed Lou in Round 3 and saw Duran with a newfound air of confidence. Quarry, however, gave the round to Lou.

"I had to give it to him because he landed the more effective punches and he did a lot of moving, and he kind of outboxed Duran that round," Quarry said.

Round 4 found Lou reenergized, drawing a comparison from Brookshier to classic actor/dancer Fred Astaire. Partway through the round, he sparred with Duran in the center of the ring. Lou caught Duran in an awkward position and hit him with a right hand. Duran went down to wild fanfare from the crowd. He bounced right back up and waved his glove, as if to say it was a slip. The referee agreed, but there is still debate about the call.

"I think he knocked him down," Don Elbaum said.

Duran was undeterred. He connected with body shots, while Lou's hyperactive strategy prevented him from landing any solid punches. Quarry gave the round to Duran.

Duran continued to land forceful body shots in Round 5. Lou attempted to exchange blows with him, which Quarry said was a big mistake.

Stan Rocky had told Lou while in their corner to stick to his strategy, so Lou continued to bounce off his toes in Round 6. Brookshier called Lou a "dancing master," but Duran was getting heated.

As the fight went on, the fighters began jawing at each other.

"You bum, you can't fight," Lou told him.

The challenger's taunt had the effect of smacking a tiger in the face.

"He understood," Lou said. "He came after me like a gangbuster. I said, 'Holy God!'"

Still, Duran couldn't catch him.

"Roberto Duran is a frustrated champion right now," Brookshier said. The crowd, too, was restless. Lou even drew some boos for continuing to move.

"It was Louie's style," Kipp said. "Louie won a helluva lot of fights with that style."

Mostly, though, the crowd stood behind Lou. There was no doubt this boosted his energy.

"I've seen fighters fighting in their hometown that are getting beat, but the crowd stays behind them and they come out with the win," Kipp said. "They get that motivation where your whole body says, 'Stop,' and you keep going."

Round 7 saw Duran again frustrated at his inability to catch Lou.

"He's fighting a roadrunner in there, and I'm sure he'd like to find out a few of Wile E. Coyote's tricks to catch him," Quarry quipped.

Round after round, Lou kept going. And Don Elbaum thought his chances of winning were solid.

"I thought Lou was gonna go the distance," he said. "I thought he had a shot to win. And in my mind, going the distance would have been like, 'Wow.'"

Quarry, though, had said one round earlier that he didn't think Lou's strategy would win him the fight. And Quarry knew that, like a single, strong gust of wind during a tornado, it might only take one heavy blow from "Hands of Stone" to take down Lou.

And yet, Duran kept missing, which only made him madder. Twice, he fell to the canvas in Round 7, but his contact both times was ruled a slip.

Whether Lou hit Duran with a hard punch or a soft jab, the Erie natives in the crowd cheered for their hero with a sound like a dynamite blast.

"I'll tell you, Erie, Pennsylvania is on fire right now," Brookshier said.

Lou kept up his blazing quickness in the eighth, drawing a comparison from Quarry to the then heavyweight champ.

"(Lou) does remind me of Muhammad Ali in 1965," Quarry said.

Still, as Lou moved, Duran stuck. He continued to connect with punches that didn't punish Lou, but still earned him points.

"I think Duran might catch him," Quarry said in Round 9.

He finally did in the 10th round. Duran hit Lou with a hard right hand, followed by a left and another right on Lou's way to the canvas.

Lou got up, but then dropped to one knee. After he reached his feet, Duran went into attack mode. He rained down blows on his challenger, as Lou did all he could to stay on his feet before falling in the middle of the ring.

"He's not going to get up on this one," Quarry said.

And yet, just before the round ended, Lou rose to his feet. He was helped to his chair after the bell.

The plan had been to wear down Duran with his speed. But Duran, as fast as he was fierce, didn't slow down.

Lou looked at Stan Rocky.

"I thought you said he was gonna get tired," Lou said.

Quarry, who in Round 11 said he thought Lou was down for longer than 10 seconds in the 10th, knew very well the impact Duran's knockdowns had had on the Erieite.

"He could not have recovered completely from that," Quarry said.

But Lou, without an ounce of quit coursing through his veins, had arguably his strongest round in the 11th. He was still moving, but he was also landing shots to Duran. The crowd roared as Lou hit him with a hard right hand.

"There (were) enough people there that saw it and knew it, and knew the hometown hero had really done it," Kipp said. "He hurt the greatest fighter in the world."

Brookshier and Quarry were also impressed, with Quarry going as far as to say Lou was winning the round.

"They've seen him dance all night," Quarry said. "Now they're seeing him fight."

As Don Elbaum said, styles can beat you. But it may have been Lou's own style that was his downfall.

Instead of following up with more hard shots, Lou reverted to jabbing and moving. Once he saw that, Kipp knew it was over.

"Would he have knocked out Roberto Duran if (he continued) throwing punches?" Kipp said. "We'll never know."

Through Round 12, Duran was fierce and Lou was resilient. It was apparent to Brooksheir that Lou must have known he wasn't going to win at this point. Instead, Brooksheir said, the goal must have been to go the distance.

As for Duran, he was throwing punches with a ferocity that had earned him his nickname.

"Duran just wants to hit him," Brooksheir said. "He doesn't care what it is."

Though Lou was cut near his right eye, he stood tall throughout Round 13. The announcers were enjoying Lou's spirit so much that they found levity amidst the brutality. Quarry noted that Lou's take was just $10,000 for the fight.

"Do you think the IRS would have the nerve to take any of it?" Brooksheir asked Quarry.

"I hope not," Quarry replied.

It appeared as though Lou would go the distance. The crowd continued to cheer on their hero.

"If you're not pulling for Lou Bizzarro this afternoon — win, lose or draw — there's something wrong with you because the champion's gonna keep his crown," Brooksheir said. "There's no doubt about that."

At the start of the 14th round, Brookshier had crowned Lou the "king of Erie, Pennsylvania" while calling Duran the "king of the whole world."

"I never thought I'd like to spend an entire afternoon in Erie, Pennsylvania," Brooksheir said. "This has been some kind of fight."

But then, Lou finally gave Duran what he wanted. He stepped in to brawl with the champ, and Duran hit him with a vicious combination of punches. Lou took a standing eight count, and Duran quickly followed a strong left with a hard right.

Lou was knocked down, but he bounced right back up. He was hurt, though, and it showed.

Johnny saw his younger brother wounded, and dashed up the steps of the ring to stop the fight. Don Elbaum grabbed him to stop him, and they tussled outside of the ring as the fight continued.

"I really thought Louie had a shot to go the distance with him, and as the fight went on I was sure," Don Elbaum said.

But Duran hit Lou with one more brutal right hand, and Lou went down. As soon as he hit the canvas, Schmidt stopped the fight.

Lou wanted to continue, but understood why the fight was halted.

"I was hurt, or they wouldn't have stopped it," he said.

Duran was victorious, and remained the lightweight champion of the world. But Lou had earned a victory of his own; he won the hearts of the people of Erie.

"Win, lose or draw, Louie was a legitimate hero at that time from that fight," Kipp said.

Don Elbaum shared his son's sentiment.

"Lou fought his heart out," he said.

Lou, though, was depressed. He said he had burned himself out by overtraining, which he said had kept him from having the speed and stamina to see his strategy through 15 rounds.

"If I wouldn't have overtrained, (Duran) would have never knocked me out, believe me," Lou said.

Jennie Bizzarro offered words of solace to her son.

"'Louie, as long as you're OK,'" Lou recalled her saying. "'You didn't get hurt.'"

She also echoed the sentiment shared by the rest of Erie: Lou had done well.

Undeniably, he had made Erie proud.

Duran went on to have a legendary career that included title victories in four weight divisions and a victory over "Sugar" Ray Leonard. His name is synonymous with the infamous "No Mas" title fight, during which he quit in a rematch with Leonard. Duran refuted sportscaster Howard Cosell's assertion that he said, "No mas," stating he actually said to himself, "No sigo," which translates from Spanish to English as "I'm not going any further."

However, he completed a years-long comeback by claiming the WBA World Super Welter Title over defending champion Davey Moore in 1983.

He went on to compile a 103-16-0 record before retiring in 2002. He joined Jack Johnson as the only boxers in history to fight professionally in five decades. In 2006, he was inducted into the World Boxing Hall of Fame. And in 2020, he won a fight of a different kind; he survived a battle with the coronavirus, for which he was hospitalized.

Lou fought for six more years and only lost one more fight. He never fought anyone as famous as Duran again, but he finished with an outstanding 31-2-0 record. He opened Lou Bizzarro's Ringside Restaurant at the intersection of Sterrettania Road and West 32nd Street in Millcreek Township, just minutes from the City of Erie.

Lou also began training boxers at his gym in Erie. He trained childhood friend and Marine Corps boxing champion Ron DiNicola, and he also helped keep boxing the family business by training his nephew, Johnny Bizzarro Jr., and his son, Lou Bizzarro Jr. Both had excellent careers, with Johnny Jr. winning titles in multiple weight classes and Lou Jr. contending for the International Boxing Council Americas Super Lightweight Title in 2002. Lou also trained his son, Joe Louis Bizzarro, who went 4-1-0 in five fights.

Lou became a staple of community philanthropy through Knockout Homelessness. The annual event since 2008 is a partnership with the Erie City Mission and raises money to increase awareness of homelessness and to support the mission's Samaritan Care Shelter. The show has featured Lou boxing with local celebrities. However, due to Lou's genuine affection for Erie, the event is much more than a publicity stunt.

Lou said that, despite pressure to move to a bigger city, he would not leave Erie.

"Erie's been good to me, really," he said. "The people (have) been good. And I like that.

"I love Erie."

Now in his seventies, Lou spends much of his time at Bizzarro's Boxing Gym at the corner of West 16th Street and Pittsburgh Avenue, which he co-owns with Erie attorney John Evanoff. When he's not there, he can often be found at the front table of Ringside Restaurant. In an era of trendy eateries for foodies, the mom 'n pop Italian restaurant is one of the last of its kind. The place is homey and nostalgic, with framed photographs of famous boxers and celebrities adorning the walls. The restaurant has been visited by household names such as Sylvester Stallone (in a meeting of the underdogs), former First Lady and U.S. Senator Hilary Clinton and Pro Football Hall of Fame quarterback Jim Kelly.

Another familiar figure also visited the restaurant. Many years after that afternoon in May 1976, Roberto Duran paid his old competitor a visit.

Lou greeted his former opponent and they chatted together. Duran told Lou he had been told before the fight that Lou couldn't punch hard. After fighting Lou, Duran thought he had been given some bad intel.

"'Lou, you were tough,'" Lou recalled Duran saying.

"Roberto, so were you," Lou told him.

It was a sentiment Duran echoed in the decades since the match.

"Duran always said Lou gave him a helluva fight," Don Elbaum said. Don Elbaum had a long and storied career as a promoter, and was inducted into the International Boxing Hall of Fame in 2019. In addition to Muhammad Ali and "Sugar" Ray Robinson, Elbaum organized and promoted fights for renowned boxers such as Willie Pep and Floyd Patterson. And yet, he considers the Bizzarro-Duran fight one of the highlights of his career.

"I've done many great ones, and this is like, 'Wow, this sticks out,'" he said.

For Kipp, who went on to become a live music promoter in New York City, the title fight of '76 is a bittersweet memory. While he called the bout "the pinnacle of Erie boxing," he said the town hasn't had a boxing event near that level since.

"It was a great day for Erie boxing," he said. "But I also think it was maybe the defining moment."

Lou, though, looks back on his title shot with a mixture of personal and communal pride.

"I was proud that I could do something and bring the fight here to Erie," he said. "That's what I did it for."

Photo by Howard Bingham
(provided by R. DiNicola and courtesy of Dustin Bingham)

Muhammd Ali gives an "Athlete of the Century" ring to Erie native Ron DiNicola, who was Ali's attorney and close friend for three decades. The rings, given to members of Ali's team, were made to commemorate multiple honors bestowed upon Ali for being the greatest athlete of the 20th century. These included *Sports Illustrated*'s "Sportsman of the Century" award.

Defending Champ

By Aaron McKrell

"The champ is here."
It was a simple enough statement, declared by Muhammad Ali upon his arrival in Kinshasa, Zaire in 1974 to fight George Foreman in what was dubbed "The Rumble in the Jungle."
To be clear, Ali was not the heavyweight champion of the world. At least, not anymore. He'd been unjustly stripped of his title and barred from boxing after refusing induction into the U.S. Army in 1967. After returning to boxing, Ali lost "The Fight of the Century" in a 15-round decision to defending heavyweight champion Joe Frazier. A few years later, he watched as Frazier was pummeled to the canvas by Foreman in fewer than two rounds.
That didn't stop Ali from arriving in Zaire (now the Democratic Republic of the Congo) like a prodigal son. He dazzled reporters and citizens alike with a self-aware twinkle in his eye as rhymes about his excellence rolled off his tongue.
"I have murdered a rock, I injured a stone, and I hospitalized a brick," he rattled off. "I'm so bad I make medicine sick."
The people of Zaire threw their arms and hearts around Ali. Yet, the vast majority of sportswriters and even diehard boxing fans around the world didn't see it his way. Ali was 32 years old, and many thought his best years were behind him. In stark contrast, the 25-year-old Foreman was renowned for his brute force, and at 40-0-0 had never lost a fight.
But there was at least one person who believed Ali had a chance: a skinny teenager from the west side of Erie, Pennsylvania, named Ronnie DiNicola.
DiNicola was in his element, advocating for Ali to his classmates at Cathedral Prep. Brought up on the lore of his uncle Carlo DiNicola's boxing career, DiNicola had been caught up in what he called the "mythology of boxing" as a young boy. It wasn't long before he laced up his own pair of gloves. And, when he wasn't landing punches in the ring as a lightweight fighter, he was delivering knockout speeches for Cathedral Prep's debate team. As both an analytical thinker and a boxer, DiNicola knew a master strategist such as Ali should never be

counted out.

The 17-year-old DiNicola became so convinced of Ali's chances that he penned a letter to *Erie Daily Times* sports editor Dick Stone making a case for Ali. DiNicola said in the letter, which was printed in its entirety, that Foreman had never faced a boxer with Ali's versatility, cunning and command of the ring.

So, when Ali employed his brilliant rope-a-dope strategy to exhaust Foreman and win by a stunning knockout in October 1974, DiNicola was delighted but not surprised.

DiNicola's optimism may have been bolstered by his own David vs. Goliath experience just months before the Ali-Foreman bout.

Cathedral Prep held its annual St. Patrick Fight Night, and DiNicola's matchup with Frank Serbati was the main event out of 15 fights.

The bout carried some extra gravitas in that it was essentially a culmination of an old-school Erie rivalry. In DiNicola's corner were local ring legend Lou Bizzarro, longtime trainer Stan "Stan Rocky" Rzodkiewicz and DiNicola's cousin, former Golden Gloves champion Vinnie DiNicola. Serbati was bolstered by area boxing legend Johnny Seaman and renowned bodybuilder/wrestler Mike Pistorio. The men in both corners were as invested in the outcome as anyone in the arena that night.

Serbati was experienced, talented and clearly the more muscular of the two. When DiNicola stepped into the ring and looked across at Serbati, he had one thought:

What the $#@! am I doing here?

But, not unlike his hero Ali — or his trainer Bizzarro — DiNicola employed his dance-like, stick-and-move style smartly and won in a split decision. What's more, the fight had been held in front of a standing-room-only crowd at Cathedral Prep that included almost everyone DiNicola knew. It wasn't "The Rumble in the Jungle," but for a kid from Erie, it might as well have been.

Both Ali and DiNicola won the biggest fights of their careers to that point, but they were at very different points in their lives. Ali was, in the minds of many, now etched in stone as "The Greatest" of all time. DiNicola, meanwhile, had yet to graduate high school, let alone do all of the things that would make him a household name in Erie and a respected lawyer nationwide.

Yet, both men were motivated by similar things both in and out of the ring: a sense of justice, a commitment to their principles and a pride that influenced everything they did. These shared values played a big part in a three-decades-long friendship between the two that was born of a professional relationship.

Though DiNicola downplays the suggestion, it is evident the two men benefited greatly from one another. Ali could count on DiNicola to be a trusted attorney, adviser and friend who would protect him from the unscrupulous. DiNicola, meanwhile, soaked up lessons about integrity, respect and the importance of living in the moment, simply by watching Ali live his life. Ali's life was so purposeful that none of it could possibly have happened by chance.

Two things happened when Ali was 12 and 13 years old that would shape his life forever. When Ali — then known as Cassius Clay — was 12, his bicycle was stolen from him. He reported the theft to Louisville, Kentucky police officer Joe Elsby Martin, who happened to run a boxing gym. Martin began to train the young Clay, who quickly showed promise in the sport. It was an encounter with a white cop who cared, and it set in motion a career that needs no introduction. Something else happened to Ali about a year later that was equally impactful. A 14-year-old African American boy named Emmett Till was brutally murdered after saying "Bye, baby" to a white woman in a store in Mississippi. Till's mutilated corpse was pictured on the cover of *Jet*, an African American magazine, with the permission of his mother, Mamie Till-Mobley.

"Let the people see what they did to my boy," she had said.

Her self-sacrificing courage proved life-changing for the 13-year-old Clay, who was shaken by the gruesome murder of a boy around his age.

"I realized that this could just as easily have been a story about me or my brother," Ali was quoted as saying in Timothy B. Tyson's *The Blood of Emmett Till.*

The story of Till stuck with him into adulthood, and even in his later years he often raised the matter with DiNicola.

"It disturbed him to the core," DiNicola said.

As a young man, Clay joined the Nation of Islam, changed his name to Muhammad Ali and befriended Islamic minister/human rights activist Malcolm X.

It was a conversion Ali initially kept quiet. The Nation of Islam was decried for its separatist views in contrast to the ecumenical civil rights movement led by Dr. Martin Luther King Jr.

King espoused the nonviolent teachings of Jesus and Mahatma Gandhi, which connected with a broader audience including white America. A grade-school-aged DiNicola, who grew up in a traditional

Italian American household, was one white kid who couldn't get enough of King. "Squawk Box," as DiNicola was called by his family for his propensity for endless chatter, would entertain his friends at Erie's west side ball fields by reciting King's famous speeches.

Chest out, head held high, the young DiNicola would let his voice ring out around the field — and later, the classroom — as he emulated his hero.

"I have a dream," he'd bellow, "that one day this nation will rise up and live out the true meaning of its creed: 'We hold these truths to be self-evident: that all men are created equal.'"

Yet, DiNicola wasn't immune to some of the misguided political views of the era. Like so many Americans, a preteen DiNicola held what he'd later call a "kid's mixed-up view" of the Vietnam War. His older brother, Louis, was a U.S. Marine at the Da Nang airbase in Vietnam. DiNicola feared for his brother's life, and didn't want to think it was all for nothing. And so, when Ali refused induction into the U.S. Army, DiNicola was confused.

"I was too young to know what Muhammad was doing or why he was doing it," DiNicola said. "I was still in the clouds of the issue."

Most of America — including those in the justice system — joined him there. Ali was convicted of felony draft evasion and faced five years' imprisonment while his heavyweight belt was stripped from him and his passport was revoked so he couldn't fight abroad. He also faced a bevy of financial issues while fighting the verdict in court.

Ali's freedom wasn't the only thing at stake. The Sixties witnessed the killings of prominent political and cultural figures at an alarmingly commonplace rate. By the time of Ali's conviction, civil rights leader Medgar Evers, President John F. Kennedy and Malcolm X had been assassinated. Even Sam Cooke, poignant soul singer and Ali's close friend, had been killed under what many consider to be suspicious circumstances. And — before Ali's case was resolved by the U.S. Supreme Court — King, Kennedy's brother — presidential hopeful Bobby Kennedy, and Black Panther Party leaders Bobby Hutton and Fred Hampton all would be killed. Ali, who was targeted for surveillance by FBI Director J. Edgar Hoover, was at significant risk of suffering the same fate.

"Given his profile, the fact that Muhammad was able to make it through a period of indiscriminate violence, high emotions and unsettled racial issues was not something he took for granted," DiNicola said.

But, as DiNicola later said, Ali was unique in that he was not trying to start a movement with his actions. It was simply a matter of principle for him.

"I will not disgrace my religion, my people or myself by becoming a tool to enslave those who are fighting for their own justice, freedom and equality," Ali said in a statement in 1967.

Ali's religious tenet was recognized in 1971 by the U.S. Supreme Court, which ruled in his favor by unanimous decision. DiNicola, who had changed his tune on the war after conversations with his friend and mentor Ronnie Maris, was doubly overjoyed. For one, he knew a free Ali meant more great fights. More importantly, he knew justice had been served.

As DiNicola later reflected, Ali changed his name in 1964, but he didn't truly become the Muhammad Ali the world would come to know and love until he risked everything he had because of his beliefs.

"We are of our politics," DiNicola said. "It does shape us, and it shapes us all the way to our character."

By that time, DiNicola was training under Bizzarro and fighting in regional amateur bouts. But his biggest fight of all would come soon enough, and would underscore yet another connection to Ali.

Photo provided by R. DiNicola

HBO announcer and International Boxing Hall of Famer Emanuel Steward considered the 1975 All-Marine Corps Boxing Team one of the best of the golden era of U.S. amateur boxing. Olympic bronze medalist Art Redden coached the team: (from left) J.C. Wade, Tony Wilson, Leon Spinks, Ronnie DiNicola, Lenis Provo, Fran Gillon, J.D. Williamson, Ricky Witt, Roger Stafford and Alvin Towns.

When DiNicola announced he wanted to join the U.S. Marines, Louis DiNicola made it a point to look out for his little brother. He mapped out a plan that involved his brother joining the Marines while affording him the chance to pursue his boxing dreams without stalling his education.

As planned, DiNicola wore his uniform every day but still spent a lot of time in his boxing trunks. He signed himself up for a series of amateur bouts dubbed "smokers." He won every match and was invited by Marine Corps boxing coach and Olympic medalist Art Redden to try out for the Camp Lejeune boxing team. His style impressed Redden and orders were cut sending DiNicola to the team full time.

He knew he had arrived when he was greeted by Leon Spinks, a national champion, and Fran Gillon, the former Golden Gloves champion of Philadelphia. Spinks was a light heavyweight from urban St. Louis who was as kind outside of the ring as he was ferocious in it. DiNicola admired Spinks' abilities and predicted that Spinks would ultimately become a heavyweight, a suggestion Spinks resisted.

Spinks didn't drive, so he turned to DiNicola to give him rides to his off-base girlfriend's house. Along the way they became friends, and Spinks paid DiNicola back in a major way.

DiNicola made his move up the ranks of Marine Corps boxing. He won the Carolinas Golden Gloves Championship in Charlotte, North Carolina, by defeating Olympic prospect Willie Adams, 47-6, in the finals.

But his biggest fight was for the Marine Corps Boxing Championship, held at the packed Camp Lejeune Field House. Spinks was not only in DiNicola's corner for the fight; he was in his ear.

"The crowd was fired up and making a lot of noise," DiNicola recalls. "Leon had walked with me to the ring. He had wedged himself against the ring apron — he should not have been there but no one in their right mind would tell Leon to move. Somehow, I could hear his deep voice clearly above the crowd. At that moment I trusted him completely, and I followed his direction."

Spinks coached DiNicola's every move.

"Right hand, right hand, again, again, — now left hook," Spinks dictated.

It was the polar opposite of DiNicola's style; he never took a step backward throughout the entire fight. It worked, and he became the Marine Corps Champion.

"I owe Spinks for that," DiNicola said.

Spinks eventually did become a heavyweight, and in 1978 beat — who else? — Ali for the title. Ali won it back from Spinks a year later, and soon retired in 1981 after showing signs of onset Parkinson's Disease. Ali's illness inevitably thrust him into a new chapter of his life. Meanwhile, DiNicola left the Marines, won two more fights and heeded the advice of his family and Bizzarro to pursue his education at Harvard University on the GI Bill. After graduating from Harvard, DiNicola went on to earn his law degree from Georgetown University and entered into a federal court clerkship in Erie and Pittsburgh. His Harvard classmate George Jackson, who would go on to become the President of Motown Records, had been asking DiNicola to come work with him in Los Angeles. Following the clerkship, that's exactly what DiNicola did.

DiNicola, who was trained as a trial lawyer, joined a prominent L.A. business and entertainment firm, and soon began moonlighting as an entertainment attorney. Jackson connected him to renowned sports photographer Howard Bingham, who was already one of the greatest photographers in American history and was best friends with Ali. DiNicola and Bingham clicked immediately, and Bingham — who took photos for the Los Angeles Sentinel — showed DiNicola around town and helped him make contacts.

"Hey," Bingham said one day. "You wanna meet Muhammad Ali?"

By the 1980s, Ali had fallen on hard times. He had lost a brutal fight to Larry Holmes in 1980, had been hospitalized for Parkinson's Disease and was facing more money woes. In 1982, he was embroiled in a lawsuit with boxing promoter Don King. The suit claimed King had defrauded Ali out of $1.2 million of an $8 million payout from his bout with Holmes. King reportedly sent an old friend of Ali's to where Ali was hospitalized with a suitcase full of $50,000 and a written agreement to end the lawsuit. Ali signed the agreement. His then lawyer, Michael Phenner, reportedly cried when he heard the news. However, Ali did have a bright spot in his life in the form of Yolanda "Lonnie" Williams. Their mothers had been good friends and they had known each other for more than two decades when they married in 1986.

Around that time, Lonnie Ali, a graduate of Vanderbilt University and UCLA's Anderson School of Business, got to work building a team around her husband that would both protect and build upon his legacy.

One of the first additions to that team? Ron DiNicola.

DiNicola and Ali met at the latter's home in the Rossmore

neighborhood of L.A. in the mid-'80s. DiNicola was initially taken by the champ's personality.

"He was very much a guy who appreciated people and lived in the moment," DiNicola said.

As DiNicola soon learned, a strong team around Ali was vital.

"Muhammad couldn't say 'no' very easily," DiNicola said.

DiNicola went about ensuring that Ali got fair deals. He took care of the contractual aspects of countless projects for Ali, starting with *Muhammad Ali: His Life and Times by Thomas Hauser.*

In turn, DiNicola learned from Ali's gracious attitude toward people. Whether he was dining in L.A. or traveling in Europe, Ali was never too busy for his fans. DiNicola would watch as elderly men and women turned into five year olds before his eyes when they encountered Ali, and saw how women just loved to wrap their arms around Ali and plant a kiss on his cheek.

"People availed themselves of Muhammad instinctively," DiNicola recalls. "Other celebrities might hang back and give off an unwelcoming vibe, but not Ali. He was so big, he was like a monument, and just like the Lincoln Memorial, people felt free to go to him and take a photograph."

Ali made time for people even in his most private moments, displaying a trait of remarkable selflessness DiNicola recalls in his favorite Ali story.

Ali's mother, Odessa Clay, had died in the summer of 1994. The church was packed for her funeral. As the eldest son, Ali sat on the aisle of the front pew. The service was almost over; attendees were seated quietly in the dimly lit sanctuary. A door opened up at the front side of the church and the light pierced the moment. In the door stood a Black kid wearing blue jeans and a T-shirt. It looked like he'd been playing hard outside. The kid made a beeline to Ali, pulled out a piece of paper and handed it to him. Everyone sat in stunned silence, waiting to see how Ali would react. Ali reached into his suit pocket for a pen. About four pens came over his shoulder. He grabbed one and signed his autograph. The kid knew the church. Without missing a beat, he walked all the way to the other side of the sanctuary and made his exit out a different door. The funeral resumed.

As DiNicola said, "That moment said more about the kind of kid that Odessa Clay had raised than anything you could have said in the homily."

As time went on, Ali and DiNicola became more than client and attorney. They became friends.

"He knew that I was gonna protect him, and he knew that I was gonna be there when he needed me," DiNicola said.

DiNicola ran in a Democratic primary for a seat in the U.S. House of Representatives in 1994. He said he'd have never had the nerve to ask Ali to come to Erie to campaign for him. As it turned out, he didn't have to. The champ volunteered.

And so it was on a spring day in 1994 that Ali strolled up and down Erie's lower east side, going door to door and shocking delighted residents with his presence as he advocated for DiNicola for congress. They made stops at Booker T. Washington Center and the Boys & Girls Club of Erie, where they were welcomed by club executive director Al Messina and board member Vic Rotunda.

As Erie attorney (and later, judge) Dan Brabender chauffeured them around, Ali gained what DiNicola later said was a positive impression of Erie. He met the city's people and performed magic tricks for kids at the community centers. Ali would always reveal how he did his tricks after he did them, as it was against his religion to deceive people.

Some things stayed mostly private, though, only to be entrusted to a select few. DiNicola was one of those people, and it was part of why, as Ali intimated to the *Erie Times-News* in 2002, they became so close.

"He's honest. He's loving. He's serious. He's a good man," Ali told the *Times-News* before quipping, "He's good-looking. I love him. I like his name: Ron DiNicola...

"He's the kind of guy you can tell your secrets to."

A higher compliment, DiNicola could not imagine.

Ali returned to Erie twice in 1996. The first time, he was there when DiNicola married his wife, Monica. Just days before, DiNicola, Monica and Lonnie Ali watched from the announcers box as Ali lit the torch for the 1996 Olympic Games in Atlanta. DiNicola and Monica were two of the few people in the world who had known Ali was going to light the torch.

When Ali had first met Monica, he turned to DiNicola and said what he often told him:

"You're not as dumb as you look."

Ali also came to Erie to campaign for DiNicola as he made another run at Congress. Denise Horton and her brother, Gary — who were active in Erie's Democratic Party — accompanied them as they made stops at Plymouth Tavern and Sullivan's Pub & Eatery.

While Ali had love for all people, he also wanted to be in Erie's African American community. So, at his request, Denise Horton drove him to Gem City Elks Lodge on East 11th St.

"You could tell that he had a heart for people," Denise Horton said. "His people, especially."

And they were overjoyed to see him. Ali's car pulled up alongside a car full of African American Erie residents at the intersection of East 12th and Parade streets. When they saw Ali, they ecstatically jumped out of the car to greet him. He met them in the street, and they began shadowboxing in the heart of the east side.

Ali and DiNicola continued to work together, including on *When We Were Kings*, which in 1997 won an Academy Award for Documentary Feature. DiNicola also played a bit role as a prosecutor during the filming of the 2001 biopic *Ali*. The scene was cut from the final version of the movie, a decision DiNicola jokes about to this day.

"The fact that I was cut out of the movie, the fact that I delivered my lines perfectly and still lost the opportunity to become a star?" he laughed, "I'm not upset about that at all."

But DiNicola had a chance to do far more important work when he went along with Ali on numerous trips abroad, including a peace mission to Afghanistan in 2002.

Ali was saddened by the anti-Islamic fervor following the September 11, 2001 terrorist attacks. He had long since moved away from the Nation of Islam in favor of what he called "true Islam," which promoted racial integration and ethnic harmony. He visited New York City following the attacks, and defended his religion to reporters at Ground Zero.

"Islam is not a killer religion," Ali said. "Islam means peace."

Ali and DiNicola, a practicing Roman Catholic, would sometimes butt heads over the interpretation of the Bible. However, Ali would say that just as rivers, lakes and streams have different names but all contain water, religions have different names but all contain truth.

So, Ali — so personable and knowledgeable about world and religious matters — was the ideal person to be the United Nations representative for the Afghanistan trip. His mission was to support the U.N. in its efforts of peacekeeping and humanitarian aid. DiNicola — who had as a young lawyer traveled with the Jesuits and human rights organizations to nations fraught by violence — went along as the primary liaison between Ali and the U.N.

Tensions in Afghanistan had quieted down by the time of the mission, but it was still a dangerous place to be. Ali, though, endured as a beloved presence. He made multiple public appearances that all went smoothly.

Ali and his team were invited by then Afghanistan President Hamid Karzai to a dinner held in a large, ornate dining room of the presidential residence. The dinner included government officials, diplomats and military leaders. Each attendee had a security detail in the form of armed guards who stood shoulder to shoulder in the shadows of the tapestry that lined the walls.

"Let's say those present were not entirely allied with one another," DiNicola said. "There was a subtle tension in the room."

Ali sat next to Karzai. He looked around and broke the ice.

"You know, I really like this country," Ali told the president so all could hear. "I like the people. I think I'm gonna go out and look for an apartment tomorrow."

Laughter broke out around the table.

"It was a moment of levity amidst a sobering backdrop that only Ali could have pulled off," DiNicola said. "It was classic Muhammad."

The day Ali and his team were set to leave the country, U.N. representatives asked Ali to attend a publicized, open-air event at a local stadium. The event was not on Ali's schedule, though, and DiNicola denied the request.

"Ali was beloved in the region, but there was still a risk, particularly considering the nature of the event and the advance press of his attendance," DiNicola said. "The mission had been a success, end of story. There wasn't any need to do anything further."

Photo by Howard Bingham
(provided by R. DiNicola and courtesy of Dustin Bingham)

Muhammad Ali sits with his namesake, Alessandra "Alie" DiNicola — the daughter of Ron and Monica DiNicola — as they celebrate their shared birthday together in his home in Louisville, Kentucky.

By the time of the Afghanistan trip, Ali was more than a friend to DiNicola. He was family to him, his wife and their three daughters — Isabella, Sophia and Alessandra — who loved their "Hommy," as they called him.

Ali came to Erie one last time in 2013, when he dined with the DiNicolas at Firebirds Wood Fired Grill. He also spent time on esteemed entrepreneur Lou Porreco's yacht, sailing Lake Erie in the company of Porreco, the DiNicolas and prominent business owner Nick Scott and Scott's family.

Ali and the DiNicolas capped off the trip by going up to Niagara Falls. There, Ali's love for the moment was on display. DiNicola's daughters taught him how to take selfies, and he was captured by the experience.

The years went on and Ali grew frailer. DiNicola said Ali handled his circumstances well, and spent some of his time preparing himself for the end. He died on June 3, 2016.

"We knew it was coming, but that didn't make it any easier for my family and me," DiNicola said. "We realized the world was not going to be quite the same."

DiNicola and the rest of Ali's team and family made sure the champ's memorial service was exactly what he had wanted: a symbol of human beings' better nature. Republicans and Democrats, Baptists and Catholics, Muslims, Hindus and American Indians joined together in remembrance of one of the most compelling people the world had ever known.

On DiNicola's recommendation, Monsignor Henry Kriegel of Erie's St. Patrick Church was among those selected to speak at the service. Kriegel, as former President Bill Clinton remarked after the memorial, was the only clergy to lead service attendees in prayer.

> Our gratitude knows no bounds as we thank You for the gift
> of this good and gentle man. Muhammad Ali opened our eyes
> to the evil of racism, to the absurdity of war. He showed us
> with incredible patience that a debilitating illness
> need never diminish joy and love in our lives.

Kriegel wasn't the only one from Erie to speak at the memorial. Lonnie Ali wanted a child's voice in the service, and all of her own grandchildren were either too young to give a speech or were adults. So, she asked DiNicola if his youngest daughter, 12-year-old Alessandra — nicknamed Alie — would speak. It was a fitting request, as Alie and Ali shared the same birthday and she was named for him, though he used to call her "The Little Greatest."

While the DiNicolas were initially unsure if she'd be able to do it, Alie came through wonderfully for her buddy Muhammad, delivering a speech that summed up in his own words how he'd like to be remembered.

I'd like for them to say, 'He took a few cups of love, he took one tablespoon of patience, one teaspoon of generosity, one pint of kindness. He took one quart of laughter, one pinch of concern, and then he mixed willingness with happiness. He added lots of faith and he stirred it up well. Then he spread it over a span of a lifetime and he served it to each and every deserving person he met.

In the years since Ali's passing, DiNicola has channeled the champ's spirit into his own altruistic efforts. DiNicola managed to make an impact on Erie in a way that was inspired by Ali's meteoric rise, which was in part due to his relationship with Joe Elsby Martin.

DiNicola spearheaded an effort to reestablish the Police Athletic League in Erie after a 40-year absence. The league uses after-school athletic programs to build bonds between the Erie Police Department and the Erie County Sheriff's Office and the city's at-risk youth.

He also co-founded Empower Erie, a nonprofit organization that crafted a plan to create a community college in Erie. The plan was approved in July 2020, and DiNicola was voted chairman of the Erie Community College Board of Trustees in September 2020.

"We finally opened a door that had been slammed shut to underserved urban and rural communities in Erie County," he told the *Times-News*. "We envision a world-class workforce development center that will serve as an economic engine to provide socio-economic mobility and equity for everyone in our community."

DiNicola is still a part of Ali's legacy. He keeps in regular contact with Lonnie Ali and provides legal representation for some of Ali's children, including former boxing champion Laila Ali.

These days, DiNicola often works from his home study, which is adorned with memorabilia from his career and friendship with Ali. On occasion, he'll stop and ponder what his friend meant to the world.

Muhammad never regretted anything, even in the most difficult days of his illness, which some would say was aggravated by his career in the ring. He had chosen the life of a warrior king, and that's the fate of warrior kings. They accept their choices and carry their wounds. As sometimes happens with warrior kings, Ali became a high priest, one who impacted the entire civilization of his time by his courage, faith and the power of his presence.

Ali would say, Show me a man who is the same at 50 as he was at 25, and I'll show you a man that has wasted 25 years of his life.'

He did not pretend to be infallible, but he would not sacrifice his principles under any circumstance for money. I saw it. I know. After the ring lights came down, he was committed to one goal — getting into heaven. That was Ali. Focused, always focused.

DiNicola and the Ali family say to each other that Ali makes his presence known to them from time to time. Not so long ago, DiNicola dreamt about Ali. In the dream, Ali was signing books and DiNicola was waiting for him in line. DiNicola was OK with that because he knew he was going to see his friend. When it was his turn, he and Ali embraced and exchanged kind words. Then, DiNicola continued on his way.

He woke up, and knew everything was all right.

The champ was still here.

the Girls and the Greatest
Phoenix 2003
by Howard Bingham

Photo provided by Craig and Vanessa Schauble

Craig Schauble (left) poses for a photo with his father, Richard Schauble, who was a Strong Vincent basketball player and an All-City Section 1 selection. Craig and Richard bonded over their love of Erie sports before Richard's passing in October 2005, which occurred just before Craig began his senior boys basketball season at Villa Maria Academy. Craig started for the Victors as they reached the PIAA Class A quarterfinals in 2006.

Predestined

By Craig Schauble

Craig Schauble, an Erie native, graduated from Villa Maria Academy in 2006. He is a veteran of the United States Air Force, an air traffic controller for the Department of the Army, and lives in Enterprise, Alabama with his wife, Vanessa, and daughter, Zoey. Together, he and Vanessa own Sixtel Bottle & Growler House, which specializes in craft beer.

To say a person is predestined for their craft or their purpose is often a cliché. Happenstance leads individuals down different paths — some fit, some don't — and the term "predestination" somehow gets tossed into the mix. However, as I look back at my and my father's love affair with Erie sports and my family's love of competition, I know I was predestined to play my small role in the lore and passion of sports competition in the northwest corner of Pennsylvania.

Even now, as an adult living over 1,000 miles away, I can still feel the rush of every big game, match and tournament I had the privilege of witnessing in Erie; the classic games between Cathedral Prep and McDowell High School in the Hammermill Center or Erie Veterans Memorial Stadium, the electricity of the McDonald's Classic or Edinboro University playoff runs, and so many state championship runs.

Erie was the premier place to spend my formative years as a young athlete and sports fan. Our city was created for it and consumed by it; a quintessential melting pot of sports and sports fans united through competition. My youth was a paradise for some time, and when that changed, it was Erie athletics which proved to be my saving grace through all of my trauma.

To understand how critical this outlet was, one must first understand where it all began. My father was Richard Schauble, a Vietnam War veteran, a long-time banker, and for this story, my basketball hero.

Some of my first memories are intertwined with Erie athletics, though at the time, I didn't know it. I was just a little boy learning the mastery of the Little Tikes basketball hoop through my dad. That evolved into watching countless games anywhere — no, *everywhere* we could. From General McLane High School to Mercyhurst College (now Mercyhurst University), Edinboro to East High, I fed right into the addiction that was the Erie sports world, especially basketball. That small plastic hoop evolved into granny-style free throws. Those became the entry into short-range set shots and layups. The evolution was exhilarating, and I had the blessing of my father molding me into the hoopster he once was, right up until the final days of his life.

My father was a swing guard/forward for the Strong Vincent Colonels from 1961-65, playing for legendary head coach Ralph Calabrese. He was named to the 1965 *Erie Times-News* All-City Section 1 team as the Colonels made it all the way to the Pennsylvania Interscholastic Athletic Association Class A western final that season. Supported by my mother and lifelong friends dating back to his youth, my father passionately loved the game of basketball. He was damn good, too, at least that's what he told me (probably a million times).

From the first moment my father was able to see me after I was born, he was thinking basketball. He returned home to my mother and sister and exclaimed, "His fingers and legs are as long as can be. He is going to be a basketball player!"

Predestined.

Now, basketball was not the only athletics-related gift I received while growing up in Erie. To be honest, it didn't matter what sport or club it was, my dad and I were going to spectate, dissect and learn about it. This was our bond and our shared passion we enjoyed together and leaned on after the death of my mother in March 1997. I was only nine at the time and unable to rationalize or even comprehend how my life would drastically change.

Looking back, I can only imagine the utter devastation my dad felt at losing the love of his life so young. In our grief, we took solace in sports, bonded through sports, and, frankly, communicated through sports. My dreams became filled with game sevens and buzzer beaters. My passion evolved through my dad's experience and acute attention to everything sports-related. I thank God that Erie had everything to offer us and more.

I will humbly introduce my athletic career with a necessary admission: I was never the best player out there. With my skin-and-bones frame and a painfully honest understanding of my lack of talent, I found myself behind the curve plenty of times. It didn't matter, though. I

LOVED it!

I craved competition. I thrived in it. Sports, academics, childhood games, it didn't matter; I wanted to win. It was that fierce nature that provided my first motivational nemesis and a wonderful lifelong friend in Dr. Geoffrey Lim. I include his prefix out of pride for his accomplishments and a little swipe at our competition-fueled love for each other. He became my partner in competition as we learned the game of basketball together, coached by my father and maturing through dedication and hard work.

Countless hours were spent honing our skills in one driveway or another. We spent many evenings watching the Chicago Bulls and debating who was the Scottie Pippen to the other's Michael Jordan. Although I will take it to the grave knowing I was Michael, we were a dynamic duo when we took the court as two small Villa Maria Elementary Blue Wings.

I would like to continue by saying we were the most incredibly talented, most outstanding elementary boys basketball squad the world had ever witnessed, but that would be a little stretch of the truth (OK, a massive stretch). We got our butts kicked plenty of times by many of the local boys I now call friends. Losing is never fun, and if you know me, saying I don't take it well would be an understatement. This was also a valuable lesson that Erie athletics helped me to grasp. However, those days are magical to look back on. I wouldn't trade the loving friends I am so humbled to know today because of the many hours spent playing a game we loved. That time was made even sweeter by being coached and mentored by my father. I would never have said it then, but I'm thankful every day for the time we had together.

I moved on to Villa Maria Academy. As I mentioned earlier, I was never the most talented or athletic guy on any team. Villa had just moved into the Metro League, Erie's elite high school league I grew up admiring. The Victors were putting together a small crop of extremely talented boys from across the Erie area. The hope was to foster a boys program that could someday match the greatness that was, and still is, Villa's girls programs. It was my chance to get into the atmosphere that ultimately developed me into the athlete I became. We were going to take on Erie's best in arenas that I held on mythical levels.

There was only one problem: I didn't make the varsity squad. I was going to be on the freshman team, developing my skills while my peers took on city and county rivals in an attempt to make a name for Villa boys basketball. To this day, I am thankful to coach Mark

Majewski for that decision he made. It was fuel for an angry fire in me to never allow myself to fall short of my potential. I stumbled through that season in the most picturesque model of an angry teen who thought he deserved more without working for it.

It was the proverbial 2x4 my father delivered that began to shape the man I am today.

"Don't fall into the woodwork," he told me. "You will not earn what you don't work for. You put yourself here, now get yourself out."

I busted my butt to make sure I would reach the same level my peers were embracing without me. To say I worked hard would be an understatement. I became the guy at practice most players probably couldn't stand. Voluntary open gyms saw me diving on the floor for loose balls and playing defense like my life depended on it.

My determination, drive and hard work finally began to pay off, and the following season, coach Mark rewarded me with the playing minutes I craved. My time began sparingly, but as the season progressed I started to see significant minutes on the court. My job was to give some of our big men a breather. I was not the best guy in Erie. I wasn't even a top-five guy on our team, but I was playing in the Hammermill Center like I'd seen so many great athletes do before me. Aspirations were coming true for me, but this was not the Cinderella story one might imagine. We got our rear ends kicked plenty of times. This was the necessary development of something brand new for our school. We learned, just as our coaching staff learned, to take on high-level talent. Well-established programs in Erie were taking on this developing group of guys from the once all-girls school.

We took our licks and moved onto the next season. Our program was improving, and I found myself trying to get into the crowd with some of the excellent players Villa had to offer; guys like Kevin Buczynski, Cory Chaffee, Ryan Dragoone and John Lowther. I needed to model my game after some of the excellent role players I had admired my whole life; guys like Shane Battier, the memorable Duke Blue Devil who out-worked any competition, and Dennis Rodman, the greatest undersized rebounder in NBA history. I was willing to do anything to help my guys, get noticed by my coaches, and, most of all, not "fall into the woodwork."

As I developed, so did our team. Villa Maria Academy had begun to make noise in the boys basketball world. Although still so youthful in our program, we began to compete with Erie's established schools. It was exhilarating and oftentimes heartbreaking to be part of such a momentous event. My final season saw the culmination of a boy not making varsity to a young man honored with the title of team co-captain. Little did I know, this would be the most life-altering season of my life.

My father had been an integral, and oftentimes, annoying part of the entire journey for me. I can't imagine the headache he must've caused my coaches, let alone anyone who happened to sit within 50 feet of him. He would even sneak into some practices to watch what I was doing, critique form or work ethic after practice, and leave me writhing in frustration so many nights. If only I had known those words of encouragement would end so abruptly, how many thoughts, words and actions would I have changed? Richard Schauble died suddenly on an October night in 2005. Part of me was lost that evening. I vividly remember, as a lost 17-year-old, notifying my family members across the country that my father had passed.

As I made these calls, I clutched the basketball he and I had practiced with just days before. I was destroyed, or at least I thought I was. That was when the concept of predestination really came full circle. That baby with the long fingers would lean into basketball harder than anything else he had in a desperate attempt to make sense of the loss of his second parent. That Villa basketball team and the athletic lessons I learned from years of Erie sports admiration probably saved my life.

Our season was starting with me, now a team captain, not knowing where I would live or even if I could stay in Erie to finish high school. How unfair can the world sometimes be? How could I have loved that place, that competition, that lifestyle so much and have it teetering precariously right in front of me? The Lord sent me an angel in the form of my sister, Jennifer Morgan, to let me see my journey to its end. She uprooted her life to move back home, allowing me to finish my senior year of school, and, most importantly to me, my final basketball season at Villa.

Everything seemed impossibly difficult for me. I couldn't relate to friends or schoolwork. I found myself depressed and lost. I stumbled upon countless negative influences and outlets in my struggle to learn who I was. The one thing that remained constant was basketball. I could get out there and forget it all. I could lose myself in the competition, sometimes becoming so engrossed that I would break down into tears. Coach Mark was there to try to help pick up the pieces while walking the tight-rope that only a man of maturity and experience could navigate. He gave me space to work through my feelings, but brought me firmly back to reality when I went well out of line.

Through the turmoil I was experiencing in my life, we as a team came out with purpose. Those Villa boys were taking on competition we should not have stood a chance against. We put together wins that sports fans across Erie never would have expected. This was going to be it: our year, my year. I would realize the electricity that was Erie athletics. I would make my mark on our city. We stumbled along the way, but we were competitive and successful.

As we entered the postseason, a district championship and a run at the state title seemed possible. At least, it did for me until something happened to remind me I was not in control. After winning a district playoff game to advance to a semifinal, I received word that my uncle had taken his life. His memorial services were to coincide with a potential district championship game. I would miss the final two games that we as a team had worked so hard to reach. I was given the opportunity to skip the semifinal and potential championship game, or to remain home and miss the final services for my uncle.

I chose to split the difference and played my heart out in our semifinal game. We won, proving a district championship was possible for the Villa boys basketball team. I left the game and drove to Hilton Head, South Carolina, to stay with family for the week. While there, I listened via a phone call to the game I so desperately wanted to be a part of. Looking back, I'm proud of the decision I made, but how I longed to be there with my team.

Although we fell short of the district title, our play had earned us a shot at a state championship. The PIAA playoffs were March basketball at its finest, and I was going to be a part of it. That was it, that was what it all came down to. We put together one win, and then another. We were going to do it!

Our next opponent was Blairsville, and I will remember every incredible and awesomely excruciating second of that game for the rest of my life. The much-higher-ranked adversary was predicted to roll over these boys from the once all-girls school. That was far from what happened. In what I would call the most electrifying game a crowd would ever witness, our small program fought with all its heart. Sadly, as is destined to happen, a victor was decided in the waning seconds — or what felt like forever — and it was not us. Our fairytale had ended. My season I had dedicated to my father, required as a lifeline to overcome the loss of him, and my Erie sports legacy were just...over.

I graduated that year, completely through the loving patience of my family, friends and wonderful teaching staff, and I did my best to find my place in the world. I took a few less-than-admirable swipes at a college education. It was actually coach Mark whose faith in me gave me a shot as a walk-on at Penn State Behrend. As Erie athletics had done so many times in the past, it was this next step which developed my life. I had learned after my dad passed that I was adopted, and my biological family was able to find me via the school athletic email information.

At 20 years old, I met my biological mother and father, and seven siblings I never knew I had. In this, my basketball career gave me another gift that I would never have expected. Unfortunately, my lack of maturity and failure to treat my mental health led to a withdrawal from basketball and higher education all together.

I worked around town for friends and family, trying to keep money coming in while I wallowed in grief and self-pity. During this time, I leaned on my other family. I was taken in by the family of my best friend, Josh Graffius. His wonderful parents, Linda and Bud, worked as surrogate parents as I tried to navigate the chaos of the world. They did all of this for me as Bud, or "Pops" as I affectionately called him, dealt with prostate cancer. He bravely battled this oppressive disease while trying to give me so much of what I had lost. Pops succumbed to cancer after my second withdrawal from college. Yet again, I felt completely lost. I began searching for solace in all the wrong places. Finally, like a freight train, the words derived from a passion for sports — in a town created to embrace them, from a father to a son predestined to be a part of it all — came to me.

"Don't fall into the woodwork."

It wasn't the basketball records or competition my passion for Erie gave me. It was a mantra, a mentality. I would use the hard work, the heartbreak and the drive to pull myself together and separate myself from "the woodwork." It was that mentality that led me to my military service. It is that mentality that has made me successful in entrepreneurship. Above all, it was that mentality that harvested my eternal love for the Lord and for my beautiful family. Erie sports and the mentorship of my family — especially my father — was a beacon to salvation and restoration.

The struggle and strife of life which I thought was just unfair and burdensome was actually the eternal battle of the world. This is a lesson that I've recently learned through the grace and restoration of Jesus. My battle with depression has never subsided. It is something that may always be present in my life. Through what can only be explained as divine intervention, I found myself embedded in an amazing organization founded to battle PTSD and suicidal tendencies in combat veterans.

Operation Restored Warrior stoked the fires of my faith, reconnected me to Jesus and showed me a path to restorative healing and redemption. This path was mine to take because of my Christian education background and the faith of my family. Erie came through again.

I now live in southern Alabama with my beautiful wife, Vanessa, and the most incredible little girl I am blessed to call mine, Zoey. I work for the Department of the Army as an air traffic controller, while backing Vanessa in her dream enterprise. Together, we run Sixtel Bottle & Growler House, which is known for having delicious craft beer. I find myself still engrossed in Erie athletics, and you can find me at a game or two on my visits home. I've caught myself looking more into Erie sports headlines than in any other place we've lived.

I look back fondly on the memories and experiences I was blessed to share with so many wonderful people in a town made to embrace competition. We live a blessed life full of love thanks to the lessons learned through pain, failure and above all, hard work, from a love affair in which I was predestined to share.

I leave you with these words…

"Don't fall into the woodwork."

Made in the USA
Columbia, SC
07 May 2021

37539642R00157